D1324433

Why Children?

Why Children?

Edited and introduced
by Stephanie Dowrick and
Sibyl Grundberg

Harcourt Brace Jovanovich, Publishers
New York and London

Copyright © 1980 by The Women's Press Limited

First published in England by The Women's Press Limited,
124 Shoreditch High Street, London E1 6JE

Requests for permission to make copies
of any part of the work should be mailed to:
Permissions, Harcourt Brace Jovanovich, Inc.,
757 Third Avenue, New York, N.Y. 10017

Irena Klepfisz's article first appeared in *Conditions;*
Karen Lindsey's first appeared in the *Boston Phoenix.*
"Waiting," from *Maps & Windows,*
copyright © 1973, 1974, by Jane Cooper,
is reprinted by permission of Macmillan Publishing Co. Inc.

Library of Congress Cataloging in Publication Data
Main entry under title:

Why children?

Includes bibliographical references.
1. Parenthood. 2. Childlessness.
3. Women's rights.
I. Dowrick, Stephanie. II. Grundberg, Sibyl.
HQ755.8.W49   1980   306.8   80-84688
ISBN 0-15-196324-X
ISBN 0-15-696362-0 (pbk.)

301.426

Printed in the United States of America
First American edition
A B C D E F G H I J

Contents

To be a mother is not a trade. It's not even a duty. It's only one right among many.

Oriana Fallaci, *Letter to a Child Never Born*

Introduction

Why do we have children?

Even to ask this question is to start a revolution. Motherhood – that 'great mesh in which all human relations are entangled'[1] – has been for so long the central fact of women's lives that the idea of *choice*, deceptively linked with such familiar concerns as contraception and the option of abortion, is almost beyond our grasp. Our thoughts and actions are shaped by the most deeply ingrained notions of what we 'ought' to do; knowing what we want is not as simple as it may seem.

Against this background we nevertheless persisted: *why children?* In asking this we encourage each other to face a major and often painful confrontation with self, upon a battlefield shared with family and custom, church and state, mythology, economic reality and an increasing anxiety about the quality of the future. History has given women little reason to expect that this future will be of our making. Our stamp upon the world has been, traditionally, our stamp upon our children. We set out to sample the effect of the Second Wave of women's liberation on women's choices about motherhood, wanting to explore further the knotty problem of 'choice', knowing that for those of us who choose to relinquish this readily accessible form of power there are terrors. Equally, that for those of us who choose to have children at this imperfect time, there are terrors too.

In seeking contributors to *Why Children?* our aim was to convey the complexity, the deep personal significance of the decision whether or not to have children, the most irrevocable and important one that most of us will make. We sought women with a wide range of backgrounds and experience. Inevitably the end result does not put forward as many different views or life situations as we would have liked. All the women writing in this book have something strongly felt to say. We opted to go with their urgency rather than attempt the impossible: a truly representative cross-section of women. Sadly, there were women whose perspectives we cherished who found the subject too painful to write about, or who felt that the honesty crucial to the project would have been too hurtful to others involved in the consequences of their 'choice'. Our contributors do include mothers in traditional 'nuclear' families, single mothers, women bringing up children to whom they did not give birth, women involved in raising children collectively; heterosexual, bisexual and lesbian women, mothers of teenagers, mothers of infants; women who have made the decision not to have children with reluctance and pain; women who have made that decision conscious of the benefits for them of a childless life; women who still hope to exercise their choice in the future. An unrepresentatively high proportion of the contributors are writers, perhaps in part because the demands of the issue are exceptional, but we did not set out to produce a 'literary' book and ultimately it refuses to be one. It is an intense and many-sided dialogue among women who speak in many different voices. Except to ask for clarification or explanation, we did not intervene in the expression of those voices.

The potential for giving birth to children unites us across barriers of class, race, culture and politics. The myths and expectations surrounding this potential, powerfully defined by Adrienne Rich as the 'institution' of motherhood[2], affect us deeply. In 1977, in her book *My Mother Myself*, Nancy Friday could write, 'most women enjoy having children, want to, and do'.[3] The reality, as this book will show, is not so simple. If the majority of mothers whose voices are heard here are happily so (and we found unhappy mothers unwilling to say so in print) it is clear that their actual choices have been hemmed about on many sides. Numbers of women with whom we have discussed this book have challenged the notion of choice which this book seeks to support. What is also clear is that the rich and dangerous reality of motherhood is not something that can be pre-imagined and that the interdependence of women with and without children is absolute. Our lives are as they are because some of us have children and some of us do not.

This book differs from others concerned with children in its unapologetic emphasis on the (actual, potential or non-) *mother*. We make the assumption that the welfare of the child is inseparable from the mother's sense of personal potency, her control over her own life's options. We assume that a woman's partnership with a man, or the absence of such a partnership, may contribute to but does not define or delimit her decision whether or not to have a child. The voices of 'experts' are absent, fathers'/husbands' voices are largely absent, and when the child's voice is heard it is as part of a dialogue which affirms that the needs of mother and child must try to coalesce and, when in conflict, to find a balance. Children emerge in this book as resilient creatures, able to survive what their parent(s) must.

We live in a society in which 'we are seen primarily as mothers; all mothers are expected to experience motherhood unambivalently and in accordance with patriarchal values, and the "non-mothering" woman is seen as deviant'.[4] Selflessness is the theme of this value system. Joss Shawyer has pointed out how inconsistently the rule is applied: 'The same people who attack childless couples as being "selfish" for not having children are, curiously, often the same people who attack single mothers for being "selfish" by refusing to give theirs away.'[5] To choose to have a child as a single woman or a lesbian is still to invite all the Furies that society can loose upon us. A woman whose identity does not include alliance with a male figure is labelled 'unfit'. The lesbian who wants a child is seen as contemplating an impracticality at best; at worst, a double perversion, a threat to the child. The world has persistently turned a deaf ear to her voice, which naturally becomes inaudible to herself also. Her voice is heard here – as is that long-stifled voice: 'I don't want to have a child'. To be able to say this aloud, without fear of suspicion or censure, is a prerequisite for all before any woman who wants to have a child is free in her choice.

Certain themes recur in this book. No fewer than three women write of 'falling in love' with their child at birth. That voices are heard to contradict this 'bonding' experience should not disturb us. Another recurring theme is that of motherhood as one form, not *the* form, of creative activity available to women. This issue is sharply raised by the writers and artists in this book. Whatever their position on the 'creativity' issue, women bringing up children are seen to be concerned with resolving the competing demands of vocation and childrearing, their compelling (and perennially underestimated) desires for fulfillment in more than one sphere. Several writers speak of their closeness to children who 'belong' to other women and the dangers of loving children to whom they are not biologically tied. Private and intense moments of warmth and closeness shared with children come through the pages. But is this exclusive relationship, and the isolation that comes with it, what we really want? Can we afford it? These are among the many questions that this book raises, for which there are no easy answers.

Although economic factors are rarely alluded to directly as a major factor in the choice each woman describes, between the lines their importance is plain. 'Choice' is meaningless in a society which refuses to accept that responsibility for the care of children should be shared by all who benefit from their existence. So we 'choose' between economic dependence within the family structure or the double load of work in the home as well as outside – or punitive welfare payments if we cannot or will not choose either. Our 'choice' takes place against a background of increasing unemployment, the persistent exploitation

10

of women's labour, shrinking social services. These factors reinforce the extremely narrowly defined structure inside which motherhood is socially approved and encouraged, in which the married mother is sentimentalised while the real work of child-raising is kept at low value.

Also between the lines, differences in stamina and temperament seem to lie behind many of the differences in point of view. Some of the writers describe vividly the exhaustion that bringing up small children entails, which each of us must confront individually. Some of us can empathise with the burst of excitement and activity that corresponded with Sara Ruddick's pregnancy; others with Adrienne Rich's stark confession in *Of Woman Born* that she felt 'boredom and indifference' towards her own work during her pregnancies.[6] The denial and deliberate suppression of the individualities underlying such vast differences of feeling and experience is among the most widely prevalent injustices inflicted upon women.

The statement that this book makes is comprised of ambiguities and paradoxes. These encompass the positive yearning, the rewards, physical euphoria, even the 'romance' of having children – all of which are memorably described and to which all deliberate non-mothers in some way pay tribute. The eighteen contributions to *Why Children?* reveal differences, disagreements, on almost every aspect of pregnancy, childbirth and the feelings that women bring to their decision for or against undertaking motherhood. There are, by implication, as many perspectives as women alive. *Why Children?* will mean different things to each reader but it is our hope that the sharing of views and experience will give each woman who reads it inspiration, reassurance and increased confidence in her own instincts.

This book was born out of a meeting in 1978 in which women concerned with the then newly-created Women's Press were discussing various projects. Suzanne Perkins, our designer and a single mother of two young children, had arrived late. She interrupted our cool discussion of theoretical subjects with a plea to remember that, out there, are millions of women with 'a damp rag in their hand'. They are the mothers, wiping up after children, wiping children, cleaning, caressing, repeating tasks, mopping up, keeping things going. The discussion exploded, became impassioned. Talk moved from theory to feelings, to experience, misgivings, longing. Someone reminded us that there is no 'we' and 'they'. Some of us had children, some of us did not. All of us felt intensely keen to share our thoughts on the subject and intensely interested to hear what the others had to say. Why were some of us mothers, what choice had we exercised, what were the consequences for us, in our own lives, of being mothers, or not? The talk spread from that room and has taken shape in this book. But it does not end here. 'We need to imagine a world in which every woman is the presiding genius of her own body,' writes Adrienne Rich in conclusion of *Of Woman Born*.[7] We hope that *Why Children?*, as much as it is about *this* world and the courage it takes to make choices in it, the courage it takes to try to change it, will encourage many women to look into themselves – and dare to imagine.

Sibyl Grundberg
Stephanie Dowrick

Notes

1   Adrienne Rich, 'Motherhood: the Contemporary Emergency and the Quantum Leap' (1978), in *On Lies, Secrets and Silence*, W. W. Norton, New York, 1979, p 260.

2   Adrienne Rich, *Of Woman Born: Motherhood as Experience and Institution*, W. W. Norton & Co, New York, 1976; Virago, London, 1977. We acknowledge our enormous debt to Rich's work.

3   Nancy Friday, *My Mother, Myself*, Delacorte, New York, 1977; Fontana, London. 1979, p 34.

4   Adrienne Rich, 'Motherhood in Bondage' (1976), in *On Lies, Secrets and Silence*, p 197.

5   Joss Shawyer, *Death by Adoption*, Cicada Press, Auckland, NZ, 1979, p 25.

6   *Of Woman Born*, p 26.

7   *Of Woman Born*, p 285.

Why Children?

JUDY WATERMAN

Irena Klepfisz was born in Warsaw, Poland, in 1941 and went to the United States at the age of eight. She has lived most of her life in New York City. She is author of *Periods of Stress*, a collection of her poetry and is founder and editor of *Conditions*, a magazine of women's writing with an emphasis on writing by lesbians. Her contribution to *Why Children?* appeared first in *Conditions: Two* as 'Women without Children'.

Irena Klepfisz

This article has grown out of my need to express some of my feelings and conflicts about being a woman who has chosen to remain childless, as well as to break the silence surrounding the general issue of women without children.

That the silence has persisted despite the presence of the women's movement is both appalling and enigmatic, since the decision not to have a child shapes both a woman's view of herself and society's view of her. I have read a great deal about woman as mother, but virtually nothing about woman as non-mother, as if her choice should be taken for granted and her life were not an issue. And though I have heard strong support for the right of women to have choices and options, I have not seen any exploration of how the decision to remain childless is to be made, how one is to come to terms with it, how one is to learn to live with its consequences. If what follows seems at moments somewhat bleak, it is because I feel very strongly that in celebrating a woman's liberation from compulsory motherhood, we have neither recognised nor dealt with the pain that often accompanies such a decision.

My intent is to be neither objective nor exhaustive. I am aware that this issue evokes many other feelings than those expressed on the following pages, the feelings of women whose lives differ drastically from mine. I hope that they too will break the silence.

The fantasy

At the centre of my bleakest fantasy is the shopping-bag lady. I see her sitting on the subway, trudging along the highway, or crouched in a doorway at dusk. Invariably she clutches her paper shopping bags close to her. From a distance, her face looks blank, her skin grey. She is oblivious to the things around her, unresponsive to sounds and movements. She is particularly indifferent to people. Periodically she makes a quick motion, like an animal automatically brushing itself free from an irritation, a tic. Her gesture is loose, flabby, hardly aimed. It is perhaps the tremor of a muscle.

I keep my distance from her, though at times in my imagination I venture closer, detecting a faint stale odour, an odour distinctly communicating stagnation. In reality, however, I have moved only close enough to discern the discoloured skin, the broken blood vessels on her legs, stained purple bruises, barely healed wounds. I have eyed her socks and stockings, her shoes, her faded dress, the safety pins which hold her coat together. I have studied the surface content of her bags, seen the bits of material (clothing perhaps), newspapers. I always want to know more, to know if the entire bag is filled with rags and papers, or if deep inside wrapped neatly and carefully in a clean cloth lies an object from the past, a memento from a life like mine. But my desire to know has never overcome my real terror of her. So I have never ventured closer.

I have a distinct fear of contagion. But it is not necessarily of disease – though there is that too, the physical fear of being touched by such a creature. My greater fear is that she carries another kind of disease. On a subway, I watch as this creature sits, harmless, self-contained, oblivious to the other people in the car, while an invisible circle seems to form around her. No one will come near her, no one will sit close to her, no one will risk being touched by her. If she has succeeded in excluding us from her world, we must remember that our response to her reflects our equal determination to keep her out of ours. It is almost as if I, as if everyone else in the subway car, were determined to classify her as a species apart, to establish firmly that there is no connection between her and us. By keeping my distance, I affirm she is not of my world, reassure myself that I could never be like her, that there is nothing she and I have in common, in short, that her disease is not communicable.

It is, I think, the most comfortable way of looking at her, for it deems her irrelevant to my life. Of course, if I were totally convinced, I would lose my fear of contagion. But this is not the case. More and more, I sense my connection to her, allow myself to absorb the fact that her world and mine overlap; more and more I dismiss as romantic the notion that some great, swift calamity, some sudden shock must have overtaken her and reduced her to her present condition. It is far more probable that her separateness, her isolation, resulted not from fire, nor from sudden death, nor from unexpected loss, but rather from a slow erosion, an imperceptible loosening of common connections and relations — a process to which I too am subject. Her 'disease' is one to which I am and will remain vulnerable. She is not an anomaly, nor is her isolation from the rest of us a freak accident. She came from the same world I did, underwent the same life processes: she was born, grew up, lives.

So I remain in a state of terror and keep myself separate from her. I fear that I will not build up the proper immunity to resist the erosion; I am afraid I too will end up alone, disconnected, relating to no one, having no one to care for, being in turn forgotten, unwanted and insignificant, my life a waste. In the grip of this terror, I can only anticipate a lonely, painful old age, an uncomforted death.

It is difficult to own up to this fantasy. I do so both because it is true that I have it, but also because I know I am not unique in having it. I have heard many other women express it, perhaps not always in terms of shopping-bag ladies, but in terms of old age, insecurity. And it is not surprising because among my friends, many in their late thirties and early forties, these issues are becoming increasingly important. It is not surprising because we are living in a period of depression when everyone is worried about money and jobs, about the possibility of surviving in some decent way. For me, the shopping-bag lady epitomises these fears, and though I often tell myself that she is an exaggerated example, equally often I think that she is not.

The myths

For a long time I believed (and on some non-rational level still believe) that I could acquire 'immunity' to the shopping-bag lady's disease by having a child. When depressed about the fragility and transience of friendships, or the inconstancies of lovers, it was the myth of a child, a blood relation and what it could bring me, which seemed to me the only real guarantee against loneliness and isolation, the only way of maintaining a connection to the rest of society. And certainly one of the difficulties for me, a woman who now knows that she will never bear children, is to let go of that myth without sinking into total despair.

That the myth is powerful is not surprising, since it is nurtured by everything around us, fostered by the media, by popular literature, by parents, by the questionnaires we fill out for jobs: *Are you married?* No. *Do you have children?* No. *Do you live alone?* Yes. *How many members in your household?* One. It is a myth perpetually reinforced by the assumption that only family and children provide us with a purpose and place, bestow upon us honour, respect, love and comfort. We are taught very early that blood relations, and only blood relations, can be a perpetual, unfluctuating source of affection, can be the foolproof guarantee that we will not be forgotten. This myth, and many others surrounding the traditional family, often make it both frightening and painful for women to think of themselves as remaining childless.

In reality, of course, I know that many shopping-bag ladies are mothers, have families, have children. What is obvious to any mature, rational woman is that children are not a medicine or a vaccine which stamps out loneliness or isolation, but rather that they are people, subject to the same weaknesses as friends

18

and lovers. I have talked to many women whose ties to their families seem to be irrevocably broken. It is common to hear stories of the prodigal daughter going cross-country, returning home after fourteen, fifteen years to parents who are strangers. Expecting a traumatic, painful reunion, the woman returns numbed by her lack of connection, by her indifference to strangers. They are people with no special relation. They follow the accepted and expected rules, in a dire crisis write dutiful cheques, and, upon their death, bequeath china to their unmarried daughters. But the emotional pull is not there from either side. There is no exchange of love, of comfort. Blood might indeed be thicker than water, but it too is capable of evaporating and drying up.

Yet despite this, despite having read Shakespeare's *King Lear* and Tillie Olsen's *Tell Me a Riddle*, despite having been taught by experience that children often come to love their ideals more than their parents (and vice versa), that children may take different roads rejecting all ties to the past, despite all this, the myth retains its power and dominates my fantasy life. And there are important reasons why it does.

First, what I have just described is what I would like to believe is an extreme, an exception. There are, after all, many warm, loving relationships between parent and child. In these relationships, one can recognise genuine affection and ties among members of the family, even if often the very same relationships are fraught with tensions and painful encounters.

Once when talking with a woman about our feelings about being childless, she began to tell me about her relationship with her mother, a relationship which for years had been filled with anger and pain. But I could sense that on some level the woman felt a deep attachment, had genuine concern and responsibility towards her mother, despite the fact that the relationship remained problematic and many painful conflicts were still unresolved. While she was describing this to me, she suddenly revealed that her mother was on welfare and receiving a hundred and eighty dollars a month. When I asked her how her mother could possibly manage on such an absurd amount, the woman laughed and said that, of course, she helped her out financially. We continued talking more generally about the issue, but then the woman suddenly said: 'You know it scares me. Being alone, without family. I think about my mother and what she would be doing now without me. I keep trying to think of her as just a woman, like me, trying to cope with the world. But there is a difference, a major difference between us. She has a daughter.'

A second reason for the myth's ability to retain its hold on my fantasy life is that I have found no adequate substitute for it. To discard it is to be left with nothing, to be faced with the void (or so I think in my most depressed moments). I admit this with some hesitancy, because certainly one aim of the lesbian/feminist movement has been to expose the superficiality of the family myth. The movement has consciously struggled to develop new alternatives for women, has, in a certain sense, offered itself as a new and better 'home', a source of the support, affection, security that many of us seek. I think, however, that for women who at one time or another were involved in various movement activities, support groups, collectives, business projects, experimental communes, for those women who as a result of these activities and groups experienced the first flush of excitement in their discovery of other women who thought that they had indeed found new and permanent homes, alternate families — for them the disappointment has been quite keen. Too often, instead of providing a new and supportive home, the collective experiments ended in frustration, bitter anger, a hard silence that severed what everyone had hoped would be permanent ties. That this occurred, is repeatedly occurring, is not surprising. Because expectations were so high, because we wanted these groups to fulfil so many divergent needs, they were destined to disappoint. For me and for many other women it was a sobering kind of experience, to say the least.

I do not mean to imply that nothing has worked or that we are standing in the midst of ruins. What I wish to emphasise is rather the sense of disillusionment and disappointment experienced by me and by many women with whom I have spoken, a sense which has contributed to a feeling of insecurity and, to some degree, pessimism. It is when these feelings become acute that I am most vulnerable, that my fantasy returns again to the concept of family and children. The old images surface again. But the difference between envisioning them now and envisioning them years ago is that now they hold no solace; they remain empty. Their uselessness in my life creates further pain, for I am without the alternatives which a few years ago, when I first became involved in the lesbian/feminist movement, I thought I had. I find the community's present and future only vaguely delineated; whatever community exists is still very young and rather shaky. The emptiness of the past, the vagueness of the future, leave me fearful, hesitant about my decision not to have a child.

Many women have had to face a similar issue on a more personal and more immediate level. They have had to face the fact that lesbian relationships are not *instantly* more stable, more secure, more permanent than heterosexual ones. And because of this, the myth of motherhood takes on added power. A woman who thought she was about to break up with her lover told me: 'For the first time in a really long time, I thought about having a child. I won't do it of course. But I did think about it'. She was clearly expressing the idea that somehow a child would guarantee her a permanent relationship.

The emphasis is of course on 'guarantee' and on 'permanent'. If the parent is good, so the logic of the fantasy goes, then the relationship with the child will withstand shock, change, growth, poverty, differences in temperament and ideals: in short, anything and everything. The woman who dreams this way may acknowledge that such a relationship has yet to be realised, but she may be quick to add that she has learned a great deal from her own experience as a daughter, that with *her* child, she will avoid all the mistakes that her parents made with her. By learning from their errors, the woman now fantasises, she will establish a far more perfect, loving, supportive relationship with her child and, thereby, guarantee for herself a permanent connection during her lifetime.

My fantasy of being a mother and my desire to have a child have been with me for a long time. It has taken me years to realise, however, that both the fantasy and the desire were to a great degree expressions of my dissatisfaction with my relationship with my own mother. It seems to me clear now that by becoming the calm, loving, patient, supportive mother that I have so often envisioned, I have hoped in effect to annihilate the impatient critical voice within myself, the voice that has kept me insecure and dissatisfied. Thus, my desire to become the perfect mother, to act out that fantasy, has in reality nothing to do with having a child, but rather with my desire to experience something I wish I had experienced. It is not a child I wish to mother, it is myself.

In my fantasy, of course, the understanding, the patience, the support are always outwardly directed, because the myth of motherhood demands that they be so. According to the myth, if I do not have a child I will never experience that caring, that uncritical peace, that completely understanding sensibility. Only the role of mother will allow me that. This is clearly a wrong reason for having a child – one which can be ultimately disastrous.

This kind of thinking, however, points up another aspect of the myth about having children, i.e. that certain qualities can only be expressed through a relationship with a child. I am not saying that a relationship with a child is not unique. It is. But some of the qualities which we attribute to it are not limited to child-parent relationships. I would like to discuss just one of these qualities. Women expressing a desire to have a child often explain that they want their values and beliefs to be passed on; they feel that by having a child they can have some measure of control, some input into the future. A child, after all, can be moulded and influenced; to a child can be passed on a whole way of life. That parents have tremendous influence over their children is, of course, self-evident. But the myth excludes the fact that they do not have total influence over their children, that they can never exert total control. As a woman once said to me about her child who was going to a day-care centre: 'Oh yes, I have great influence. I send her off in the morning looking like a human being and she comes back in the evening with green nail polish because green nail polish is some teacher's idea of femininity.'

There is something extraordinary in the idea of being able to participate so immediately in the shaping of another life, no matter how much other factors attempt to undermine that influence. Nevertheless, it is not only through a growing child that a woman can influence the world around her, though in the interests of the traditional family, women are taught to believe that it is the most direct and most meaningful way for them. Obviously, a woman taught to think this way will think that her life, her work, are totally useless and ineffectual if she does not have a child, an heir to her ideals and values. This is another real impasse for many women who decide to remain childless. I was interested in a conversation I had with a woman who told me she was considering adopting a child. One of her main reasons was the one I have just discussed. Later in the conversation, she told me about a talk she had had with a friend. Sometime after the talk, her friend told her that she had had a tremendous impact on her, that the talk had helped her in making certain basic decisions about her life. The woman told me: 'I was really stunned. I always consider conversations with friends just talk. It never occurs to me that anyone really listens to me, or that what I say has any effect on anyone.'

This is not to say that for every aspect of a relationship with a child we can find a substitute, and women who decide not to have children can somehow 'make up for it' by looking elsewhere. I believe a relationship with a child is as unique as a relationship with a friend or a lover. Each has its own special qualities. But myths about having children do prevent women from seeing just what it is they want from having a child and from participating in such a close way in another life. It is something which needs closer examination, so that when a woman decides not to have children, she knows what she is giving up — both the negative and the positive aspects of being a mother — knows it in a real, concrete way, and not in the foggy, idealised, sticky-sentimentalised version with which we all are so familiar.

The consequences
Myths and private fantasies are not the only obstacles in the way of women coming to terms with their childlessness. There are

also the very real, and often harsh, circumstances of living in a society where a woman who does not marry and, above all, who does not have a child, is stigmatised, characterised as cold, as unwomanly and unfeminine, as unnatural in some essential way. I wince when I recall how throughout my twenties, when I was certain that I was destined to marry and to have children, I would assume with total confidence that a married woman who did not have children must either have physical problems or deep psychological ones. And I remember with some shame the freedom with which I would mouth these opinions.

Today, many of us know better. But although we may understand that a woman has a right to choose to remain childless, the society in which we live still does not, and most of the time it is extremely difficult to be a woman who is deliberately *not* a mother. On the most immediate level, a childless woman must deal with the painful confrontations and equally painful silences between her family and herself. Let me use myself as an example. I am an only child, a survivor of World War II. My father was killed during the war, as was his whole family; my mother was the only family I had. Most of her friends were, like us, surviving members of families which had been wiped out. It was an unstated aim of the individuals of this circle to regenerate the traditional family, thereby making themselves 'whole'. And over the years, most of them were quite successful. Some re-married; those who did not had the satisfaction of watching their children grow up and of knowing that they would take the 'normal' route. Soon there were in-laws, then grandchildren. The nuclear family seemed to reassert itself.

It has been extremely difficult as well as painful for me to live with the knowledge that I willingly, deliberately never produced the child who could have continued 'my father's line', that I never provided my mother with the new family and the grandchildren she was sure would appear, which she thought were her right to expect. I know that other women, coming out of different circumstances, have experienced similar difficulties and pain – women who were raised as only children, who were given the burden of providing their parents with the stereotypical props of old age. These women have complained bitterly about how their parents' disappointment in *them* (as if they had failed at something) has affected them. The 'You're-the-last-of-the-line' argument always makes the woman who chooses not to have children appear perverse, stubborn, ungiving, selfish. Equally painful can be the excitement of parents when they inform the childless daughter of the birth of a friend's grandchild. I have heard this kind of excitement in my mother's voice, and have often resented the fact that nothing that I could achieve could elicit that tone of voice, that kind of lasting, enduring satisfaction. Her envy of her friend is clear; and underneath it, I know, lies a silent, unstated criticism of me. I have held back.

A woman who is not an only child is often relieved of this kind of burden and pressure when one of her siblings marries and gives birth. But this too creates its own problems; often the childless woman feels resentment and jealousy because the parents seem so pleased with the sibling for making them grandparents. A woman once told me how her sister, who had recently given birth, said to her that she was glad she had been able to provide their mother with the pleasure of seeing her first grandchild. The mother was dying. The woman felt deeply hurt, not only because of her sister's insensitivity to her feelings, but also because she felt she had nothing comparable to offer her mother.

At moments like these, women often yearn for the perfect excuse which will relieve them of the burden of having chosen to remain childless, which will convert them back into 'warm, loving women'. The choice seems too great a responsibility, seems too much against the values of our society. I remember a few years ago, when I had to have surgery on my uterus, how frightened I was at the prospect of having a hysterectomy. I told the doctor that, if at all possible, I wanted to keep my ability to have children. What I did not express to anyone, and barely to myself, was that a part of me wished that in fact a hysterectomy would be necessary. By becoming sterile, I would be relieved of having to make an agonising decision. Remaining childless would no longer be a result of my 'perverseness'. I would be childless because I could not bear children. What could anyone possibly say to me after I had had my hysterectomy? I have heard other women reluctantly confess similar 'secret thoughts', women with raised feminist consciousnesses, who nevertheless find it difficult to make the decision not to have children, and also to take full responsibility for it without feeling defensive and to some degree unjustified.

In the end, I did not have a hysterectomy and my childlessness is a result of my own decision. The process by which that decision was made is in large measure difficult for me to trace or reconstruct. To a certain degree, I think I made it over a long period of years, during many of which, on the surface at least, I was not consciously thinking about the issue. Certainly, for a long time I thought there was no decision to be made; I was sure that I would marry and have a family. Furthermore, I never doubted my intense desire to have a large family, never stopped to question whether I really wanted this, or whether it was something I thought I should want. Looking back, I find that often, in order to appear 'normal' to myself, I adopted attitudes and values which were clearly not my own. In this particular case the unconscious argument went as follows: A normal woman wants children; I am a normal woman; I want children. This kind of short-circuiting of real feelings is quite common with many women, women who cling to fantasies created by others. These fantasies, many women think, will keep them in the mainstream, will prevent them from appearing different or conspicuous.

I fantasised about my future family for a long, long time, though in my actual life there was nothing to indicate that I was moving in that direction, that the fantasy would become a reality. I never married, never became pregnant. Yet I continued to assume that it was simply a question of time, that of course *it* would happen. *It* did not.

At the age of thirty, I was finally able to admit to myself that I did not want to marry. That realisation, however, did not resolve the question of whether or not I should have children, and so I began to think about the issue in more real, more concrete terms. Two years later I became involved with a woman, and a year later I had to have my operation. At that point I was already thirty-three, was beginning to realise that I had to make a clear decision. And I made it by doing nothing about it. I thought a good deal about children, my need for them, my intense longing for them, my fears about being without them. But I did nothing.

The long years during which I was making my decision were extremely difficult. Most of the time I felt inadequate and incomplete. I was conscious that many people around me thought it peculiar that I was not being swept away by 'a normal woman's instinct' to bear and rear children, an instinct which should have overriden any of my qualms about marriage. The message communicated to me was that I – a woman alone, without a partner, without children – was enigmatic at best, superfluous at worst. In those years, I was unable to articulate to myself or to others that I was following other instincts. The best defence that I could muster was to say: 'I'm too *selfish* for that life.' Nevertheless, I evolved my decision and stuck to it.

Conclusion

This past April I became thirty-six and I think it is not accidental that it was around that time that I began thinking about writing this article. Though most of the time I really do not know what to make of my age, what to think of its significance, it is around the issue of having a child that my age becomes real to me. For if I do not feel thirty-six (whatever feeling that is supposed to be), I certainly know that biologically my body is thirty-six, that the time for bearing children is almost over for me, and that once I pass a certain point, the decision not to bear a child is irrevocable. That the decision has already been made is very clear to me, though I cannot pinpoint the exact moment when I made it. No matter what my age, the issue is closed.

Often, of course, I wish I had done *it*, done it in those unconscious years when so many women I knew were doing it. They are now mothers whose children are almost real adults – eight, ten, twelve years of age. Frequently I find myself envying these mothers for having got it over with in those early years. That certainly seems to be the perfect solution: have the child in the

27

past, so you can have it now. Fantasising in this way, I can easily skip over all the hardships and frustrations that many of these women have experienced in the past ten or twelve years of raising their children under extremely difficult circumstances, hardships which they continue to experience, and which I can only partially understand.

Still, there are moments when I can actually assert a certain amount of pride in the way I have chosen to lead my life, when I can feel extremely good about the fact that I did not succumb and did not keep myself in line. I am pleased that I withstood the pressures, that I kept my independence, that I did not give in to the myths which surrounded me. I know of course that there are various reasons why I did not and others did, which include conditions over which none of us had very much control. Nevertheless, I do experience momentary delight in the fact that I escaped and did what I wanted to do (even when that was somewhat unclear), that I did not give in to the temptation to please my mother, did not give in to the pleas of my father's ghost to keep him alive, did not conform with the rest of my friends, but instead kept myself apart and independent in some essential way. In moments like these, I can easily take responsibility for my life and say it is the life that I have chosen.

None of this is ever very simple. There are pleasures that one gives up when one decides not to have children. But as I keep telling myself: you can't have everything. Choices have to be made, and consequences have to be lived with. The act of choosing inevitably brings loss. It is a difficult lesson to understand and accept. I keep trying to relearn it.

While writing this article, I saw my mother, who had just discovered, stuck away somewhere in a closet, my favourite doll. I was surprised by my instant sadness at seeing and then holding it: the sweetness of the face, the smallness of the head against the palm of my hand. I felt as if I wanted to cry. But in touching it, it was not a baby that I envisioned, but rather myself, five or six years old, cradling the doll in her arms and rocking it gently to sleep.

Lucy Goodison

When I was twenty-one, I wanted to get married and have a baby. When I was twenty-three, I wanted to have a career and have a baby. When I was twenty-five, I wanted to live in a commune and have a baby. When I was twenty-six, I became active in left-wing politics and was too involved in finding myself and understanding the world, in the joy and release of creative collective action, to think about babies. Gradually I became involved in the women's movement and realised that anyway having children is a source of oppression for women, limiting our strength and freedom. Women who already had children from pre-movement days were supported, but how could we consciously choose this burden now we knew what it meant? My yearning for a baby returned, but was channelled into looking after friends' children and starting a local playgroup. I felt it was a yearning too selfish to be indulged when there were already so many mothers needing relief.

I was nearly thirty when the urge for a child returned so intensely as to become almost an obsession. Looking back, it is

JILL POSENER

Lucy Goodison has been involved in the women's movement and in
Red Therapy since 1973. She teaches self-help therapy skills, does
massage, dance and dream workshops and lives in East London.

still hard for me to understand exactly why this happened. There were many sound reasons. I was still in a relationship with the same man I was with at twenty-one. I was living in a warm and committed collective with several children and shared childcare: the kind of situation I had been half-consciously looking for over years to have a baby in. I was afraid that over thirty was too late to start childbearing safely. At some deep level of sureness I knew that I wanted children to be an ongoing part of my life: I value their energy, directness and anarchy too much to imagine a life without them. But my experience of shared childcare had shown that other people's children retained a primary relationship with their parents and moved on with them. After a few painful separations I realised that if I wanted a continuing and close relationship with a child, I needed to give birth myself. I had a picture of myself at forty: lonely, childless, bitterly regretful at having passed by a significant experience open to me as a woman. I didn't want to spend my life without trying this experience. I wanted to live my life to the full, to explore everything my body could do: dancing, making love, having babies . . . I felt readier to have a child than I had ever been. I had done a difficult job for several years and acquired some skills and confidence which would be there to come back to. I had done some self-help therapy and felt less neurotic, less likely to damage the baby or lose myself forever under a pile of nappies, than I was in my early twenties. I had been intensely active in the world for a number of years and was ready to look inside and try a different kind of experience. There was also a political dimension: after some time in a Leninist political group I realised that I didn't want to be a 'revolutionary cadre' separate from others and 'serving the masses' in a self-denying way. I had been more effective and creative politically when I simply lived my life like other people and let my politics grow out of my life instead of the other way round. Living my life included doing other things I enjoy like gardening, and having a baby if I wanted one.

There were also emotional elements in my decision which were not all rational. It was a rebellion against my bloke, who had refused to have a child all these years and still did not feel ready. 'It's all right for you', I thought, 'you can have a child when you're sixty. It's about time I asserted what I want now!' The situation with him was confused. At this point, as at various times before, we were involved in other sexual relationships: it was a complex and difficult web of interrelationships. Looking back I can see how I denied my feelings in that situation, like believing 'I shouldn't be jealous', 'I should be able to share in all my relationships', and so on. This made it hard for me to ask for what I needed in my relationships. Maybe the baby became, unconsciously, a symbol for those things which I needed – an ongoing closeness, security and a 'special' intimate contact with another human being – which I was ashamed to ask for. It felt competitive, as if I said to the people I was involved with: 'See, you can't hurt me, I'll have a baby who I'll be close to instead.' In that painful chaos I somehow felt I had lost everything else, only the baby seemed sure.

Looking back I can see all these reasons good and bad which made me feel the way I did; at the time I simply experienced a burning desire to have a child. The conception was not easy. People in the collective were unenthusiastic about my having a baby. They did not want the responsibility of another child and found the idea upsetting. I felt surprised, hurt and a bit aggrieved ('I've looked after other people's children, now nobody wants to look after mine'). I did not realise to what extent the mention of babies brought up difficult feelings in almost everyone, reminding them of their own upset or ambivalence about having or not having babies of their own. I felt frustrated at the irony of my situation: for many women who marry young it is difficult to decide *not* to have a baby, whereas for me it was beginning to seem the hardest thing in the world to actually *do*. My bloke did not want to cooperate. When I refused to use contraception, he refused to make love. Angry scenes. I withdrew. Our relationship deteriorated. My other relationship seemed too unstable to carry a pregnancy and baby. I abandoned the whole idea, then found myself unconsciously sabotaging contraception. By the time my bloke agreed to the idea, our relationship was in tatters. It was a mess. When I finally became pregnant it was at a bad time and was a source of upset and disruption for several people close to me.

The pregnancy . . . I can remember the woman in the clinic who carefully sat me down and was surprised when the news she broke with such tact turned out to be wonderful news to me. I felt like dancing as I walked out down the street. That joy never left me, and grew with the baby's first movement, the first heartbeat sound, the first contractions . . . My body felt strange and sensual, as if I had lost my virginity all over again in a different way. Once the pregnancy was established, my bloke greeted the news with joy. But there were also difficulties. I do not think I had ever realised how much the pregnancy would affect my relationships. My women friends felt jealous, or excluded, or replaced, or simply sad that my life was taking a different path from theirs. Several of them were very honest about their feelings; saying, for example, that they were afraid the baby would be a rival for my attention and I would have less nurturing energy to give to them. Some friendships were built on the understanding that she had a child and I didn't, and my pregnancy upset the balance. To share my feelings about the baby I found myself spending more time with women who, like me, were pregnant. During the early months of the pregnancy I felt exhausted, headachey, very vulnerable. I could no longer cope with the tensions, the stormy highs and lows of multiple relationships; the other people involved also found the situation increasingly difficult. After a few months the child's father and I found ourselves back in a monogamous relationship, and the pregnancy was tinged with the pain of separation. It also became clear that no one else in the collective wanted to live with the baby. The only person who was really willing and able to be close, to share the physical experience of the pregnancy and early months, was the father. We found ourselves pushed back on to one another at a time when things between us were very shaky.

I loved carrying the baby, and felt healthy and strong during my late pregnancy. I prepared for the birth and survived without taking any drugs. It was excruciatingly painful and I was disappointed that after a period of my pushing, the hospital staff swooped in and pulled her out with forceps. The feeling was a mixture of shock and triumph as I lay there finally holding in my arms an amazing breathing Buddha-like toothpaste-covered child. But for all my experience looking after children over the years, I had not been able to imagine what it would be like to come home with a small baby. For all my debunking of the 'perfect mother' myths, I had a lurking fantasy that a pink haze would spread over the first months of my baby's life. Instead I moved into a strange netherworld. After forty-eight hours in the hospital, I came out feeling that I had been away six months and everything had changed. In the street things looked unusual and different, as if I was abroad. I have heard that your hormones after giving birth are similar to the pre-menstrual period, and to me this figures. Picture six months of pre-menstrual tension combined with sleepless nights, the physical depletion of breastfeeding, and at the same time a complete upheaval in your life-style and difficulties in all your relationships: looking back it seems like a weird dream. Intermixed in the dream were magical episodes: times of looking at her in her cot and feeling the moment so precious that I wanted time to stand still. Times of charmed contact with her when I wept for joy. But it was all somehow disorientating. The bond with the baby – which again I had not expected – was a blinding, intense physical longing rather like falling in love. It put all my other relationships out of focus. It tugged at my gut painfully as if I was emptying myself of her. Later I read in Castaneda the idea that you give your child an edge of your luminosity which you never recover; at the time I certainly felt that I had had the 'stuffing knocked out of me', as if all the energy which had been in me had gone into her. In the months close after the birth, death also seemed somehow near, and I experienced sudden panics that she might get hurt, irrational fears when I was crossing the road. I felt fragile, emotional. My confidence to act in the world seemed to have vanished overnight. As soon as I was a mother, many people believed themselves entitled to give me (usually conflicting) criticisms and advice about how I looked after the baby. As a 'mother symbol' I became a target for frustrations people had about their own mothers; some criticisms turned out to relate mostly to what they themselves did or didn't get from their parents in childhood. I was often told about other babies who didn't wake in the night and never cried. I badly needed someone to believe in me, to tell me I was doing it okay. Giving so much to her, I needed to be mothered in turn, and missed deeply the friends who had done that in the past. Sitting breastfeeding, or lying awake crying in the early morning hours, I felt my life to be very bleak and lonely. The father was himself tired, disorientated and needy, and we found it hard to give one another enough. Lovemaking was difficult for many weeks because my body felt like a bomb-site. We cared for each other as best we could, we talked and enjoyed our mutual love for the baby, but I had little to give him left over from her. I in turn desperately needed his support but could not let it nourish me; I was afraid of becoming dependent, of losing the autonomy which I had won so hard over the years.

I had not anticipated that the baby would pull us together as much as she did. After his reluctance over the years, I had imagined that I was undertaking the main responsibility for the baby, against the background of the collective, and that he would be a kind of weekend father. But in the event he asserted clearly his wish and right to have an equal relationship with the baby. I found this idea unrealistic and threatening in the early months when she still felt like part of my body and was breastfeeding almost continually. As she grew older the idea seemed a really good one, but I insisted that it meant him doing as much work looking after her as I did. This was difficult: he actually needed support to gain the confidence that he could look after a small baby in the face of his conditioning. We each found it hard to support ourself while doing part-time childcare; money became a problem. I now feel very grateful and appreciative of this sharing, but the struggle to organise and equalise childcare proved a whole new arena for arguments, resentments and involvement with one another. I had not only taken on the baby; I had taken on a whole new dimension in my relationship with him. My free time depended on his baby time, I couldn't arrange to go out without making sure he would be in, and vice versa. From being a free single agent I suddenly found I had to operate as a unit of three. The collective was still a caring and supportive framework, but for complicated reasons was slowly dissolving. At the same time grandparents came forward with offers of love, interest and practical help for the baby. Blood-ties re-asserted themselves. At moments of claustrophobia and panic I felt my situation was becoming that of a nuclear family. There was not enough time, space or emotional energy to put into other friendships. I felt enmeshed in a grey web of tiredness and responsibilities, desperate to clear my mind, to write, to think, to create, to have adult contact: anything to assert my existence outside the small frail world of home and baby.

The picture I am painting perhaps sounds negative, but at no time did I regret my decision to have a child. In the early months of her presence I felt a passionate gratitude, which opened out as I regained my strength and balance into a calm and joyful delight that this child is sharing her life with me. Before the birth, I had some small idea of the burdens of child-rearing ('Poor So-and-so, she never gets any free time from them . . . ') but I had no idea of the rewards. It seems strange that even now some people regard it as 'selfish' to admit that children bring any joys apart from those of self-sacrifice. But they give so much love. And honesty. And tenderness. My relationship with her is sustaining like any close loving relation-ship. And the closeness, which is physical as well as emotional, is different in quality from almost anything I have experienced with adults. I am not denying the daily hassles, demands, con-frontations, boredom, and the times when you feel like murder-ing them. I am not trying to drown the real oppression of childrearing in our society in a flush of sentimental feeling. What I am saying is that there is more to childbearing than is easy to experience in this society, just as there is more to work, to feeling, to sexuality, than the conditions of capitalism often allow us to experience. When we think of having children, we think of isolation, nuclear families, deceptive 'motherhood mystiques', economic dependency, exhausting work; but these are conditions which our society has attached to childrearing, they are not what childrearing is actually about. There is another dimension to it. In other societies it has apparently even been a source of power for women. We can throw out the baby with the bathwater; or we can consciously take on the difficulties attendant on childrearing under present conditions in the hope of fighting through to gain some of that relationship's joy, which is our birthright. I am interested in the ways in which we as mothers are not martyrs saddled with guilt and resentment (which someone will have to pay for later on). I am interested in the reasons why we might choose to have children as a positive choice for ourselves.

Our child was under a year old when we saw the first clear signs that she was not developing as fast as other babies her age. There was a kind of unspoken competition between parents as their children in turn reached various landmarks on the path towards growing up; our baby never even joined the race. I don't know which upset me more – when people kept persistently and over-solicitously bringing it up ('I'm very worried about her', 'She's backward, isn't she?') or when they had tactful discussions of 'the problem' behind my back. They said I was hard to talk to about it, and were surprised I wasn't more anxious; was I being admirably calm or was I just blanking out? Having a handicapped child seems to remain one of the great unmentionable subjects which none of us could approach clearly. Though she was not walking at eighteen months, or two years, I still felt she was just a slow developer. I did not want to be pitied, nor did I want to be bullied into taking her on round after round of hospital tests, though I did. I felt pained at the playgroup as she clung for support while babies half her age ran, jumped and climbed. I felt irrational anger at her: why had she come out 'wrong'? I felt humiliated by the endless tests and cross-examinations at the hospital where they treated her as an 'interesting specimen' and me with contempt ('You're not married, are you?', 'Do you *play* with your child?'). My heart sank at the idea that she might really turn out to have some physical malfunction; my sister has a handicapped child and I had some small idea of the pain in watching your child not fulfil herself, the anxiety and the back-breaking work. But all the hospital tests turned out clear. After eight months with a good osteopath she started to walk and is slowly but surely learning to talk, toilet-train and so on, many months behind her contemporaries but still steadily gaining ground at her own sweet pace. People still sometimes talk to me about her 'development' in a special hushed tone of voice as if it was a dreadful affliction to have a slow child. But I do not feel it that way. In our family children tend to be very quick, intelligent and over-verbal. When I was a child, I won attention by being precocious: I sought to be accepted for my achievements rather than for myself. I had feared that my child might be the same. But she is so clearly the opposite, and in her measured flowering, her refusal to conform to external expectations, I feel a kind of balance or healing for the experience of my own childhood.

Being with her in these early years has often felt like a way of reclaiming and coming to terms with my own early childhood. I have been more aware of my relationship with my own mother. I have felt more a part of the procession of generations, cycles of life and death, the passing of time – those areas of life which are often ignored by people on the Left. Crude Marxism (not Marx) reduces the world to a series of economic and social relations. There is little language on the Left to talk about illness, death, birth, animal life, the natural world, the place of our planet in the galaxies . . . By bearing a child I have lost some of my freedom and some of my pride, but I have gained a deeper sense of belonging to humankind, sharing the human experience as generations of women have experienced it, being part of the world as it evolves through plants, animals and people living and dying over the centuries.

I have also been forced to change. I feel sadder and wiser – but stronger. The toll of childbearing does not end with the lines under my eyes, the stomach muscles which aren't quite what they were, the episiotomy scar which twinges like an old war wound from time to time. It has been a testing experience on many levels. It has involved adapting to real changes in my social identity. I have to accept that I am now a person who sometimes needs to be helped, whether I am getting on a bus loaded with baby, shopping and pushchair, or asking friends to babysit and hating the feeling of being indebted to them. It seems that I am no longer so threatening to men: the baby suggests that I have accepted my role as a 'proper woman' after all. Sexual insults in the street are muted, shopkeepers treat me with respect, old ladies on the bus strike up conversations about their grandchildren. Even though I am not married, to many people I seem to have 'done the right thing'. Among contemporaries, it is more complicated. Many women in the movement are strongly deferent to the needs of mothers as an oppressed group. Others seem to resent the power which children bring, and in their dealings with you clearly wish your child ignored or removed. Sometimes I find myself patronised, or left out of serious conversations as 'just a dumb mother'. Compared with political work serving the mass of people, serving one (very small) individual in a private way does not seem significant. On the Left you are often regarded as handicapped or a drop-out from the real action of class struggle; rarely are you recognised as a person who is doing an important job. These changes in social roles and the way you are treated do affect your image of yourself and your identity. But I have also had to adapt to some basic changes in the patterns of personality by which I live my life. Over the years I had unconsciously developed certain ways of acting and relating which protected me from loneliness, emptiness, despair: things like having a lot of friends, achieving in my work, supporting and 'mothering' other people, being very active, running away when things got hard . . . After the birth, the demands the baby made and the changes she brought meant that I could no longer follow these patterns. I was drained and immobilised. There is no running away from a screaming baby at four o'clock in the morning; you just have to face yourself, to look inside yourself and find what resources you have for coping and surviving. There are no rewards for doing this either, except knowing that you can do it. I felt as if many of my external props had been swept away and I had to rebuild again from base. At the same time I had to start again to rebuild many of my old friendships. I could not escape the reality which stared me rather grimly in the face. I felt tied down, but *by my feet*. I realised one icy morning as I clung to the baby's pushchair to stop myself falling over on the way to the shops: she anchors me to the ground. She grounds me. She has taught me a lot.

My child is now three years old, and the question arises: 'Shall I have another?' I always used to imagine having many children, but at the moment one child seems enough. I am too much enjoying recovering my strength, experimenting with new work projects, watching her strike out on her independent path, willingly to plunge back soon into the misty world of childbirth. I imagine her growing up – a plump schoolgirl, a wilful teen-ager, a self-possessed adult scolding me when I am a silly old woman – and it seems delightful, absorbing, enough, to watch this process with just one child. I gaze with enormous respect at mothers I pass in the street, knowing how much work has gone into feeding, washing and clothing each of her children and herself before she even left her home. And yet one day I expect I will feel the desire welling up in me again with an undeniable sureness, and I will know as clearly as I did the first time around, and as clearly as I know in all the big decisions in my life (leaving a job, ending a relationship), that the time has come when the way I need to move and grow is by having another child. I am less clear in what situation I might have one. I did not have my first child in the most ideal circum-stances, but I can put this down to my inexperience and ignorance of what the decision meant. Now I have to take more responsibility for choosing or creating a good environment for a second child to enter. One child is one more person, but two children seems dauntingly like a decision to 'settle down' and produce a 'Family'. Do I want to perpetuate indefinitely our present life-style living together as a couple? We share a lot of love in the relationship, and I have come to terms with some of the restrictions. But the idea of living happily ever after with two point four children (family holidays, breakfast round the table like in the ads . . .) fills me with horror. Several of my friends who are separated do a good job of bringing up their children split between two homes; but this does not seem an ideal option to choose at conception. And watching a friend who had her baby completely single-handed I have been impressed by what a very heavy undertaking that can be. What other choices are there? My thinking turns back to collectives, seeing the resilience of friendship and loyalties from that time.

But the collective childsharing seems to work better with slightly older children who can develop strong relationships with other collective members, and are rewarding to look after; babies do not seem able to know many adults at once, nor is changing nappies and waking in the night rewarding for non-parents outside the baby's small range of intimacy. It seems that the situations which we need to have babies in do not exist. If we wait for the 'right' circumstances or the 'right' time, we could wait for ever. For all the difficulties, and for all my own confusion, I feel certain that at some point I will have another child. The whole experience has been too amazing not to enjoy again in my lifetime.

Barbara Hanrahan is both a novelist and a printmaker. She was born in Adelaide and studied printmaking in Australia and then in England. Her prints have been shown in Australia, Japan, Italy and the United Kingdom. Her books are: *The Scent of Eucalyptus* (1973), *Sea-Green* (1974), *The Albatross Muff* (1977; reprinted by The Women's Press, 1978), *Where the Queens all Strayed* (1978), *The Peach Groves* (1979). She is at present living in Adelaide working on a new novel.

Barbara Hanrahan

My father died when I was a year old and my child-hood was spent in a household of women. My mother was the elusive one, who smelled of Blue Grass perfume and wore her hair in a Victory roll and went off each day in the tram to draw wirelesses like Aztec temples and tiger-striped lounge suits — she was a commercial artist in one of the department stores in Rundle Street. Nan was my grandmother, a big lady who was happiest in her garden, whose pale mouth kissed good-bye when I went to school and turned Cyclax cerise to welcome me home. Reece was my great-aunt — the small person with eyes like a Japanese spy who swept the floor and boiled the hankies and cried 'Cease' if I talked too much (she was a mongol, but I wouldn't have recognised the word).

Adelaide was home. It was a little city that seemed full of statues. Pale Venuses and bronze Amazons smirked coyly in the Botanic Gardens; Robbie Burns was outside the Public Library; explorers were frozen in hero poses about the Queen who lent Victoria Square her name. It was a proper place in the forties and fifties. Matrons clutched raffia baskets in their white-gloved hands and waited to meet others exactly the same on the Beehive Corner at the dot of twelve. Lunch would be ham sandwiches with parsley garnish at Balfour's, where the waitresses wore butterfly caps and fig-leaf aprons.

Magic was everywhere. I walked down Rose Street to school and each house – Ricks' with its tortuous fretwork trim and romantic garden of weeds, Wrights' with its sinister verandah and moist green fernery – had a personal history; each crack in the asphalt was part of the plan. The bell rang and we marched into school and Miss Cox, the Grade Seven teacher, was a hundred years old and had hairs on her chin; at lunchtime we sat under the peppertrees and shared out bites of our apples and told each other what we'd do with our lives. Janet was going to be a spangled lady in a circus and ride one-legged on the coal-black stallion's back. I'd rival Sonja Henie on skates in a short skirt that showed my pants. It was allowable to dream, anything could happen: we were only children.

Yet, even then, in the primary school playground, I was conscious of my difference from the girls about me. Home for me meant three women; in my family the roles were reversed. My mother was more truly my stylish big sister; the part of Mum was played out by Nan; Reece, with her myopic eyes and starfish fingers, her lisle stockings and shell-stitch cardigans, could be made to play any part I chose – the Japanese spy, the handmaiden who brought me breakfast in bed. I was glad my father had died. It was comforting to know reality couldn't get him, that the photograph album's Irish face would always stay young and fresh.

It was an original life. I sat at table with a book propped before me; I read my grandmother's *True Confessions*; there were no secrets. When you had a baby the pain was awful; men were dirty buggers – you should never trust them. I sat on the slatted seat under the fig tree, and my grandmother put her head in my lap and I nipped at the hairs above her lip with the tweezers. She yelped in pain and Reece started to cry. I slept in the sleepout in a bed that was twin to my mother's. For a while her cigarette would glow in the dark – I was asleep before she stubbed it out.

44

Because I was a child, I was a person; nothing was expected of me, I could be true to myself. The girls at school were people, too. In Grade Seven, twelve years old, we were big and brave. Menstruation was only a word you whispered; it could never happen to you. Boys existed, but they didn't really count.

Everything changed when I left the primary school. Suddenly I wore a uniform, the last remnants of childhood faded away in a dull haze of navy blue. There was a headmistress who spat as she told us that young ladies did not run, that we must wear our straw hats in the street (though it was permissible to remove your blazer in the heat-wave). At speech days they called us the Mothers of Tomorrow: it was a technical school, and you were taught how to mash potatoes into tidy pyramids, how to smock a baby's dress to perfection. Now Janet and I practised shorthand. Sonja Henie and the spangled circus lady were forgotten – it would be interesting being someone's secretary.

My mother remarried and the old perfect life came to an end. We moved from an inner suburb to an outer, new one. Now there were no desert ash trees springing from cracked asphalt; no Milk-oh, Ice-oh, or Golden Crust baker. All that, and so much more – old trees, old roses turning to briars, old ladies in dusty black – were exchanged for lots of little pink babies. New mothers wheeled prams across plushy lawns sprung from closely scattered seed.

It seemed like a different country. My mother had married a man with a moustache and a Returned Services League badge and two little girls, and now we were a proper family. Things were different; there were rules. You said 'May I leave the table?' when you finished your tea; you were supposed to call the strange man Dad. But I couldn't do it – a man was funny, it was odd to see them together in bed: they compromised by letting me call him Uncle. And you couldn't say what you thought any more, and at night the grown-ups quarrelled – it was being part of a family; there was a car, now, and a fridge and a television. It was living a proper life – neat and clean and normal. Reece's belly rattled at meals and you felt embarrassed. She didn't go with the new things. She was too strong, too potent to fit into a regular way of life.

I side-stepped shorthand and typing by turning into a student teacher. Adelaide, 1958: Queen City of the South, where God plays fair and villainy doesn't venture, but is conveniently engaged elsewhere (maybe wicked Sydney or Melbourne, though usually overseas). In Adelaide the Union Jack flew over Government House and you walked to the teachers' college in your royal-blue blazer with the flaming satin-stitch torch on the pocket, your briefcase swung against your leg – but when did you begin to live? What did the lives inside the books in the college library have to do with you? D. H. Lawrence had lived a life that was different from yours – somehow he'd broken the rules.

The ladies I'd grown up with were different now, away from the old street. My mother was linked to someone other than me. My grandmother looked older, shrunken. Amongst all the glossy new things, a mongol was someone to be hidden away.

I learned to be a teacher; I went to dances at the Palais in my fake fur cape and ballerina. The first dance where I sat alone all evening was terrible. Afterwards, at the railway station, pausing by the chromium refreshment counter to check the platform, I realised I'd never be safe again; never exist free if I went on with this game that all the others played so well. A game where you satisfied your mother and Vanity and someone called *them*: a game calling for coquetry and pretty dresses, little steps and a smile upon the mouth to secure the price of popularity – a boy. It was then, for the first time, that I felt the burden of being falsely female, and knew what it would be like to play by those rules. Yet pride wouldn't let me call quits.

I wasn't strong enough to hurt those I loved by setting myself physically apart from all those little Adelaide lives about me; yet I wasn't strong enough to betray the child I'd been by forgetting the old original life. I solved the problem by neatly dividing into two. I taught in a school five days a week in my sheath frock and high heels; I came home and wiped off the lipstick and wandered in the garden and read my great-grandmother's books. Bits of bridesmaid's fern pressed to tissue-paper frailty fell out as I turned the *Girl's Own Annual*'s pages. Inside covers like that I found a world that suited me exactly. The

46

juxtaposition of the concrete and the immaterial was fascinating; under the whimsicalities and Willy-wetleg pieties was a harshness I could relate to, a cruelty — little white girl is constantly threatened. Surrounded by pressure from the people I loved to lead the conventional life they'd failed at themselves, I was saved by a fantastic world. Art and poetry came out of the books' inconsistencies. I liked my angels weighed down in marble; I relished the marvellous absurdities, the hypocrisies, the terrible extremes.

I was saved, too, by the art school on North Terrace. Three evenings a week I'd walk towards the domed Exhibition building covered in Virginia creeper. In the printmaking class I could forget the rows of identical redbrick houses with their pocket-handkerchief lawns and hairy-stemmed Iceland poppy borders. Suddenly I had something to spend my secret passion and boldness upon. I felt as brave and free as I had as a child, when I drew my own imaginative world upon the litho stone or scratched at the etching plate with my needle. One night I walked from the class along the dark Terrace, past the War Memorial angel to catch the nine o'clock train — I wore gloves to hide my fingers that were stained with ink, I carried a folder full of my prints — and suddenly the feeling of freedom came stronger than ever before, and I knew I'd escape the smallness of the city and the lives about me; that somehow I'd be strong enough to be myself all the time. That night I knew that art was what I cared about most; that because I cared enough to be dedicated, I would be put in the way of living a life that was really mine.

I blundered on: I taught, I worked at the prints, I read; occasionally I went out with nice boys in sanforised shirts. In the Regent or the Majestic lounge I played my part well. Sometimes the agreeing little-girl voice surprised even me — was I really going to wear that diamond cluster . . . and become a Catholic for the sake of the kiddies? It was ridiculous, of course — eventually I'd write them a letter. The 'No' was always easier to say on paper. For I knew, though I wouldn't admit it, that the marriage, the child, had never been meant to be mine. That world of happy families was more of a fantasy than the one in the Victorian books.

At night I'd cry, for I didn't understand myself. I felt guilty, ashamed. There was no one to help by pointing out my difference. Loneliness, the Depression, years of playing at dutiful daughters had made my mother and grandmother afraid of recognising their own originality, their difference from those about them – how could they help me? There was only my ignorant, unstated, belief in myself, and in the feeling of freedom that came potently now and then through my work, and which I felt linked up with what I called God. I didn't want to marry anyone; I didn't want a life as soft and dulling as the lives that surrounded me. I remembered the old untidy, uncommon life with longing. The garden, my mother and Nan and Reece as they were in the beginning seemed part of a lovely dream.

Slowly, the realisation grew that my real world could only be an inner one; that a real child for me could be more truly created by making contact, spiritually, with the child I once was. The decision made, that art was what I cared about most, I felt quite positively that for me to compromise, to sacrifice that art to something else, would be wicked. It's an unfashionable idea today – the artist as hero, but the writers I have related to strongly – like Lawrence, Katherine Mansfield, Virginia Woolf – have been people who have made their work the most meaningful thing in their lives; their artistic integrity has been absolute.

When I had taught long enough to save enough money, I left Adelaide for London. I believed in myself as an artist, but I had no idea what the outer circumstances of my life would be.

London meant freedom. From the first, from my reading, it seemed a familiar place. I loved the stimulation of a huge city, the anonymity – the way I felt small and unimportant. I was no one, and because of this I came alive, I had a chance to explore myself; I wasn't pinned down and placed because I had an image to live up to. I loved the city because, once known, its vastness was never dull or flat, but could be broken down into endless fascinating detail. Fantasy was everywhere. I found the greyness and grubbiness invigorating after the healthy mediocrities of suburban Australia. The extremes of living I'd always been drawn to were all about me. I relished the basement bedsits, the crumbling Shepherd's Bush stucco. It was the year people played the soft sad Beatle tunes and Marianne Faithful sang 'Yesterday'. How lucky I was. I had a silver dress and I'd seen snow and been in the Zambesi Club at Earl's Court.

I cared about art – when I was alone with my etching plate I was strong; but outside the art school's easy camaraderie I was vulnerable. The women's magazines' glossy pages sometimes seemed true – even in London. I was still weak enough to feel something was wrong with me because I was different. There were days when I was stalked by all the falsely feminine phantoms; when time ticking on was my enemy. I was an artist, I knew, but even art couldn't make me fit in: I seemed more serious, dedicated, than the others at the school. When I was strong, aloneness was stimulating; when I was weak I wanted to be part of a pattern. I was twenty-six; the magazine ladies (really, I didn't think of them as women) were different from me. At twenty-six you were supposed to be married. That little pink baby I didn't care for could still reach out to taunt me in London – didn't a baby make you a proper person? Art was the only true thing in my life, but wasn't it shaming that I spent Saturday night alone?

I was still a half thing; I kept on pretending. Regularly, I put on my silver mini-dress to court a fate I didn't want.

And then I met Jo Steele, the man I have lived with for the past twelve years. For the first time I was with someone I respected as much as myself. He was from Adelaide, too, though his background was different from mine. He hadn't spent Saturday arvo at the Odeon matinée, or barracked for Torrens at the footy in a blue and gold beanie. School for him meant St Peter's College, Adelaide's equivalent to Eton . . . all his life he'd been a misfit in an Establishment family. From his earliest years he'd reacted violently against rigid family pressures that had sought to restrict his physical as well as spiritual development. He was always in rebellion; his hands were scarred from the home-made explosives he'd experimented with as a child. He was an engineer who drove a racing-car at weekends.

Our life together began in a tatty flat in Fulham. Now and

then I'd wonder about marriage and all the other happy-ever-after predictabilities – the old worn-out ways of thinking were a habit. But I sought the conventional reassurances with little feeling; really, the phrases came automatically off my tongue.

Together, we each became whole. It was important that we both came from the same small city – we understood each other and all we'd left. London was necessary for us both. Jo's life in Adelaide had become so reactionary that he'd built up enough momentum to propel himself far enough away to be able to find his true self and values. The drinking, the racing-car, the friends who were part of the old way of life were dismissed; his false hardness dissolved. The pressures of conforming that had made him rebel were removed by a big city's vastness; he rediscovered the gentleness within himself. His strength, his blunt refusal to compromise by treating me as a lesser person – someone to placate with easy promises and half truths – got rid of the dangerous saccharine insipidities, the glib banalities that so often imprisoned my mind. Life became heady. We were a pair of people who lived together, yet we were individuals who were separate, who realised that our first faithfulness must be to ourselves. It was stimulating to be treated as an equal. All Jo's early romantic attachments had culminated in matrimonial pressure and expectancy – the girls had never been strong enough, individual enough to match him . . . he was the sort of person their mothers had warned them about: when the girls started yearning for soft options the relationship ceased.

I became strong enough to voice what, in the past, I had only unconsciously felt. I stopped paying lip service to all the crippling conventionalities I'd never really believed in. It was as if through our life together, I cancelled out those times when I'd been untrue to myself. I stopped caring about age and all the other falsities. That phantom proper woman who had never stopped shadowing me, shaming me, was finally wiped out. In a big city it is easy to be alone. Through isolation Jo rediscovered himself; I began to read again, I remembered. The Adelaide of my childhood still existed inside my head. In London, while snow flew at the pane, I recalled the quince tree by the fowl-house, the geranium by the lavatory . . . Nan put cucumber peel on your forehead in the heat-wave, Reece made a perfect Japanese spy . . .

It was a romantic existence in that dusty room with its brass bed and unlikely chandelier, its threadbare Indian rug. We were free; we were adult enough to know decisions had to be made. It wasn't enough to leave things to chance – Jo was gentle, but a realist, too. Where I'd come gradually to the realisation that a child could never be part of my life, he'd determined the fact early on. The family structure with all its expectations, the pressures of an older generation to live on through their children and grandchildren were the epitome of all he loathed. A child would turn us into a family unit; the constant complementary interchange of thought and stimulation that was so important to us would be reduced to a lower level by the addition of family concerns. Jo held fiercely to the child he'd been – really, though in the beginning we'd only sensed it vaguely, we were alike. We knew we weren't fitted by something deep and basic in our natures, by the examples of family life we'd experienced, to be cast as parents. The attendant accessories that are part of having a child were unnatural to us, abhorrent. We wanted to live a poetic life, therefore it was necessary to be realistic. It was only logical that Jo should choose to have a vasectomy.

Because we were together, responsible only to ourselves and each other, our lives were able to change and broaden. Jo gave up engineering and was accepted for a degree course in sculpture at a London art school. I began keeping a diary.

I wrote in it each day – long letters to myself, inner explorations, descriptions. The diary was my friend and confidant; writing became a habit. As well, I read. Unconsciously, I identified more and more with writers. Heroes have always been necessary in my life. In the Hammersmith Library I discovered a host of strong-minded people I could link myself with.

Then, in Adelaide, my grandmother died, and a flood of childhood memories surfaced. The old world seemed so real that it was unbelievable that, in a physical sense, it no longer existed. Without deliberate planning or decision I began to write of the old places, the old people. I created a child that was more truly my own that any other might have been, when I recreated myself. I wrote without thought of publication, it was something that had to be done. I was writing for my grandmother, my mother and Reece. Eventually it was finished, and I found that, without meaning to, I had become a writer. *The Scent of Eucalyptus*, a memoir of my childhood, was published in 1973.

So many young people jell young; early on they limit their expectations. The girls who were so alive at twelve are old and deadened at twenty. Jo and I have both developed slowly – we have been so many different people on the way to finding ourselves. Because the life we have chosen is lived largely alone and apart; because we do not regard the newspaper world as the real one, we have been left free to develop at our own pace. For both of us, the real world is an inner one; we refuse to be fettered by an ordinary, accepted vision. We are two people who exist harmoniously together; we share out the tasks of our common life. One respects the other. We are both free to be as dedicated to our individual artistic aims as we wish, to explore them at the deepest level of intensity.

Only since we have distanced ourselves emotionally from the crippling influences of our past has it been possible for us to return to Adelaide. It is a different city now. Some of the old things are still there; much is new. Adelaide is a dream city. Our pasts are everywhere, yet they have no power to harm us. The rich natural world of Australia has proved wonderfully stimulating to us both creatively. Yet London with its vast resources, its humbling enormities, its variety of lifestyles is essential, too. Together, we have found it possible to achieve the freedom of physical movement which would have been impossible for us with a child. We have decided to set up bases in both cities.

When I tried to be the same as the people about me, the world ceased being original, Adelaide shrank smaller. I was lost in a hostile, foreign place. I have found through my prints and writing that the true world is the one that travels with me, inside my head. I have found that mere chronological age doesn't count: the true artist is as fresh at seventy as at twenty.

Writing is my religion. At its best, what I create should be a bigger thing than myself. The task of creating needs discipline, sacrifice. If I had chosen to have a child I would be a different writer; for the type of writing I strive for, and the intense concentration over long periods of time that is necessary to achieve it, a child would be a handicap. It is not what I was meant for, or equipped for. I work for those times when what I create is powerful enough to stand by itself, without relating directly back to me. To achieve this sometimes is rewarding; it is what answers the need in me that other women fill with a child.

Katherine Mansfield, Virginia Woolf, Anaïs Nin, Flannery O'Connor, Jean Rhys, Christina Stead, Janet Frame, Eudora Welty are all writers to whom I relate. They are all dedicated women whose lives were lived out, are being lived out — sometimes against their will — without children. It is an insult to these women and their work to judge a woman who has produced a child and writes, too, as somehow being more whole. We would never apply the same notion of wholeness to the male writer — it is allowable that he should be childless.

Yet I am fascinated by the structure, by the strangeness and absurdity of family situations. I love writing of others' real worlds which are my fantasies. But to do this I must be apart; I must be free enough and alone enough to remain true to the child I once was, that I am still. Because I do not mock it, because I do not forget or replace it with another, the child in me remains alive and strong. It is the source of all my creativity.

Spes P. Dolphin: 'I was born 37 years ago in the midwestern plains of the US. Although I live in England now, I am most at home near the sea and mountains of Oregon and British Columbia. I love being on the water, growing vegetables, women, dogs, children, photography and fighting the System. I have supported myself by a variety of jobs from teaching literacy to carpentry. I almost always live with groups of women in the country.'

Spes P. Dolphin

In one of the first women's rap groups I belonged to we had a discussion in which every woman in the group expressed the desire to give birth to and raise a baby — except me. I felt very strange as I had in fact given birth to a child and given her to another woman to raise. I stated my experience and was met with silence — to savour my oddness alone.

Both of my grandmothers died in childbirth, although I did not know this as a child. At any rate I only occasionally thought of raising children. I was always going to do great feats when I grew up like being a famous scientist, the first woman on the moon, or a professional baseball pitcher. I grew up around boys and identified with the things boys do. As the oldest of three girls I helped my father out doing the more physical things on our land like roto-tilling the garden, helping to build our new house and cutting up wood.

I do remember having a mental picture of myself raising five children who were adopted. So I can guess that I must have had negative images of giving birth. I can't remember my mother talking about childbirth, but perhaps there was a repressive atmosphere around the whole issue of sex and having babies. I don't think that either of my parents really wanted to be parents. They took care of us quite well, but I think on some level my mother wanted more from her life than just raising children. Neither of them subscribed to psychologies of child-rearing and, living in the country where I could roam freely without them fearing for my safety, I had a lot of independence.

During high school and university I had various intensely emotional relationships with women and none with men. After university I joined the civil rights movement and from 1964 until the end of 1965 I lived and worked within the black community in the Delta in Mississippi and in 1966, in the Cree Indian community in northern Saskatchewan, Canada. I shared the lives of these peoples – their poverty, hopes and fears – as we struggled together to change their conditions for the better.

During this time I was part of a group that was questioning everything about society – political power structures, racism, poverty, the ways groups are organised. Questioning about sexuality went so far as to say that everyone could/should sleep with everyone else regardless of marital status or race but, of course, no one ever considered or hinted that men could sleep with men or women with women.

Before I was part of what came to be known as the New Left I had felt tremendous pain and total isolation as one after another of the women I cared about fled from our closeness to look for the socially approved safety of relationships with men. Nothing in our upbringing in the fifties in the midwestern Bible Belt had prepared them to challenge the assumptions of their parents and teachers. We grew up in the town next to the later infamous Kent State University and in the seventies one of Portage County's two judges was to proclaim that the county had no homosexuals. Fleeing this milieu, seeking to lose my isolation and feeling the pressures of the 'movement', I began to try to be 'normal' and to enter into sexual relationships with men. This was so alien to me that when I was actually raped, while hitch-hiking to a nearby city, I didn't really distinguish the experience from the other cold-blooded sexual encounters I was having. And I never even considered that I might get pregnant — so, of course, I did.

I was living and working in northern Canada. Two months after the rape I had missed two periods. I saw a doctor and she did a test. When she said I was pregnant I got very scared and angry and said, 'Well, I'm not going to have this baby.' She said, 'Yes you are. Abortions are illegal.' I ran out of her office yelling at her: there was no way I was going to have this baby.

I talked to women around me and met one who had had a legal abortion and who told me how to go about it. I was able to find two psychiatrists who would sign statements saying I needed an abortion for my mental health. In the hospital a doctor examined me and found that I had actually been pregnant two months longer than I had thought. Naturally I was very confused. It turned out that I had had two periods while being pregnant.

I freaked out, celebrated my twenty-fourth birthday and got a ride 1000 miles west to Vancouver, BC, as far as I could go. Knowledge of the suction method was suppressed in North America in 1966. I wasn't willing to take the risk that an illegal abortion would have been at this point, even though I'd found a friend to lend me the money.

So I just kept hoping that somehow the birth wouldn't happen. I went horseback riding and hoped I'd have a miscarriage. I thought that it didn't show until I saw a picture of myself in a bathing suit. I didn't even think of applying for welfare. I marched to the US border on Hiroshima Day to protest the involvement in Vietnam. I kept on ignoring my growing belly. Eventually a woman friend came to visit from the States. We became lovers and she helped me to face up to the fact that I was pregnant and to eat better.

My new lover left and I felt my isolation again. An older couple I knew came to visit from the prairies and I returned to Saskatchewan to live with them.

Winter comes early in the prairies and it was quite cold. My pregnancy was by then six months along. I got on welfare by chance. A doctor I had finally gone to see gave me a number to ring up to start the procedure for adoption, and the next thing I knew I was on welfare. I continued to be involved in fighting against the war in Vietnam. I took a few courses at the university, typed theses, and took lots of long walks.

I was totally immersed in political movements. I still believed that the revolution was coming any day. Since I had left university my life had been intertwined with the struggles of communities of very oppressed peoples. I expected that involvement to continue and did not see any way that having a child would allow me to do that. Being pregnant and raising a child was a total disruption of my life. I must have thought about it before I returned to Saskatchewan because as soon as I got there I talked to some friends who, I knew, wanted to adopt an Indian child.

When I had discovered that I was further advanced in my pregnancy than I had thought, I realised that the father of the child was a Cree Indian. That seemed even harder. I had a distressing picture of my illegitimate child having a hard time growing up in 'legitimate' society. I imagined that a half Indian child would have an even harder time because he/she wouldn't really be accepted by either culture. (I actually assumed the child would be a boy – I think because subconsciously I couldn't even consider that with all these other disadvantages she might also be a girl.)

I wanted whoever adopted the child to have some knowledge of and pride in the Indian heritage. So I did talk to this couple, but they wanted a child the age of their own daughter who was then nine. I then wrote to an Indian couple I knew who had adopted a child. There were also quite a few young unmarried white women who wanted my baby. This was a dilemma for me. I wondered about the single women as I felt they didn't see the long-term commitment and were carried away by the idea of having a tiny baby. I didn't think any one of them could raise a child any better than I, except that they weren't gay. At this time I accepted the myth that homosexuals are sick. I was ready to live with this sickness, but did not feel that I should raise a child. Also it seemed to me too hard for *any* woman to raise a child alone. I didn't see many alternatives around me in 1966 in the prairies. It was quite straight in a lot of ways. I had known a lot of black women who were raising their kids without men, but they had their mother's help.

Some part of me was putting myself in another category from these other women – just as I never thought of getting on welfare, although I'd helped many women apply for it. I was still a product of white, middle-class society, in which an unmarried mother is to be condemned. It had never occurred to me to have my mother help me. I hadn't even told her I was pregnant (and it was years before I did tell her).

In black communities women who do not raise their children themselves, or at least give them to their mothers, are seen as inadequate. There isn't a stigma of illegitimacy in these communities. For women to raise their children, rather than giving them to the authorities, is seen as a necessary survival technique for maintaining the race in the face of threatening genocide. Through the institutions of poverty, the courts, welfare laws and police violence the power structure is trying to reduce the numbers of peoples of colour in North America. I know it is a big problem for the Indian peoples particularly who too frequently have their children stolen (all legally, of course, often for their lack of an indoor toilet) and raised to be white.

As for choices, there are many women in third world communities for whom raising children is an occupation and an identity. Generally speaking they don't have the options that we white educated women have. A black woman in Mississippi isn't likely to go much further than being a maid or working in a factory, so she might as well raise kids and have something to show for her life. Me, I can dream about making films.

For most of my life I hadn't seen myself as fitting into white society and I also knew that as a white person I didn't fit into Indian society. But I did want economic security for the child and so I felt apprehensive about letting my child go to the Indian couple who were really poor. They were in a starvation situation in which too many people were fishing from one lake. I knew they loved kids, but I felt that I would worry for the duration of her/his childhood that she/he wasn't getting enough to eat. I had never had more than enough money for myself.

One day the woman I had originally approached about adopting the baby rang me up and said, 'I have these friends who want to adopt a baby and I really trust them. If anything ever happened to me, I'd want them to raise my child.' So I went over and met John, whom I'd met during a previous political encounter (we were on different sides). Later I met his wife – and in the first minute I knew she was the right person to raise my yet-to-be-born child. Laura related a similar experience of being an unwed mother, which made me feel at ease with her as she understood my situation and had no judgements. She already had four sons and had tried unsuccessfully to get pregnant again. She loved being around children, bringing them up. She was involved in helping native women form a weaving co-op using traditional Indian designs and I could really feel her strong connection with Indian peoples, particularly the older women. It was quite a relief to have finally decided who would take the baby.

Meanwhile I had to deal with the legal bureaucracy. My social worker insisted that I couldn't decide for myself who the baby's parents would be. According to good social work practice the mother of the baby should never know what happens to the child and the child should never know who her/his biological mother is. She said that what I wanted to do would mess up the child's life. I might decide to take the child back or the adoptive parents might want to give her back to me. But she did tell me I had the legal right to do what I wanted.

The birth was terrible. Besides various bureaucratic hassles in the hospital because I wasn't married or a Catholic, I asked to have a picture of Jesus taken off the wall in front of me when I was in labour and they were very offended. But the worst was the pain. I had grown up thinking I was impervious to pain and had assumed I wouldn't need any drugs. I quickly found out that I was wrong. When I did ask for drugs it took them a long time to get any to me. Finally, I went to the delivery room and the doctor who had originally refused to give me an abortion was there to deliver the baby. I felt helpless and battered. They strapped me down and wouldn't give me anything to drink until I 'pushed harder'. The birth itself felt like having a large bowel movement. Then, it was over. I had been through a lot of pain. I had been in labour for fifteen hours.

I was awake for the birth, but because I was strapped down I couldn't see the baby. I asked to see it and I saw that she was a girl, not very dark. Then they took her away. I went to a ward with three other women who talked incessantly about their husbands, other children and Christmas presents. I persuaded my doctor to get me out after two days. The baby had to stay because hospital procedure required all babies to be watched for five days.

Laura went to the hospital to get her, but in the end I had to return there to sign a form officially identifying her as the correct baby – to protect the hospital from lawsuits for giving the wrong children to the wrong parents. Of course I didn't know what she looked like any more than Laura did. She got the baby and took her home and on Christmas Eve I flew 2000 miles east to forget.

In Toronto, despite the fact that every movie I chanced to see and every book I chanced to read were about unwed mothers, I threw myself into renewed political activities, including one of the first women's liberation groups. We produced pamphlets of what feminist literature was available in 1967, wrote some polemics ourselves and campaigned vigorously to change Canadian abortion laws. My lover eventually came to live there too and we were as happy as we could be considering that no one was supposed to know we were anything more than room-mates. We both thought we were wrong to be homosexuals (neither of us would have dreamed of using the word 'lesbian' in those days), but I was determined to try to live with my disease. She still wanted to escape it. We were both highly paid supply teachers and had our own flat – a change for me from years of sleeping in other people's living-rooms.

Because Laura and John were not quite the ideal couple (in what I imagined to be the eyes of the adoption agency) I was still afraid they might not be accepted and I would get the baby back. I still might have to take the baby before a judge and state, 'I relinquish all claim to this baby to the Province of . . .' – a horrifying prospect. I didn't want her to be given to nice, respectable, middle-class folks.

Every time I saw a child who seemed about her age, I would wonder if she looked like that. I worried that she might not be happy, or healthy, that I might have made the wrong decision. I didn't actually see Penny again until she was three. Once I saw her and knew she was happy, I didn't worry about my decision any more. I wasn't feeling any 'motherly instincts' or any great loss that I had experienced this birth and the child wasn't there, but I did decide not to take a job that would have filled my life with children. And I did have pangs when I saw her with Laura and realised I was just another stranger to her. I had fantasies of her coming to see me when she was in her teens and wanting to know why I had given her up. I hoped that I would be a success-ful person and that she would be glad to know I was her mom.

The next time I saw her she was six and seemed a little dis-appointed that I didn't do my hair up and wasn't more feminine. I've since learned that six is the dressing-up stage of little girls' lives. When I saw her two years later we talked about her being adopted. She said she felt 'a little funny' about it. Laura and John had adopted another Indian girl about a year after Penny and had told both girls that they were 'special' because they had two moms. Penny and Diane both like this.

As for the legality of the adoption, it hasn't seemed to matter. No one has ever asked Laura for any papers. Once we went to the welfare office together to sign the forms and the workers were so stunned that the 'real' mother and the adoptive mother were together that they couldn't find the forms. Laura wanted to adopt both girls at the same time, so one summer I helped her find Diane's mom. I think that the adoption has gone through by now.

During the time that I was making these biennial visits to Canada my political interests moved from working within the women's movement in the cities towards finding the means to provide country bases in which women can learn new skills, breathe fresh air, grow our own food and take better care of ourselves. A small group of us came together to start the first women's land trust, and one year later we made the down payment on a lovely 150-acre farm, open to all women and children who want to visit or live there. Penny and Diane came to visit during our second summer. They were eleven and ten at this point. I was very excited as for a long time I'd wanted them to visit me and be in an all-women environment. Because there were a great many women and children staying with us at the time, some with vastly differing needs, we set up a girls' camp on a river in the nearby mountains with seven girls between the ages of two and eleven, and ten adults. Four of the children were Indian and one a Chicana; three had been adopted.

Penny really loved being in this environment. She loved doing what the adults did and was the most faithful attender of our sometimes endless meetings (circles). At first she stuck close to Diane but eventually she realised that the other women could take care of her sister and struck out on her own. She got quite close to one of the women in particular.

But Penny and I felt shy with each other. We don't have any models to look at to see how to be. I think we were mainly appreciating each other from afar. We went rafting; I showed her how to take pictures; we went camping on the coast with Diane and another woman, and to the city to be around some more kids their age. A lot of my old friends reinforced my new feeling of being a 'mother' and talked about how Penny and I looked and moved alike (interesting, as we've spent very little time together). I started thinking that I would like the two girls to come to live with me for a year, sometime before they are sixteen.

I had wanted Penny to experience one of the cultures of the women's movement because in her remote home environment she is constantly exposed to the assumptions of nuclear family and heterosexual relationships in school and the media. I was afraid she would automatically become a suburban housewife. Now that she's had a sampling of another way of life I hope she will be better able to make her own choices.

Penny will also have to cope with her mixed racial identity and decide whether or not she will try to meet her father. She is now thirteen and I imagine old enough to make her own decisions about meeting him. He never knew I was pregnant and I have no idea if he still lives in the same community.

If I had been pregnant in the context of a strong women's movement – even five years later – I might have done many things differently. I might well have kept my child if I'd had support for doing so from other women. I would certainly not have felt so alone and isolated during the pregnancy. I did not really talk about it or how I felt about giving up the child at the time, so I had to make my decisions with little feedback. I would have known about eating wholesome, natural foods rather than supermarket plastic and would have used natural childbirth methods. I would gladly have skipped the hospital experience. But as things are I am happy with the choices I made and that I have the chance to share in my daughter's growing up to some extent without the restrictions of constantly caring for another being.

For the last ten years I have lived with children both in the city and (mostly) in the country. I have had a great deal of experience of helping to raise other women's children which has aroused mixed emotions. On the one hand there is the joy of being with children without being tied down; on the other hand, the biological mother still has the power to decide to take the child away with her and often seeks to control how others relate to the child.

During the two years we've had the open women's land many women have arrived ready to change their relationship with their children. They have wanted to stop being a 'mom' and become a friend to their children. After many struggles about the necessity and processes of collective childcare, the caretaking collective of the farm now assumes that all children are cared for by whoever is living there. This change seems to be quite good for both the mother and child. Other women are there to meet the child's needs and the mother can experience the freedom to spend time with her child because she *wants* to. This might result in nights of a child screaming for his or her mom, but eventually the child learns that any one of a number of women can give her/him support and loving – and to give and take these things with the other children as well.

As one of the 'non-biological mothers' I have experienced the frustrations of being told how to relate to children by their biological mothers (sometimes in conflicting ways by different mothers). I have also had the more painful experience of getting really close to a particular child who is then taken away from the farm by her/his mother and I have no idea when and where I might see her/him again. Separations like these have at times led me to be closed to other children. At present I am trying to be open to whatever children I am with and somehow accept the temporary nature of these relationships. Sometimes I have wished that the biological mothers would listen to women (often long-time lesbians) who have made the choice not to have children, and would respect our reticence about assuming responsibility for the child of another woman who has made a different choice. Even more, I wish they would see the security they have with their children and the insecurity we non-biological mothers have about the children's movements and emotional ties to us, especially as they change and grow so quickly away from us. But despite all these frustrations (and I know the biological mothers have some also) it does seem to me that collective childcare is the best answer for women wanting to raise children without losing their identities as individual people. I now know that revolution is a long time coming, and that learning to raise children in new and creative ways is an essential part of that struggle.

JILL POSENER

Stephanie Dowrick was born in Wellington, New Zealand, in 1947. She left New Zealand in 1967 and now lives in East London. She has worked in publishing since 1972, has written two books and is founder of The Women's Press.

'My work for this book has been deeply inspired by Adrienne Rich's beautiful and important book, *Of Woman Born*. I am also grateful for the inspiration and love of my friends and, towards this subject especially, to Luise Eichenbaum who listened with such care.'

Stephanie Dowrick

Motherhood, inside the patriarchy, is bound by institutional forms. As a revolutionary, committed to the liberation of women and the overthrow of the patriarchy, my relationship to motherhood is very special.

I want to have a child.

I don't need to have a child to please a husband or cement a marriage. I have no husband; there is no marriage.

I don't need to have a child to give my life a purpose. It is already filled with purposeful activity: work, politics, friends.

My family have no expectations of me as a mother-person. My friends do not expect me to confirm dubious notions of womanliness by childbearing. On the contrary, I see their picture of me much more clearly as a childless woman, an attentive midwife at the birth of books.

The choice to have a child is mine alone. The luxury to have a child to please only myself is real. The privilege is mine; the work will be mine; the support — financial and physical — will be mine. I hope others will love my child and the more complicated person that I will become. But in the dark of night and in the light of day, it will be up to me. And why not? I want to be filled to the limits with pregnancy. I want to stretch myself with motherhood beyond any proscribed group of activities which the world might call enough. I do not want to choose between work, lovers, a child. I want everything.

It is precisely 'everything' that the patriarchy has forbidden us to have. Even next-to-nothing has sometimes seemed too much. The choice between madonna (good virgin mother) and whore (woman daring to take a place in the world) is a non-choice. It binds us tight. A few roles, all active in nurturing the male, are called 'natural' by the patriarchy. They have become axioms for nature itself. In the name of nature, laughingly called mother, the patriarchy has delineated and diminished our lives from birth to death.

Those among us who would seem to have had more choice (access to money, tortured and expensive though this access may be; access to self-determination, hard won though this always is) have, still, to a greater or smaller degree internalised the gritty messages of the patriarchy. Brigitte Berger is quoted by Adrienne Rich in *Of Woman Born* (p 58) as saying: 'Until now a primarily masculine intellect and spirit have dominated in the interpretation of society and culture — whether this interpretation is carried out by males or females . . . fundamentally masculine assumptions have shaped our whole moral and intellectual history.'

So, the patriarchy tells us — and enforces via its institutions of church, state and culture — that:

we cannot be good mothers alone

every child must have a father

without a husband, a woman's child is not legitimate.

Children are, in patriarchal terms, property. Property may, properly, be handed only from one man to another, even if a female channel is used. A woman alone cannot make legitimate her 'property'/child. The growth of the child within the mother and the child's journey through the body of the mother are not enough. They are in fact as nothing when compared to the journey a woman makes up the aisle to be joined to a representative of the patriarchy. Without this joining, she is unfit to be a mother, her child is outside the laws and protection, so-called, of the fathers. The price she is required to pay — whatever her degree of volition — has often been as high as life itself.

When we can act consciously against the patriarchy, when we can move towards self-determination using the light of female experience and values as our guide, when we can work towards the creation of a society based on those female values of life giving and respect for life, then we are making a revolution.

I will not make a revolution by having a baby outside patriarchally approved limits. However, feminism has given to me the vocabulary, the confidence, the examples to understand that I can approach motherhood on terms which seem to reflect my own reality: that motherhood is not synonymous with marriage and dependence on one hand and poverty and shame on the other. Each of these leaps of understanding, each *action* based on that understanding, diminishes the power of the patriarchy, loosens its bullying grip, is a step towards creating an alternative to a most *un*natural order of things.

My reality is that I want to have a baby. I want to work. I *must* work. I have worked constantly since I was sixteen, to support myself and to find my place in the world. At no level could my becoming a mother mean the end of work. I will have a child to support, a self to support, in all those ways of which financial is only one.

It is not my mission, my destiny, to be a mother. In the choice between mother and whore it is impossible to know if motherhood is ever destiny. In choosing to be a mother I am not, I hope, a victim of biological determinism. I would prefer to see it as a conscious act of gainful adventure. But I don't know. As we begin slowly slowly to throw over aeons of male control, there are so many more questions than answers. We are throwing our voices to each other more and more clearly, opening our lives out wide. Our messages are louder, hurled over back fences, tossed from street end to street end, carrying across oceans. Our common experiences join us far more surely than our differences separate us, yet still our corners of freedom are only corners and none of us is free while so many are shackled by the daddies.

But where I can take charge of my life, I will. I do choose to become pregnant. I can yet be foiled by nature (oh mother) but not by the rules of the fathers. I want to be judged, if at all, by women's understanding and experience of my choice. Even after I am dead, I am told, a father in heaven will decide whether to take me in or toss me out. The judgements of the patriarchy are harsh, and unfit to shape my reality.

My inspirations for motherhood come from women. My pictures of motherhood come from books, from talking, from art, from listening, from watching. My sister's experience has specifically inspired me. She has not experienced motherhood in an especially safe harbour but the positive flow of love and pleasure between her and her sons, whom I too have found so easy and rewarding to love, has given me confidence in my capacity to love and sometimes filled me with an envy that I long to replace with the complicated emotions of motherhood. One does not understand the indefinables of sexual love by reading and watching. It takes practice. In that same way, loving my nephews is not enough. I want to experience motherhood with a baby of my own.

When I was thirty I learned to swim and to drive a car. The further I have moved away from a distorting and unconfident adolescence the more rapidly my physical confidence has grown. My relationship to my body has also changed profoundly since I ceased to anticipate or care how I was being viewed by men with their strange and once intimidating judgements. My daily world is a world of women. I now see myself through the eyes of women whose ideas of beauty and strength are – when undistorted by the competitive censorship the oppressed are taught to wield with such effectiveness – unexpected in their breadth, disarming in their unexpectedness.

I like myself; I like my body. I am delighted to find new strengths still unfolding to me. As my mind and spirit grow stronger, so does my body. (We are one.) I expect to enjoy harbouring a life inside my strong body. I expect to like the life my body produces. My spirit of adventure has never tingled more forcibly than since I gave myself the freedom to acknowledge that I want to have, and will have if it is possible, a child. I seem to have wanted it forever, but am liberated by my acceptance that an ideal time will never come. I will not get rich. I will not have more friends eager to help. I will never, ever *have time*. Now – or when I become pregnant – that will be the time. It has to be. My sense of adventure is fuelled by self-love and curiosity and carnal longings for baby flesh and smells and sounds. I want to combine pleasure of the body and mind. My body will change, so will my life as I give my baby life; and she will be making a mother out of me.

Why would I want to be a mother when this is the role which has so concretely expressed and reinforced the dependency of women, which has led to the intertwining and infantilisation of women with their children?

Because I believe it can be different. We are truly victims if we cannot create those new realities. We are undone unless we break those rules which can and do make of motherhood a prison and a burden. I would be undone if I had to forsake the rest of my life as a price for motherhood. The twigs of a nest would soon rub me raw. I want to expand my limits by having a child, not reduce my world, no matter how precious my fellow-occupant. I must work. I want to organise an environment in which care and love is given to my child by others. There is no single person in the world, no matter how beloved, with whom I could possibly contemplate an indefinite, unbroken togetherness. Nor would I wish myself on another with that same excess.

I have role models to encourage me. My mother taught and I moved between home and her school as two naturally linked environments, learning from both. My grandmothers also and always worked. One combined the labour of groundbreaking New Zealand farming with the labour of pregnancy and birth eight times over. The other bore three sons and gardened from morning until night in the nursery and floral business she ran with her husband and, after his death, alone.

I want what is familiar: work, politics, relationships. Out of these known familiars, out of my body increasingly known to me, I want to create what will be only in part familiar: my child. I hope to be open to whatever transformation this synthesis of the familiar and unknown brings.

This chosen journeyer through my body, this unwitting co-conspirator against the rules of the patriarchy, will not spring from my cells alone. She will not be the product of concentrated thought, parthenogenesis or cloning. She will be made up not only of the cells and genes of my pioneering foreparents, but also those of her father.

There has never been any doubt for me that she should have a known father. Artificial insemination is not a choice I could accept. I have no reasoned thoughts on this. Words come to mind: fear, vanity, lack of history . . . but more powerful than that, I want my child to have another parent. My arguments against the patriarchy are not arguments against men as actual or potential parents, nor against those women who choose to live with men. I do, however, believe that too few men are willing to foresake being fathers in all those ways which allow the patriarchy to flourish, to be duplicated and reinforced in countless households and outside them in the world at large. The basic institution of sexism remains the family, with father at the head and mother and children in a lump together dependent on father's goodwill. There are other ways. There are some men joining our efforts to find them.

I combine a passion for life with a high regard for and aware-ness of its fragility. I have no belief in my immortality. I do not want my child to experience a world in which she can depend only on me, to fear that in losing me she would find a world empty of anyone who really cared. I want her to learn to know and be known by those friends whom I love. Among them will be her biological father. He may or may not be especially close to her. Loving him as I do I hope it will be so, but that will be a choice each of them will make. He is my chosen fellow-traveller into parenthood but his life — lived abroad — may be less changed by this event which means so much to me. With ten years of love and mutual interest behind us, I see him as clearly visible in this adventure. I look forward to seeing in the child reflections of the man, and loving those reflections. Without him my desire for a child would be still-born. It is clear to me though that the *force* of the desire is mine: it is to please myself. I have still to learn what it will mean to us separately, and in our relationship to each other, to be parents of the same child. I have still to learn what it will mean to the women who share with me not biological parenthood, but love and interest and vital commitment to the changing realities of my life.

In considering the decision to become a mother, I have also been considering what it means to be the child of a mother: first, I am a daughter. For three-quarters of my life my mother has been dead. The space she vacated when I was eight remains empty. I feel my connection to that space as part of my daily life, shaping but not misshaping it. I have tried to fill it up, more recently with my increased knowledge of and love for women, women at large and also individual women, valuing their connection to her and to me. I have memories of her, good and bad. I was not powerful when she died and experienced acutely my lack of power to protect her from distress, from death itself. I beat against the dragon of disaster and the scales of the dragon were untouched by my hand.

She has danced in my dreams, my mother. The space she vacated on one side of me was balanced by the waiting space on my other side, waiting for my child not yet born. We have danced together in my dreams, my mother, my self, my child. When my child is visible, real in the world's understanding of the word, then my relationship to my mother will change again. I do not want to *become* her by becoming a mother, but I expect to increase my knowledge of her; I would welcome that.

The strength that I have contacted in my developing relationships with the living and the dead is real. But it does have dents. I am writing these words on papers of different colours. The confidence that I express is hard won. The neatness of my situation is self-built and the foundations have yet to be tested.

I have a house. There is room for a child.

The mortgage company is an insatiable monster. Suppose the roof needs replacing?

I have a job. I can pay for childcare. I can continue to work.

Suppose the Press collapses? What if the baby is ill and needs me full-time? I may be too exhausted to combine work and motherhood. I am already so often so tired.

I live in a working-class neighbourhood. There is community feeling. People will help me out.

My child will be different. Their ranks may close against me, against her.

I have always been loved. I expect my change in circumstances to be accepted by those who love me. I expect to have a lovable child.

I may change for the worse. My fantasies involve a healthy child. My reality could not incorporate an unhealthy child.

My family will understand.

This time I'm going too far.

My act of reproduction is consciously chosen. My sexuality is not about reproduction; the two acts are distinctly chosen, even when harmonised.

I will be alone, unloved except by the child, discarded by others who have loved me as a non-mother. In choosing reproduction I will lose my sexuality.

I put some yellow paper back into my typewriter.

The curious thing is that although I can summon the voices, order their chorus, they do not convince me. They buzz around my ears but don't go in. In my guts – in my waiting womb – I contact different voices, joining me to a uniquely female experience, a potentially joyous female adventure. Those are the voices I give credibility to. I add my own. My baby is not my entrance into the world, not my raison d'être. I am inviting her to share with me what is precious: my life. I anticipate with pleasure that the sharing will be mutual: that her life may be open to me too.

Friends ask, with concern: 'What if your baby is a boy?' My real voices know that I would love my child, not *anyway*, not as an acceptance of second best, but with caring for individuality and determination that with a boy too I could share much, including my passion to change a world which has such little regard for women. And not love him only as a potential revolutionary, spooning texts into his mouth along with rusks. I want to *learn* from my child, whatever its sex; to play with, fondle, feed . . . whatever its sex. I could more easily accommodate a girl into the life I have consciously structured, but what I long for is a healthy child, a child who will like me and respond to my concerns, who will want to share and create, whatever its sex.

This last realisation was a big step towards knowing that it is a real child that I want and not a second fresh self. I had a dream in February 1978 which was important. It came to me the night before the first Women's Press books were to be published. In my dream I was sitting up in my bed, lots of cushions behind my back, giving birth. At the end of the bed stood a caring woman, all grey, indistinguishable features but familiar to me and clearly there to show care for me. There was no real fuss or strain at this birth. I am – awake – a total coward, fearful and resentful of pain. I was conscious, in the dream, of real satisfaction at how little fuss I needed to make and how much in control I felt. The child was born, quite quickly. It was a boy, creamy in colour, who lay rather still. I was calm (I, whose emotional range is considerable) and got ready to deliver the afterbirth when instead a second boy was born. Again, he was quiet; again, very creamy in colour. I feared that this stillness indicated that the babies were dead but my grey protector signified mutely that this was not so. The birth of the second baby took me by surprise. I was not unhappy, not at all, but realised that having had two boys I would never have the daughter I had always expected. That was simply how things were to be.

The grey protector entered a dream on a second occasion. This time I fled from hideous chaos and desperate confusion as a fire raged and found her alongside a lake, holding what looked like a tray of dead babies. But on the tray, one baby was alive and she gave that one to me. I felt she was entrusting it to me.

The significance of those dreams has felt considerable, but

especially that first dream. It is 'real' to me that I was so unafraid. I am happy that I could accept so quickly the sex of both children. I have considered the symbolism often. I was, after all, metaphorically giving birth the next day to a project which was, to date, my most important work: The Women's Press. But why two boys then, not one? Why boys?

My guess is that they symbolise two lives: work and motherhood, that I will grow through my acceptance of each, overturning the patriarchal scale of justice which would allow me work if I accept lesser rewards and would joyfully give me motherhood in exchange for submission to its institutions and abandonment of my independence. I will have to breath life into both lives. They will be inert without my energy. They don't come to me full-blooded and kicking; they are, however, alive.

The symbolism of giving birth to male children seems to represent a positive surprise, rather than the usual attributes given to the appearance of males in the dreams of women (strength in the world, worldliness and so on). I have made contact with those strengths within myself. I intend to bring them to my practice of motherhood. I practise them in testing situations, fearful enough of invisibility to shine up my visibility with conscious effort. To stretch this image of surprise a little further: I knew that I was giving birth and at that time would only have expected to give birth to a girl. I work to create order in my life but am learning to accept and welcome a new understanding that sometimes my most creative moments have come when the order allows something to emerge which I had not looked for, felt capable of, or even expected.

There are no adventures without surprises.

Sara Maitland

This is a love story.

Like most good love stories it is about disillusion and compromise and joy. Much of what I have to say is highly critical — of me, of my daughter, and of the society which forces guilt, inappropriate behaviour patterns and grief on both of us — and despite all this I want her, and the world, to know that this is a love story and I love her. In fact she is the great romantic love of my life. As I strongly disapprove of romantic love, I do not feel complacent about this: but I know that the feelings I have for her respond more nearly to the women's magazines'/mediaeval poets'/religious mystics' descriptions of love than anything else I have ever felt. I find my daughter movingly, passionately beautiful: when I see her running naked, or coiled sleeping, I feel something which is not (I hope) lust, but alarmingly akin to it — a physical delight and recognition and excitement; and a desire to elicit from her an equal response. And I like her: for her energy and tenderness and sturdy independence; for her wit and intelligence and her passionate sense of her own selfhood.

Sara Maitland, who was born in 1950, is a writer and, among other things, a Feminist and a Christian. She was part of the collective that wrote *Tales I Tell My Mother* (Journeyman Press, 1978), and her first novel *Daughter of Jerusalem* (Blond and Briggs) was published in 1978. Currently she is reviewing for *Time Out*, publishing short stories where and when possible and working on a book about Women and Christianity. She lives in London with her daughter Mildred and her husband who is a parish priest.

As with the most traditional romantic love there is a darker side to all this. My daughter draws out of me other responses, which I hate: some of these are personal between her and me; some of them are between me and my world. She has changed parts of my understanding so radically that I have difficulty recognising the person I was before she was born. She has forced upon me an unwelcome self-knowledge; she has made demands on me which I resent fiercely. She has opened up painful and apparently unresolvable differences between me and my husband, and has affected all the other relationships I have, even with my closest woman friends. She has forced me to confront dark places in my own soul — my desire to possess, to own; selfishness, or egocentricity; real doubts about the purity of my past loves, past actions. And above all she has compelled me to feel both an anger and a bleeding impotence about the position of women in this society, such as I never truly felt when I was far more 'on-the-street' politically active than I am now. I have been obliged to recognise in myself feelings about biology and gender difference and social relationships, which I was able to evade in the years before she was born, and which I cannot analyse away into the accepted modes of feminist orthodoxy. Emotionally, psychologically, politically, socially my daughter has forced unwelcome changes on me. I feel bullied and victimised — intellectually, emotionally and practically — in precisely the ways I swore I would never be by any man. And I chose that oppression, and do not regret it; indeed I embrace it with love and joy.

I find little real support for these confusions within the women's movement. We are getting better at the practical support and articulation of the bad sides of motherhood, but we do not really seem to be coming to grips with the reality of that painful, wonderful, destructive, liberating love that many of us feel for our children. I am left, apparently isolated, swinging impotently between the old poles of romantic love — a desire to be with her, alone with her on a desert island, to cherish and love her forever; and a mean darkness in which I never want to have to see her again: a painful biting furious tedium which makes me scream and snarl. Oh so intolerably different from that rich, carefree, generous, liberated motherhood I espoused before I met her.

So why did I get into all this in the first place? Why did I, in the face of being told that marriage and motherhood were the symbols and actualities of women's oppression, choose to have her? Certainly she was conceived and born in a blissful ignorance of what was to follow. But it was a clear choice: by the time I stopped taking the pill and started consciously to try and get pregnant it was what I determinedly wanted to do. I lusted after a baby almost exactly as I had lusted after beautiful lovable adults. I wanted a child, a family of my own, someone to need and want me; and also I wanted to do that thing, called pregnancy and childbirth, with my body – my own beautiful and brilliant woman's body. I saw having children as an essential part of my deliberate and clear plan for my own life.

I had spent about seven years running as fast and as far from my own childhood as I could. I totally rejected the social milieu, the religion, the family structures and the hieratic morality of my infancy. I wanted to be a great writer, a 'real' feminist and a sexual libertarian. The year I was twenty-two I stopped short; the same year that I had my first short stories published, I also became a Christian, got married and conceived a baby. The events are in chronological order, but in fact they all go together absolutely and were culminated and completed in pregnancy.

Looking back now, I know I had been searching for a situation in which to have a baby for several years. The painful conflict between rejection of my family and the longing for one landed me briefly in a mental hospital and also in a number of infantile relationships in which I selected (male) victims to lavish my maternal urges upon. I was saved from this destructive and not very original course by the women's movement, and by a woman who demanded more from me than all that, and who loved me and taught me that there were better ways of securing love than by reducing other adults to infancy. She also changed my sexuality into a joy instead of a weapon, taught me how to laugh at myself without too much self-hatred; would not tolerate disguised or sloppy thinking and indeed bullied and loved me into some semblance of adulthood. I loved her, and I still do. She and the women's movement began to show me the extent to which I had deceived myself and others, how tough and sane I could be if I wanted. But I also learned then a dangerous and deceptive optimism: that I could claim control over my own life; that we were free and had 'A Woman's Right to Choose'. I could be a writer and a lover and a politically active person *and* be a mother if I wanted to. For the first time I was able to become conscious of how much I wanted a baby – as a legitimate sexual option, and a new person in my life who would grow naturally through dependency, loving me without having to be trapped there as I had trapped, or tried to trap, adults. I realised very strongly that this was something I wanted to do a lot, as much as I wanted to be a writer, and there was no reason why the two should be mutually exclusive. This newly articulated desire was one of the things that broke up the relationship. I know that there are gay women who manage what we could not manage and I admire them – but I could not have done it then. Perhaps it might have been possible if I had been content to think of one child, but with my own special gift for exaggeration I was immediately thinking of a brood. I was in fact, although I did not know it, thinking of my own childhood family, which I believed I had spent all these years working out of my system. If this sounds like a simple regret that I am not still gay, it is not meant to; but I come to recognise increasingly that what society would like us to see as a pure, inspired 'love choice' of sexual orientation or life partners is so complicated a thing, so tangled with other desires, sexual and social, that we must be always cynical about that magical 'falling in love' which is supposed to justify the most preposterous social arrangements.

I met a man who, although not politically active himself, was gentle and open and supportive and who himself really wanted to be a father. He offered me a new sort of heterosexuality, a new sort of religion and potentially a new sort of family. The three went very closely together: I am often asked if I became a Christian just 'because of him' – luckily this is not a book on 'Why Faith' because I do not fully know the answer to that yet; but certainly we have had a very profound effect on each other's thinking and understanding, we have been able to offer each other truths – or what we believe to be truths – that we could neither of us, perhaps, have received from anyone else. What we did first of all was, apparently, make possible for each other a whole range of fantasies and hidden desires which we had both previously thought we would be forced to abandon. Blinded by a recognition of each other we were perhaps not as honest or realistic about ourselves as we should have been, but there was a lot of love going for us – as there still is.

Reader, I married him. And for us, with our brand of religious faith, we both believed that heterosexual love meant sacramental marriage and sacramental marriage meant parenthood. At least we were spared the problem of making two separate decisions about it.

I really did believe that I would be good at motherhood. I liked children; I liked caring for, nurturing people; I felt I was now sufficiently tough not to be conspicuously bad for a child; I was interested in childraising and the politics that surround those aspects of women's lives; I had a father available, willing to participate in all of that; I had a very demanding physical urge to be pregnant. I must also have believed that there were thirty-four hours in every day; that I had the concentration and tenacity of a bulldog; a special saint instead of an ordinary lovable man; and the maternal instincts of the Primal Earth Goddess. I think I did believe all that actually: I did think I was pretty special. I thought I was Superwoman.

I was brought up in a large family. My parents had five children in the first seven years of their marriage, and another one later for good measure. We were planned, wanted, loved children. That family was the centre of our emotional life for an unusually long time. We knew we were all hot stuff: we needed little emotional support from outside; in the last count there was no one so able, charming, clever and emotionally committed to each other as we were. We loved and fought and grew within an arrogant and emotionally charged community. Even now I feel one of the most difficult things about living with my husband is that he really does not enjoy a good fight; does not get any emotional titilation from brawling with the people he loves.

And that was the family I wanted. I did not want the Victorian discipline, the Presbyterian moralism, the sexual repression or the closed front (probably precisely the elements which held the whole unit together); but I wanted the intimacy and emotion and energy. I quite seriously planned to educate my eight (I had to do things more extremely than my mother, of course) proposed infants all by myself, which I deftly rationalised as a desire to keep them from the corrupting influence of capitalist, sexist society. I would breastfeed them till they weaned themselves, teach them to read before they were toilet-trained, and be a *very creative* mother: educational play, and natural spontaneity and long rambles in beautiful woods. I was going to bake bread and boil soup on the back of the stove and be a great writer.

I got pregnant within four months of marriage. I was thrilled. My happiness was endorsed by my husband and enough of my friends for me to ignore the warnings of others. There was an added bonus which I had not consciously been seeking, but which had probably appealed to some sneaky part of my psyche: I was miraculously restored to my mother's love, and approval. I was having a baby: for her that meant I was a good girl and a good woman. Having, in her view, been neither since I was fifteen, I basked in this new state of affairs.

About one thing I had been absolutely right. Physically I loved being pregnant. I loved my own body in a new and cherishing way. I liked its new shape — I bought pregnancy clothes long before I needed them. I felt well and bodily contented. I do find pregnant women very beautiful; here was one image of female, traditional beauty to which I could conform. I was also high on pregnancy: far from losing energy and gaining weight I reversed the standard process. I was extremely active. Spring 1973 was the time of the anti-discrimination legislation campaign and I demonstrated and marched down Whitehall and sat up all night talking about it. In Oxford we were setting up new, more locally-based women's groups to cope with the growth of the movement. I met other feminists who were pregnant or already mothers, and found a concrete encouragement. We were most of us University-connected people:

middle-class, intellectual and, above all, in an environment where we had not just the inclination but the time to be sisterly. I had spent most of my independent life in this sort of atmosphere – and my childhood in one where there was at least the money to buy the next best thing to sisterhood: paid childcare. Intellectually of course I knew that this was abnormal, but emotionally I had no context for realising what the lack of it might mean.

I do wonder now if some of my energy and certainty sprang from a desire to vindicate my choices: I could be a feminist and a mother. I could be happy and liberated and active and still be married and pregnant. It was emotionally necessary to me to justify myself. I lost over a stone while I was pregnant and was certainly tired by the time my child was born so perhaps this high was neither as natural nor as healthy as I thought. But I was happy, and had no conscious worries. Or only one: I wanted a girl. I still do not know entirely why, but it was clear in my mind: it was a daughter not just a child that I was wanting. I never actually expressed the feeling, 'I don't want a boy'. I was simply absolutely certain that I would have a girl and I never considered the alternative. I know still that if I had had a son I would have been profoundly disappointed. I never put this into any context with the continuing conviction that this was just the first of many pregnancies. It never occurred to me that I would be freakishly lucky to pull off a girl eight times in a row.

The most exciting thing that has ever happened to me, physically and emotionally, was giving birth. Although it was not a technically easy, nor a remotely painless delivery, it was and remains one of the high points in my life. I was lucky: the maternity provisions in Oxford were very flexible. I had a general practitioner delivery, with my own non-interfering GP and a wonderful feminist midwife. I had some supportive natural childbirth classes, run by a non-fanatic, who never made me feel 'responsible' for the success of 'her method'. (And I do know women who found that this fear of failing their teacher totally ruined their own experience of birth.) My baby was also born on a quiet night at the hospital, so that I felt no pressure to 'get on with it', or that anyone else might be needing the personnel and time that I was consuming. Because of the relaxed approach of my midwife I was not shaved, was free to walk about and choose my own pace, position and responses. My husband was wonderful: never made me feel guilty about him, or tried to claim the emotional energies of the situation. All these things cannot be estimated in terms of what contribution they made, I know they were important; but I also know there was something completely internal: I felt very committed to labour, strong, in control in one sense, and carried away by the pure strength of my body in another. The actual moment of birth was the ultimate orgasmic experience of my life, completely demanding and completely satisfying. My husband put this naked triumph into my arms and she reached for my nipple with extraordinary spontaneous enthusiasm. Something happened to me right there on the delivery table that I had never expected, especially after all the properly given warnings: I fell in love. It was absolute, sudden and total. Not with a baby, not with an abstract plan for my life. I fell in love with Her. Because our cord was not cut until she was breathing naturally there was no screaming, no violence. We were allowed, all three of us, to celebrate her birth — with whisky, cigarettes and cheers — in a way that most delivery staff do not seem to allow. We were also given a lot of peaceful time together without being moved. Again all these things certainly contributed to our early relationship, but I do not believe that they fully explain the very powerful and passionate delight that I felt.

I was 'in love' with all the stars and glitter. I was also confirmed in my ideas about myself — I was a neat mother, I loved my baby and she was happy, beautiful and well. I gained an immense confidence and security: I did not need to isolate myself from the world. I wanted everyone to see how good I was at this. Before she was three weeks old my baby was travelling round the country. I felt confident enough to feed and change her as publicly as I needed to; or to leave her with other people, or let them share in caring for her. This confidence was enhanced by the fact that it was I, and only I, who could feed her, and I loved doing it. We had this very special thing going together, so we could afford to let other people have relationships with us as well.

I was also in a very strong position socially. She was born in July and her father did not have to go back to college until October. He could not work because he was an alien without a work permit. This not only meant that he had a lot of time to spend with her, and with me, and with us; it also meant that it was economically vital to us that I should start working again as soon as possible. Although I was working, from home, and only part-time, my work had a real priority in the family: an advantage most women do not have. So we were all delighted, happy, proud. Our friends were admiring and we were complacent. Before she was two months old we were already talking about having another baby; the only hesitation was a feeling that it would be impossible to love another child as much as we loved this one, impossible to do anything as perfect again.

Of course reaction set in. My husband started college and simultaneously my daughter stopped being a sweet sleeping bundle of love and started screaming all evening. The long Oxford summer was over and everyone had other things to do than sit around my house drinking coffee and chatting. I was all alone with her for hours and hours. The man who had shared our house with us for two years went back to America and I missed him, and missed the balancing effect he had had on my relationship with my husband. I was lonely. I was also under stress: it is one thing to stop working to feed a clean and happy baby whom someone else has changed and brought to your desk; it is quite another to have to work with one ear cocked for sounds that will disrupt a smooth morning. And of course she was sleeping less and less, wanting more and more; more, suddenly, than I had ever given to another human being, in terms of time and attention.

I discovered I was selfish and mean, even towards this beloved person. I felt guilty. When she screamed sometimes I could not comfort her even with my warm, milk-filled and loving breasts; I could not make her happy and I felt guilty. My husband was not just out during the day: he came in tired, he had a lot of new things to deal with, and he also started to assert the importance of his work as well as mine. He ceased to be centred on us, and as his day filled up it became apparent that he had real personal difficulties in responding to sudden emotional demands: he liked, needed, to have his day organised. He would do, generously and gladly, appointed tasks, but found it very hard to respond to unanticipated needs. I do believe this is a socially encouraged deficiency in most men, because they do have control in the majority of situations and simply do not *have* to respond emotionally as women do, but it was the first time I had encountered it as a practical problem in my own life. He was also being far more rewarded for being a 'good father' than I was for being a good mother. Even if our contribution in hours had been exactly equal (which it was not) we would still not have had equal childcare, because he was getting so much praise and psychic support for doing simple things which, had I not done them, would have been considered gross inadequacy in me. We fought about this; or rather I yelled at him, he retreated and I felt guilty.

There was another problem. I found to my surprise, and to the shattering of a crucial self-image, that she was, as a companion, extremely boring. I was still reading enthusiastic books about sensory play and early learning, but I could find no corresponding pleasure when confronted with the reality of waving coloured beads under her nose. And she never wanted to engage in these jolly activities between four and six in the afternoon, when I was ready and willing, but when *she* chose. She was selfish, autocratic, demanding. She was tiny, vulnerable and beautiful and I loved her. I was confused and angry and I felt guilty.

Sometimes I would go to pick her up feeling furious and resentful and at the touch or sight of her, I would collapse, melted by physical love and tenderness. Sometimes I would be playing with her quite happily when a complete and profound anger would come over me and I would want to kill her. The confusions began to get out of control and I was frightened. I went to see my doctor and told him that I was suffering from post-natal depression and he said 'Rubbish'.

I am deeply grateful to him. He did in fact say more than 'Rubbish'. He was the first person to articulate clearly that it was perfectly sane to have strong difficulties in adjusting to being a mother. He said that small babies were indeed demanding, annoying and boring. He said it was like marrying a male chauvinist pig, except that one felt bad about fighting back, guilty about either winning or losing. I am sure that he was making an important point. Before post-natal depression was properly recognised I know that women were made to suffer intolerably and feel guilt-wracked failures. But now there is a reverse trend: even sensible worries about concrete realities like housing or money are dismissed as 'Baby Blues'; a definition which can and does prevent women themselves coming to face the realities of motherhood. It is still important to society that we should consent to be nuclear family mothers, and enjoy it. If we are failing to enjoy it, it is easier to say we are poor sick things and some nice drugs will make us feel better, than face up to the fact that mothering is an impossible and treacherous job in our society. Mothering is a job which not only demands a unique combination of management responsibilities, manual labour and skilled work, but also goes on seven days a week, twenty-four hours a day and is completely unpaid, unrewarded, and undervalued. Moreover it is a no-win arrangement nowadays: if you devote yourself entirely to the child, you are failing yourself in your duties to self-development, damaging your husband's frail ego and probably 'over-mothering' or 'spoiling' your child. If you do not so devote yourself you are depriving your child of her/his emotional needs. Either way you are isolated and either way, whatever happens, it is *all your fault*.

The doctor did not himself say all this, but he said enough for me to feel liberated into working some of it out. The problem was put into a context which was not completely private. Another important factor was my husband suddenly revealing, one evening, that he did find that the 'joys of fatherhood' were wearing thin. It was easier for him to say it, but it did relieve a lot of my guilt. The final breakthrough into some sort of self-knowledge and a willingness to tackle the situation came when my daughter was about eight months old: I thought I was pregnant again. The misery and multi-dimensional fury that I felt were so profound and total that they broke through even my powers of self-deception. I had to face the facts: I was not going to make it as an Earth Mother. I sat about dealing with the guilt and trying to find a life-style that would be more suitable for all of us. First I acknowledged that it would have to be me who did it. I could not look to my husband to change himself radically: it was too easy for him, as a man, to escape from the intolerable bits of his domestic situation. Nurturance was part of his occupation, so he could too simply place its priorities so high that he could make me admit that he *had* to be unavailable to his wife and child in some ways. He gets so much support from his colleagues and from society at large that I do not blame him, much, for his evasions. But I had to accept, and it was a painful parting with a high ideal, that the ultimate responsibility for children lies with, and solely with, women. It was me who had to change. I determined to change myself from a lousy, nurturing mother, into something else: a competent, administrating mother.

The whole dream that we had for our life was effectively shattered. Luckily the disillusion was equal for both my husband and me: we were not who we had hoped to be, who we had fantasised about being. We were two people who could not cope with a lot of emotional intrusion into our lives; we both put our professional ambitions too high. We did not want an intense tangled emotionally vibrant life with eight children making demands on us which we were generous and loving enough to respond to. We wanted instead something much more orderly and unthreatening; we both had enormous needs for time and privacy. With this clarity I tried to look at my daughter: first I accepted that at least for the foreseeable future she was going to be my only child. This released a great deal of affection; I ceased to feel that I had to keep some love or time or energy in reserve, that I could adore her and commit myself to her totally without that worry that I would not have any love 'left over' for her little brothers and sisters. I realised that, this being so, it was important for her as it was for me, that she should acquire independence and friendships of her own. The best thing that I could do for her was to orchestrate a life that would provide her with the best facilities for finding social skills. In the first instance this meant a babyminder, meant a search for good nursery schools, meant creating space into which she could bring her own friends. I have learned that it takes great personal and emotional skills to be an administrative mother, certainly as great as, though different from, those of a nurturer; there is nothing to be ashamed of. (I can still too easily be made to feel guilty, worry that I will be found out as 'bad', but I can and will fight that.) There is a price to be paid, by her, for my choices: she has not had that high focus of attention from a single source that small children are supposed to need (although I rarely see that in traditionally 'nurturing' households). At five years old she lacks the skills that sort of attention does develop, early reading or handicrafts for example. But I do believe that, in her case, and because of who her parents are, she has had overwhelming advantages. She is very independent, self-sufficient and sociable. She is verbally sophisticated because of having to communicate with a larger assortment of people. She is accustomed to and flexible about a large range of social situations; from my mother's large country house where she spends part of every summer without me, to the battered women's refuge where she spends both days and nights with me when I'm working, or on her own with our friends there. One of the best things about acknowledging one's own personal deficiencies as a mother, and having faith that one's child will survive them, is that one ceases to expect perfection of other people. Women have said to me 'You've always been so lucky finding babyminders' or 'You're so lucky having a mother you can leave Mildred with'. I do not think that this is luck – once you have admitted you are not wonderful yourself, it is easier not to demand perfection from the other people you 'let' care for your child. I really always did look for the 'best available' knowing I *had* to have someone, rather than looking for some ideal substitute. I do not agree with everything that my mother expects from, or offers to my daughter, but then I do not agree with everything I expect from or offer her either. Somewhere in the variety I hope she will find what she needs.

The best thing, I believe, that we offer her is a model of ego-centricity; the acknowledgement of her parents as people with real needs that we must and will fulfil. I believe that this is a vital survival tool for her as a girl growing up in our society. She must, and at the moment does, demand from us what she needs. We do try very sincerely to fit this into the complicated pattern of our lives. We are a family of egotists, but we need each other in a back-to-back-facing-the-world relationship which is filled with respect, humour and enormous affection.

She has taught me to love her in my own way, rather than in some way dictated by social norms, and I sincerely hope she will be free to return the compliment. She has shown me that our way works, by being happy, healthy and lovable, and by loving me. Because I no longer feel obliged to be 'all-in-all' for her we can develop those unique qualities in our relationship which we both want. We have a great physical togetherness and love, and a quality of indulgence and humour that I value enormously. She is, quite seriously, the favourite person in my life.

But I have bought this really delightful relationship at a price. Above all I have had to recognise that I cannot do it again: I see pregnant women in the street, or cuddle the babies of my friends, and I am consumed with a physical jealousy. I engage in maternity and childbirth campaigns and am desolate that I will not be able to use the facilities I am fighting for. My daughter has confronted me with reality and toughened me so that I will never be able to fall in love again with such an innocent and openhearted joy. I know how much she has cost me in terms of self-esteem: I am obliged to face the fact that I am not Superwoman. I never regret that I had her, when I did and how I did. I never regret the fact that I love her very much – but I also know that I have neither the energy nor the naiveté to love any more people so much. She is the great romantic love of my life.

Brook d'Abreu: 'I was born in 1951, attended a London girls' school and, later, art school. I am a sculptor and a feminist. My life and my art are dedicated to the attempt to create a context for the expression of women's rediscovered wholeness.'

Brook D'Abreu

As soon as she had spoken, the small child realised that she had made a terrible mistake. The rough texture of the cloth and the strange, pungent smell of pipe tobacco told her that her impatient 'Daddy' had been directed not at her father, but at a total stranger. It wasn't the absence of her father that was uppermost in her mind as tears began to burn her eyes. It was the knowledge that she had done something out of place, something unforgivably naughty. The anonymous grey suit which dilineated an apparently familiar adult, male form had seemed a reasonable target for her outstretched hand. But the man's down-turned scowl informed her that it wasn't at all reasonable, as far as he was concerned, and effectively hastened the withdrawal of her grasp from his trouser leg. Why should such an unremarkable error have moved the child to tears of shame? Why is childhood inevitably punctuated by numerous similar incidents which, despite their triviality, are capable of producing a flush of embarrassment when recalled years later, still potent to evoke the painful experience of being small and vulnerable and the wish that some miraculous dematerialisation could remove one from the disapproval and ridicule of adults? But wait: I who was the child am now the stranger, disconcerted and embarrassed by the approach of a child.

Throughout my childhood I can remember adults saying to me, 'Oh, I was your age once too, you know'. The statement was usually backed up by a chuckle that was supposed to sound reassuring but which was invariably accompanied by some sort of nervous twitch. It was difficult enough to believe that it was physically possible that this hulk of a person had once been small. Still, I might have been able to muster the necessary leap of imagination if the adult in question had made the banal comment with even a modicum of conviction. But I always had a sneaking suspicion that the whole idea was equally incredible to us both. It might also have helped if the phrase had been intended to communicate a real feeling of empathy, to affirm the reality and importance of what I was feeling. But all too often it was used as a subtle put-down. The message that came across was 'Yes, I too used to be over excitable, silly and childish but luckily I've grown out of it and it'll be a damn good thing when you grow up and can understand just how trivial and unreasonable your feelings are'. The assumption that adults, through their own experience of childhood, can easily understand the pains and pleasures of a child doesn't ring true in practice. What is it about growing up in our society that makes the concerns of children and those of adults seem worlds apart?

The London suburb where I grew up, though dreary, was rough enough to make street play forbidden and before we reached school age my sister and I had virtually no contact with other kids. My whole world revolved around my mother, whose own isolation contributed to keeping my contact with other adults to a minimum. Having escaped the strictures of paternalistic colonial society, only to replace them with marriage, rather than endure the struggle to survive alone in post-war England, my mother devoted herself to the uninspiring task of homemaking with nervous compulsion. Married to a man with whom she had little in common except the depersonalising experience of war, she remained friendless and frustrated. My father's family, who might have helped alleviate her isolation, only added to it by their inhospitable attitudes. They didn't take kindly to my mother's middle-class values, nor to her threateningly un-English complexion, deeply tanned by years of exposure to the eastern sun. Staunchly working-class and proud of it, my father's relations couldn't include someone so alien as my mother in their ranks and regarded the match as a 'mixed marriage'. My mother compensated for her loneliness by becoming 'housewife extraordinaire', a cleanliness fanatic who hoovered and scrubbed and cooked and cleaned relentlessly and devoted herself to her girls with clinging protectiveness – just like most mothers. Consequently my relationship with my mother, through its very closeness, emphasised my lack of communication with other adults.

Perhaps the aphorism 'familiarity breeds contempt' is appropriate to describe the conventional mother/child relationship. The child sees the mother in a contemptible situation, totally responsible for the child on a practical level but lacking power in relation to the father in his traditional role as head of the family. The child learns to expect what in any other relationship would be considered unreasonable: total attention and self-denial. Such a relationship, which denies the autonomy of the mother so completely, fosters self-centredness and inhibits the development of children's sensitivity to the needs of others. Children are often criticised for their lack of consideration but the capacity to appreciate another's separateness and to be aware of her or his needs is actively suppressed by the stereotypical mother/child relationship. Furthermore, the stifling intimacy between mothers and children forms a paradigm for other 'love' relationships and is to a large extent responsible for the debilitating dependency and selfishness thought to be normal attributes of conventional romantic love. But that's another story – or more accurately, another aspect of the same story.

To return to my own childhood. Despite its ambiguities of class, ours was the archetypal nuclear family, with all the familiar features of this idyllic little unit, so highly commended by our civilisation. The cosy nest (an ugly semi-detached), the happy couple (a lonely, manic woman and her uninterested spouse) and, to complete the picture, two nice children ('rather painfully shy little girls, but they're bound to grow out of it'). Unfortunately I didn't grow out of it. The rigid peer group segregation of school inhibited communication between children of different ages and I remained inordinately shy even with children my own age. My contact with adults, other than my parents, was confined to what superficial proprieties duty demanded of my begrudging relatives, who only ever bothered to address me to say, 'My, haven't you grown.' This gem of adult wisdom, tossed from on high with monotonous frequency, seemed to express the sum total of adults' perception of me: that I had a tendency to get physically bigger. It took me until my early twenties to feel reasonably comfortable with people of my own age; and my childhood unease in the company of adults changed to an equal inability to relate to children when I reached adulthood.

If, then, I look to my childhood to supply an answer to the question 'Why children?' I find little of use. No evidence of the possibility of meaningful relationships between people of different ages, apart from the limiting and overdependent mother/ child relationship; no experience of the process of birth which might provide some insight into my own participation, either as a child or as a potential mother; no acquaintance with mother-hood in any form other than the prolonged hysteria caused by imprisonment in a meaningless marriage 'for the sake of the children'.

Perhaps the Victorian sentiment that children should be seen and not heard has not entirely disappeared. Attitudes towards children may have changed (although, come to think of it, I was allowed to speak but I'm not altogether sure that I was often *really* heard), but everything about growing up in this society still seems geared to keeping adults and children separate and children cut off from a sense of their continuity with the adult world by their regimentation into peer groups. When I try to recall the feeling of being a child, it isn't the unique and mysterious complexities of childish perception which come to mind. On the contrary, it is incidents such as I have described, trivial incidents which recall to memory hurtful, uncomfortable feelings caused by socially determined factors rather than those intrinsic to childhood. Seen and not heard; my memories of childhood are like a mute pageant. I see the cryptic gestures of a procession of events whose meaning evades me. I do not hear the voice of my childhood telling me the secrets of growth and change. In the goal-oriented, linear time of this male-dominated, materialistic society one looks only forward. Childhood is behind and its messages are forgotten. If not to my childhood, where should I look to elucidate the mysteries of generation?

Although my projected husband and offspring seemed to feature prominently in the thoughts and conversation of my relations, teachers, prospective employers, casual acquaintances and even total strangers, they certainly didn't in mine. The world at large may have regarded my biology as my only important attribute but somehow I had arrived in adulthood singularly lacking in all the inclinations and expectations thought to be appropriate to my sex. On the contrary, I had by then developed a strong lesbian identity and serious intentions as an artist. Children in general, let alone my own capacity to conceive, couldn't have been farther from my mind. Instilled with the deceptive individualism of a middle-class education, I attributed my lack of motherly feelings to personal peculiarities of inclination, consistent with being a lesbian and with my aspirations as an artist. All the experience that had informed my adult self-image confirmed my expectation that I would remain childless and for a long time I was content to ignore issues which I regarded as irrelevant to the direction of my life.

Getting involved with the women's movement rid me of the conviction that I was an isolated freak of nature. Through meeting women who felt similarly isolated, I realised that I was not alone in my refusal to conform and that it was men, not women, who had decided that a woman's place was in the home surrounded by children. But even though women's efforts to rediscover their real selves, unfettered by the limitations of socialisation, included the re-evaluation of motherhood, feminist analysis of the problems of mothers seemed only peripherally relevant to my own development. I felt that I had made a choice which automatically relieved me of the burdens of motherhood and my involvement with the women's movement served to reinforce my rejection of motherhood as a restrictive stereotype, inappropriate to a lesbian feminist life style. Being a lesbian meant that I didn't have to cope with the problems of contraception or unwanted pregnancies. I was thereby protected from any reminders of my capacity to conceive other than the monthly rumblings of what seemed a dispensible bodily function. Being an artist meant that I had a purpose to my life incompatible with the activity of childrearing. My interests and circumstances contributed to confining my social interaction with other women to those who had also chosen to remain childless.

Alongside my practical dissociation from children, I developed an ideology which questioned the existence of a biologically determined nurturant impulse in women and thereby ensured that any disturbing hints of motherly 'instincts' in myself could be neatly disposed of under the heading of natural human (as opposed to specifically female) concern for the young, the expression of which I had foregone in favour of a career. Thus insulated by both circumstance and ideology from the concerns of motherhood, I might have continued to ignore my own potential for childbirth had I not been prompted to examine my assumptions in the light of what seemed like a veritable epidemic of pregnancy among feminists of my age. Profoundly afraid that I too might suddenly be overcome by an irresistible desire to conceive as I approached the 'now or never' age group, the problems surrounding motherhood began to assume personal significance. Was I suffering, in some dark and dusty corner of my psyche, the damaging deprivation of a uniquely female experience?

As my concern propelled me, almost against my will, on a painfully revealing journey towards deeper and deeper levels of my emotional responses, I found that I was indeed suffering — not from a lack of children *per se*, but from a deep-seated inability to embrace that aspect of being a woman that is defined by the capacity to conceive. I began to realise that my refusal to identify with the role of mother was nothing so simple as a purely personal disinclination. Although I had never relished the physical discomforts of pregnancy, my acute fear of motherhood could not be explained away by the threat of physical invasion that childbirth poses: the nature and magnitude of my fear suggested that I felt threatened by a far deeper and less specific invasion of my person.

It began to be clear that my rejection of motherhood involved more than a refusal to be defined by my biology; it involved the virtual denial of my biology. My image of myself as a strong, independent woman was in some way inextricably linked to the condition of childlessness. To view myself as a potential mother, regardless of whether I were to realise that potential or not, appeared to undermine the integrity of my personality, as a feminist, as a lesbian and as an artist. I had, despite conscious denial, subconsciously internalised the patriarchal definition of motherhood as being incompatible with a career and with being a lesbian.

I was dismayed to discover that my apparently 'sound' ideology was providing a support system for underlying unsound attitudes. Ironically, my feminism was itself the barrier to perceiving the extent to which I had internalised conventional definitions of motherhood.

Superficially, my reasons for assuming that I would remain childless seemed adequate. As an artist, my creative energy was focused on my work and the demands of childraising would impose impossible limitations on the mental and physical freedom that my work necessitates. I had never considered myself to be cut out for motherhood; I seemed to lack the qualities to which children respond with warmth and ease, and always felt somewhat confused and often irritated by their presence. But these are precisely the excuses men have used to justify their non-involvement with childraising and to perpetuate the myth that childcare and work are mutually exclusive activities. It is only under male dominance that motherhood is a full-time occupation demanding absolute commitment, and it is convenient to the mysogynist intentions of patriarchy that women who decide not to bear children continue to accept the idea of motherhood as a vocation and to view themselves as exceptions.

The view that *not all* women are destined to become mothers and that their biology should not exclude them from stereotypically male preserves, though on the surface 'ideologically sound', fails to challenge the view that mothers are bound to be mothers above all else. The assertion that not *all* women are destined to be defined as mothers implies that *some* women are. The false logic that defines women by their capacity to bear children and identifies motherhood as the ultimate expression of femaleness is essentially the same whether it is applied to all women or just some. Although I had mouthed platitudes bemoaning the lot of mothers, arguing that childcare should be shared, that the nuclear family is not the ideal environment in which to raise children and similar clichés of popular 'liberated' thinking, my underlying inability to identify with mothers negated the possibility of such paths of thought leading me beyond theory towards radical alternatives.

As long as I persisted in seeing myself as being of a different constitution from mothers, my perception of my role in relation to childcare could be seen as analogous to that of a father figure. Patriarchal thinking is capable of absorbing any number of 'pseudofathers' without essentially altering its misconceptions concerning motherhood. It is clear to me now that in order to challenge the oppressive bases of such attitudes, I need to achieve a positive relationship with my own reproductive capacity; to acknowledge that the capacity to conceive is non-definitive of femaleness, *both for mothers and non-mothers*.

Identifying the patterns of deception which have led me to experience my potential as a mother as a threat to my identity has provided me with the means to re-evaluate my attitudes towards bearing children. The illusion that I have made a choice to remain childless, *when in reality I have made no such choice*, emerges as the crux of the deception in which I have unwittingly colluded.

In order to make a choice it is necessary, firstly, to be equipped with adequate information on which to base a decision, and secondly, *to be provided with conditions that make that decision viable.* Under the existing social system neither of these two essential conditions are present. Even if my experience had equipped me to make an informed decision, a choice in favour of bearing children is still, by implication, a choice against doing anything else. Conversely, to choose not to bear children is to relinquish any opportunity to participate in childraising. Such 'choices' are not really choices at all. I had been duped into believing that I had made a choice just as surely as a woman who unquestioningly accepts motherhood as her destiny is deceived into believing that she is acting upon a personal desire to bear a child.

Of course, many mothers refuse to make the 'choice' by deciding to do both, with varying degrees of success. But since important aspects of my self-image had become mistakenly associated with childlessness, I lacked the motivation to tackle the many problems facing women who attempt both to pursue a career and to bear children. Although I feel that I have begun to establish a more positive relationship with my potential as a mother, I still don't view the alternative as personally viable or even desirable. My fear that beneath my ideological veneer I would discover a seething pool of animal instincts, urging me to experience childbirth, has proved to be unfounded. Though I feel more fully in touch with emotional states associated with the capacity to conceive, it is children, as separate living beings, that are missing from my life, not foetuses.

The trouble is that identifying the absence of children in my daily life as something I regret and wish to change is easier said than done. I still feel inept, confused and shy with children and my lack of experience makes it difficult to know to what extent I am willing or able to involve myself with childcare. It is a circular problem with multilayered complexities. I am aware that it is not enough for women who decide not to bear children to assume a 'pseudofather' relationship with other women's children. Through their non-involvement with the day-to-day responsibilities of caring for the young, fathers have had access to the enjoyable aspects of being with children without sharing in the mundane, wearing, daily routine that mothers are expected to cope with single handed. The problem is further complicated by its social context. Since the nuclear family is generally considered to be the most suitable environment for children, and biological parents best equipped to raise the children they have borne, the patterns of social organisation which reflect this view are very difficult to break. Many others are understandably reluctant really to share all aspects of their role with other women knowing that when the chips are down, ultimate responsibility for their children falls to them, legally and 'morally'.

Practical solutions to such problems remain to be tried and tested. I do not feel equipped or inclined to propose a blueprint for successful childcare sharing. I do feel committed to trying to break down the barriers imposed by both circumstance and attitudes which keep mothers separate from non-mothers, children separate from adults, and theory separate from practice.

Through realising that the problems of motherhood are crucially relevant to my life even though I do not wish to bear a child, I feel that I can begin to exorcise some of the myths concerning motherhood that have influenced not only my perceptions of mothers, children, and my own reproductive potential, but also seemingly unconnected aspects of my personality, such as my identity as an artist. There is another level to the myth that a career and childcare are incompatible when it is applied to creative activities. There is an underlying assumption that creativity itself is incompatible with being female; that because women are 'naturally creative' in that they can give birth, they do not need (and therefore are unable) to be intellectually creative. Thus in one fell swoop women are reduced to baby machines — and art itself is reduced to a mere substitute for the 'real thing'.

Although I have always found the analogy between art and birth, expressed by such phrases as 'pregnant with meaning', highly offensive, I never fully understood quite why. Though I hate to admit it, I think part of my inability to identify with motherhood stemmed from this insidious equation. In some unnamed way I felt that to identify as a mother would sap my creative energy. The question is, to whom is the analogy appropriate? Surely it is only applicable to those who view both children and art as vehicles for their self-perpetuation. I am sure that most women will agree that self-perpetuation has nothing to do with caring for children. Nor is it responsible for women's intellectual creativity.

But an analysis of the parallels, real or fabricated, between birth and art would be out of place here. My point is that motherhood is not an isolated issue, but has hidden ramifications in all areas of experience. I feel that rooting out these invisible influences is as important as, for example, redistributing childcare, in determining the kinds of solutions we find to the problems surrounding motherhood. It seems to me that it is not ultimately important whether individual women decide to bear children or not. It is the degree of awareness that we each bring to the decision, on all kinds of levels, that really counts.

JAKE WILSON

Melba Wilson was born in Virginia, USA, grew up in Texas and has lived in California, where she was active in the civil rights and campus movements of the 'sixties. She now lives in London where she works as a journalist. She is a member of the Black Women's Group, Brixton, South London.

Melba Wilson

I suppose that in order really to sort out my feelings about having or not having children, I have to go back to my own childhood.

I am the oldest of nine kids. For eighteen years, my mother kept up a biennial tradition of having babies, spending a year or two with each, and then leaving us with her mother for the remaining time to adulthood. It was the extended black family in the flesh.

What little money there was was stretched to the limit in feeding, clothing and otherwise trying to take care of basic needs. I can remember sometimes hating that there were so many of us. Occasionally, when people came over to visit, they would cluck sympathetically to my grandmother and tell her how it was a miracle she managed to take care of all of us with so little help. Then they would look at us and tell us how we should be grateful that we had a grandmother who didn't mind sacrificing so that we could have food to eat.

That would make me mad. I and, I'm sure, we, didn't need to hear that from them! Their saying such things implied we were only there on sufferance and should never, or more accurately, would never, be allowed to forget it. I resented their intrusions.

As the oldest, I had to help out with my brothers and sisters. From about twelve onwards it fell to me to take charge of things like making sure their hair was combed, the beds made and jobs around the house done. I sometimes even had to be disciplinarian. My job was a precarious one because I, not being all that much older than most of them, alternated between being the mother figure and big sister who, after all, couldn't really tell *them* what to do!

By the time I reached my late teens, I had had enough of being 'mother'. My grandmother had come increasingly to rely on me as she got older and less able to do so much, and although I wanted to make things as easy as possible for her, I wanted a rest. I wanted to be more like my friends, who didn't have to rush home after school to start dinner or spend their weekends making sure the washing and cleaning was done. Why did I have to be the odd one out?

I blamed my mother. I resented her not being able to handle things any better than to have all us kids and not take care of us properly. She thus became for me, in this and other ways, the antithesis of how I wanted my life to be. I was determined to make a better go of things. (As I've grown older I have tried to understand my mother's position then, and have come to realise that she just couldn't cope with the responsibility of having us, and that her answer was to run away from it.)

While I didn't think then that I would never have children, I knew they would be a very long way off. I was first and foremost going to make a life for myself before I even thought about children. I didn't want to have the same kind of situation develop with my children as had happened to us.

Also my grandmother, who not surprisingly had a major influence on me, always kept at us to make something of ourselves. She used to say it was hard enough being black, without making things worse by having a whole load of children to take care of. She repeatedly warned my sisters (I have six) and me, as we got older, not to 'get in trouble' with boys and bring more babies home for her to look after.

106

I had heard so often that all a boy wanted to do was 'have his way' with a girl, and knew from my own experience the hardship caused by having unwanted children, so I was terrified if a boy even asked me out. Above all else, I would not get pregnant. I spent the remainder of my teens and early twenties shying away from close contact with the opposite sex, as a result.

I can remember once, when I was about eighteen or nineteen, being positively shocked to see my neighbour kissing a boy. It was the first time I'd seen anyone kiss in that way, apart from television. She was about three years older than me and had a reputation for being 'fast'. A few years after the incident she had an illegitimate child, and in the late sixties in the small Texas town where I grew up, this was still considered a scandal and disgrace.

By the time I went to college two of my sisters had become pregnant. They had no money, no education to speak of and no place to go except to my grandmother. This meant that just as the last of us had gotten out of diapers and into school, allowing a breather for once, there was to be a new lot of babies to begin the whole damn process all over again! It was too much. Looking back on it now I suppose the appearance of their kids (subsequently added to by those of my other brothers and sisters in quick succession) made me even more determined that I was not going to end up the same way.

When Jake and I met and started living together in 1973, there was no doubt in either of our minds that children were out of the question. Although at twenty-six I had begun to work at sorting out some of my own problems (especially as to my long suppressed sexuality), I was still far too insecure both about myself and our fledgling relationship even to think about complicating matters more with a child.

We were living in San Francisco. Before that I had spent two years in college — a lot of it taken up with grassroots community activity and burning campus issues of the time. I had dropped out a few years earlier, doing a variety of things, and was now working as a secretary. I had made up my mind to go back to college, however, and so when we started to live together my energies were divided between enjoying this new relationship and trying to work and save up enough to go back and finish.

We had the usual quota of good times and hassles, I suppose. One big headache was the opposition we encountered because I, a black woman, and Jake, a white man, chose to live together. Although it posed no problem insofar as our relationship with each other was concerned, it did have to be dealt with when we came in contact with some others – my family especially. Most of them saw our being together as the rape of the black community all over again. This time, though, it was worse, because here I was voluntarily submitting. Their insistent disapproval precipitated painful and sometimes violent encounters. It wasn't an easy time.

At this point, even if we'd had any intention of having children, such a climate would have forced us to think twice and even three times before deciding yes. For instance, one of my sisters once told me during an argument that she didn't want to have what she called 'half breed' children in the family.

These kinds of things hurt us a lot, and I was damned if a child of mine was going to be subjected to that kind of nonsense. No, if we had children, and after three years together it was still a big 'if', the race issue would have to be sorted out with my family. Eventually it was, but it took a lot of time, energy and perseverance; and it was a time best spent without children.

Another thing contributing to our not considering seriously or very much about having children was the thinking of many of our friends. Many were couples and, like us, childless, and they enjoyed life, as we did, without children. I mean, you could decide on the spur of the moment to go to a film or whatever, without worrying about either keeping the child up (if you took it along) or finding a babysitter (if you didn't). Two people are cheaper to take care of than three, and on the whole life was fine just the way it was.

We knew some people who had had a child, and had split up because of it. Not being on as firm a ground as it could have been, their relationship just couldn't stand the added strain of bringing up a child. Then, too, we spent time with children of friends and family and so didn't lack having them around.

The plain and simple truth was that we just weren't ready emotionally or any other way to have children. Nor were we pining to.

It was and is very important to Jake, for instance, to feel free enough to pick up and travel or not work or whatever, and not be a slave to circumstances. If we had had a child then, he would have accepted the responsibility of it, but it could have been at the expense of our relationship. That I knew I didn't want. Our being together was more important to me than anything else. Besides, the idea of being dependent in the way I would almost certainly have to have been, didn't appeal to me either.

There were still plenty of things I wanted to do and I had only just begun to scratch the surface. I was busy with school and had begun to think about a job afterwards. I was looking forward to the prospect of earning money again and doing work I enjoyed. I had a life as a woman, separate from being Jake's partner or a mother, and I liked it. I wasn't ready to trade all of that for the fairly restricting and constricting job of motherhood.

Added to this was the fact that I had begun to want to be part of the women's movement, which was well underway. I had always seen myself as working more outside the home in a career of some kind anyway. So the women's movement, for me, served to validate my choice of the outside world over the confines of home.

There was one other reason why I was put off having children – the pain. I was scared to death thinking about having that huge bulge forced through my vagina. I knew they could drug you so that you didn't feel a thing, but that didn't appeal to me either. Added to this, I had the benefit of hearing my sisters' stories about the pain they experienced in childbirth, all told in graphic, grisly detail. I didn't talk much about my fears. Most women survived it all right and I guess I knew if it came to it, I would too.

I was twenty-nine when I finally graduated from college. We

moved to England shortly afterwards and I found a job. As it was mainly my responsibility to support us (Jake having done it while I was at college full-time), children were still not considered.

I surprised myself though, because I became aware of an ever-so-slight shift in my attitude about the whole pregnancy-childbirth-childraising issue. I'd catch myself looking at women with babies, for instance. One time I was standing behind a woman holding her baby at a supermarket checkout counter. She was caressing it and cooing to it and kissing it with such obvious tenderness that I almost felt too embarrassed to watch.

Pregnant women also came under scrutiny. Before, if I'd noticed them at all, it was to be glad I didn't look like that. Now I looked at their bodies without revulsion. I looked at their faces to try and figure out if they were happy or sad or aggravated or what, by their pregnancy. I watched how they carried their big bellies – some waddled laboriously while others seemed to have a somewhat easier time. A friend of mine who was almost due let me feel her baby kicking. It was one of the strangest sensations I've ever had.

I was also having new feelings about children themselves. I think my years of forced motherhood had made me build up a resentment against them which they invariably picked up on. For a long time I never really liked them and had to pretend friendliness when I was around them. Most times I tried to ignore them altogether. They usually reciprocated and didn't show much warmth towards me either. It bothered me a little, but not enough to change the situation.

Now however, I felt less antagonistic towards them. I started to look at them less as burdens to be fed, clothed and sacrificed for, and more as people who, like adult people, also had a lot of good things to offer. My sisters, for example, enjoyed their kids, even given what I considered their less than ideal circumstances to bring them up in. I began to envy that. Amazingly, too, kids began to respond more positively towards me and I found I liked having them around – talking to them and generally enjoying their company.

Being in England also contributed to this favourable

attitude. It seemed to both Jake and me that there was less of an anti-children attitude than there had been in San Francisco. Lots of people our age had them here, whereas before, the reverse was true. They weren't regarded as intrusions but as welcomed additions.

Another thing was that many of the women I now knew either were trying to get or were already pregnant. There seemed to be fewer and fewer people opting for childlessness. I'm not sure if I put myself in situations where I would mainly meet pregnant women to reinforce my own changing feelings.

As most of us were in our late twenties and early thirties, I think it must have dawned on us at roughly the same time that we *were* getting older and fast coming up on the time when we would be past the childbearing age, and that we would soon have to decide one way or the other about children. I know my age was a big consideration for me in starting to think seriously about becoming pregnant.

I didn't say much to anyone about my new feelings. People were so used to hearing me say how much I didn't want children, that it would have been too much to try and explain what I now felt. *I* wasn't even sure why I felt this way. Besides, as Jake and I hadn't really talked about it, I didn't know what he felt, and was not yet ready to ask.

Instead I fantasised about having a child, savouring my thoughts a bit longer before bringing them out into the open. For instance, I thought about its colouring — what would it be? It would be nice to have coffee-coloured children like those I'd seen from other interracial unions. Another thing I thought about was breastfeeding — the idea of the baby seeking out my breasts to eat was so intimate and sensual. It would need me, be dependent on me, and I would love it.

I began to read about pregnancy and childbirth. I sought and even initiated discussions with women friends about it. I came to realise that despite my years as 'mother', I knew very little about the whole thing. I'm still not sure why I decided I wanted children. Maybe I always did and denied my feelings because I felt I needed to prove I could be different from the rest of my family. I knew I no longer felt this way. I had even come round to the idea that maybe the extended family wasn't such a bad idea after all.

Maybe it was not wanting to miss out. In fact I know that had something to do with it. In the back of my mind there was the feeling that no matter how well I performed in other ways, if I didn't have a child there would be a part of life that I could never experience or really understand; and I wanted to. I wanted to feel the bonding everyone talks about that takes place between a mother and child — the maternal instinct, if you like. I wanted to be pregnant. I wanted my own baby. I suppose, too, that like a lot of people, I wanted to leave something of myself behind. Maybe I decided yes because now, unlike before, I felt more secure about myself as a person, more on top of things. Whatever the reason, I was ready.

I broached the subject with Jake and to my surprise he had also been thinking about it and even liked the idea of having children. What about feeling tied down? money? my career? shared parenting? and the race issue? We talked about all these things and to be perfectly honest, we didn't come up with any hard and fast answers to them.

Jake still likes to feel he can chuck his job and travel, if he wants; so do I. What we've said is that although things are bound to change after we have a baby, we'll try as much as possible to integrate its life with ours, so that we can continue (both of us) to do many of the things we like to do.

Of all the considerations, money was probably the easiest to deal with. We'll probably never have enough to do all the things we want, but we've managed okay so far, and will most likely continue to. So we're just not going to worry too much about it. As to my career, well, I think I'll want to be a full-time mother for maybe six months to a year. After that, I will probably want to resume working again, in some way, maybe on a limited basis at first. Fortunately, I'm doing the kind of work which allows me to make such an arrangement work without too many hitches. In a sense, therefore, I can have my cake and eat it too. And why not? Also, as Jake will have more than just a token role in bringing up our children, that makes things still easier.

As for the race issue, well, the opposition from my family has all but ceased. I've noticed that the younger kids of friends of ours in mixed relationships seem to have no problems in getting along with black and white children. Although, not long ago, I asked a friend who's a teacher, and also in a mixed relationship and planning children, how she felt the school situation was. She said she was apprehensive because it had been her experience that as they got older, racially mixed children had a much harder time in school than either black or white kids. They weren't all that easily accepted by either group and to a large extent were isolated much more. On the other hand, I have seen racially mixed children managing to find common ground with black and white kids, so it can be done. There are no easy answers as far as this is concerned. We'll just have to deal with the situations as they develop.

I became pregnant about a year after we decided. It's impossible to describe how happy we were. Up until then, neither of us was sure we were even capable of producing a child, but we'd done it and were over the moon. We went to see the R.D. Laing film about birth without violence, which helped to ease a lot of my fears about childbirth. I think it helped Jake too, as it was the first time he'd seen such a film.

We told everyone we knew about the pregnancy — and they were all almost as happy as we were about it. Surely there was no baby that would be more wanted or who would be born into happier circumstances than this one.

About two months into my pregnancy, I started to miscarry. It was the day before New Year's Eve and I was so scared I was sick, more from worry than from the actual miscarriage. From my reading I knew there was a chance I could stop it if I got into bed immediately, which I did. I phoned the doctor, told him what was happening and he said I'd done exactly the right thing and that I was under no circumstances to attempt to get up. I was in bed for the next three days, and still the bleeding didn't stop.

I was eventually taken to hospital for more bed rest — and I still bled. After three days, during which time they'd done tests to try and detect a foetal heartbeat (and found none), the bleeding had increased and was now coming out in big clots. I prayed and prayed that the inevitable wouldn't happen. But it did.

On the fourth day in hospital they told me they would have to do a D & C (dilation and curretage) on me in order to get the rest of the aborted foetus out. They could not tell me why it happened, only that it occurred sixty per cent of the time with first pregnancies.

I cried so much I didn't think I had any more tears left. Even now, when I think about it, the tears want to come. I wasn't in very much physical pain, maybe it would have been better if I had been. Then I would have had something else to concentrate on besides that terrible feeling of emptiness sinking over me.

And poor Jake. I felt so sorry for him. He never cried once or showed any kind of emotion except to hold my hand so tightly it hurt. I knew though that inside he was going through almost as much hell as I was. When he came to visit me in hospital he looked so tired and bedraggled and confused that it was almost too much to take.

I felt sorry for *me* when it came to it. One day I had a baby growing inside me and the next day I didn't. My breasts, which had grown bigger and were the only outward sign of my pregnancy, quickly went back to their normal size. It's hard to describe the sense of devastation and loss I felt. Even though I knew I would get pregnant again, I was not comforted. *This* baby, my first child, was not to be.

All the people we'd told so happily about the pregnancy only a few weeks before now had to be told about the miscarriage. That was painful. It was bad enough having actually to live through it once without reliving it through repetition to others.

We were completely shattered. It was like a bad dream that we knew would not go away. We had been primed for that baby – planned for it, wanted it, made a space in our lives for it, and then suddenly it was no longer there. The life we had created was now scraped away. We had to start all over again.

We tried to get me pregnant almost immediately, but my body physically wasn't up to it. I was still having pain and some bleeding two months after the operation. Our hasty efforts only served to make us more depressed; each time we thought we'd done it again, only to have our hopes dashed when I got my period.

Since then, we've done a lot of talking to friends who've had miscarriages, and that has helped us both a lot. I was amazed to find out just how many had had them. They were all very comforting and understanding and did a great deal to help us through those dark winter months.

We're now trying to relax more about my getting pregnant. We don't have intercourse around the time of my period because the doctors say the contractions could cause me to miscarry again if I am pregnant. I don't lift heavy things for the same reason. I don't like the restrictions, but I don't like not being pregnant more, so I try to do all the right things. We try not to build up our hopes every month, but it's hard not to.

Postscript
On 12 February 1980 Melba gave birth to a son, Joel.

FINE ART DEPT. PORTSMOUTH POLYTECHNIC

Flora Dutton was born in Birmingham in 1940 and moved to East London in 1946. She studied at the Royal College of Art and at the Courtauld Institute, has travelled intermittently and has been teaching art history at Portsmouth Polytechnic since 1970. She now lives in Portsmouth.

Flora Dutton

As a child I remember how, when I tried to imagine
my own future – myself *married* that is – I used to be seized by a
kind of sick dread. It was the fear of failure I think. My
daughter at one stage used to worry herself about how her body
would get to Heaven. 'How do you get the wings?' she would ask
anxiously and I saw that same sick feeling of unreality in her
face. It arises when one is impelled to attempt some impossibly
difficult and unimaginable feat. She was hoping for the name
and address of the suppliers, but, as she already suspected only
too well, none was forthcoming.

Her question was not answerable and was set aside. It lost its
power, was defused. For me the power of that demand which is
made on all women in our society – namely that we should live
closely and happily with a man and if possible produce children – has now been defused. I accept what I have and what I am
and try to live it out.

One way in which I am described is as a Single Parent. My
child was produced in a deviant manner by devious means. I

have been asked to write about my situation, how and why it arose, how it has been for *me*. I realise that the description I give will inevitably be a kind of *explanation*. I also realise that the explanation that I give myself is continuously changing in the light of my present experience. I experience a central void, or loneliness, in which I converse with myself. A constant inner dialogue possesses me, a kind of perpetual novel is being recited in my head to which I am closely attached. I must prevent myself from speculating on the nature and meaning of this obsessive activity now, and concentrate on the matter in hand.

After a certain point in my childhood I imagined that my mother had rejected me. Why? Briefly, I loved her but I could not accept her view of the world; that view I rejected. I think I often perceive my own rejecting as a rejection of myself. This is not surprising. I became lonely and desolate within the very bosom of the family. The others clustered around my mother. As I remember it, they were all always literally clustered around a glowing fire in warm companionship. There was another member of the family rejected by, or rejecting of, this group and that was my father. But we were off at different tangents and had no contact with each other. Perhaps it is significant that our house was large enough to enable this to happen.

Looking back it seems to me that once I felt I had lost the central emotional support of my mother's love and approval, I was like a building with no proper foundations which has to be supported by some magical act of will. Without my mother's love I felt unreal, unconfirmed. From then on I had to perform a series of magical acts in order to stay alive. I grew up with an overriding need to control my *own* life which masked an abject fear of losing it. This is how it seemed, and seems, to me in fantasy.

This need to *control*, to *make* things happen by individual acts of *will*, 'to pull oneself up by one's own bootstraps' (to use that neat description of the supposed modus operandi of capitalism) coincided with the values of the educational system to which I was subjected. It is paradoxical that it was partly this attitude in my mother that I had consciously rejected. It nevertheless became highly developed in me. (My sister has

pointed out to me how much I resemble my mother in 'character' despite our violent antagonisms of belief.) As a modus
operandi, it was in some ways easier for a man to attempt
than a woman, but I didn't really discover this until I left
school and was faced with knotty problems concerning sexual
conduct.

To begin with I was sent to a small private school to be
prepared for the 11-plus examination. The headmistress used
to whip the backs of our knees to make us stand in line and in
winter we could not drink our free milk because it was frozen in
the bottles. Intensely thin, I suffered agonies from the cold, but
these were nothing in comparison with the mental pain I
endured. Emotionally, I was passionately attached to my
schoolmistresses successively. My greatest pleasures in life came
from their praise. Also I had a very intense relationship with a
'best friend' who was in competition with me academically. The
boys, who played separately, seemed very distant from me, and
of little interest. I almost thought of them as a different species,
in a world apart.

I remember my state of mind concerning the 11-plus. If I
failed, I was convinced that I would cease to exist, that my life
would be over. I would hang miserably around the classroom
after hours, longing for help and reassurance. My teacher, who
was a kindly soul, finally told me that if I didn't pass the 11-plus
she would eat her hat. This helped. I managed to cross that
hurdle and, unfortunately as it seems to me now, all the subsequent hurdles set in my path. That is until my marriage at
twenty-one when I fell hard and flat. Until then each success
that I had seemed to me to result from a supreme and magical
effort of my will. The more I succeeded the more unimaginable
failure seemed and the more inauthentic I felt — it was as if I was
somehow managing to cheat my way through life by a magic
trick. Naturally I never told anyone about this. I knew that it
would break the spell. In fact I was terrified of being found out.
By the time I married, I believe I was really mentally very ill.
Probably I was fortunate not to have been diagnosed and
'treated', it would have been ECT (electric shock treatment) in
those days. When I married I attempted above all else to

maintain my separateness. I wanted to remain hidden because I felt safe that way. I couldn't risk another rejection having so narrowly and miraculously managed to survive my mother's. So I withdrew continuously and only emerged on my own terms at certain moments when I felt I was in control. After the marriage, I continued to present a mask – I could only allow the perfect part of myself to show. But relationships on these terms are almost impossible and I continued to be neurotic, anxious, unhappy, demanding. Ever since that catastrophic event – the marriage was very short and a total disaster – I have been trying to pick myself up and understand what *happened*. This was when the inner dialogue that I mentioned earlier really got started in me. I felt I had been the victim of a collision of forces far beyond my comprehension. And I wished to comprehend them, so as to control them, I suppose. (Freud describes himself as having a similar compulsion as a small child to understand what was happening to him, and why.)

In the years that followed I was lucky enough to find one or two wise and kind lovers, to make a few good friends, to become involved in certain things which helped to strengthen me and allowed me to grow together again. Of all the good things that happened, it was probably having my baby which really saved me by giving me an emotional stability and a stronger sense of the reality of my existence. I didn't consciously have the baby to this end – in fact nothing could have been farther from my mind – but that was the result. Having Emma helped me shed many fears – I *had* to be strong, I *had* to be able to bring my feelings forward and let them show (often in anger, often in gratitude), in order that we might *both* live. In fact I felt very strongly for a while after the birth that Freud's fantastic idea of the child being a substitute penis for the woman, and capable of making her whole and complete at last, might be the case. And there *is* a kind of symbolic truth in this. The child makes the woman strong, it gives her a certain measure of status, power, responsibility, all the things that are denied her in society at large because she is a woman. It makes her important. But Freud's formulation is only another rationalisation of the status quo. There is no reason why a child should be the only thing capable of making a woman feel strong and complete. Many other kinds of social function could do this for her.

There is still a great deal about my own past which I don't understand, which fills me with confusion and a sort of bafflement when I try to think it through. I accept Marx's dictum that social relations determine consciousness – yet 'What do we know of shoes when we know they are produced by the shoe industry?'

This has been a very lop-sided description of what happened. Everything did not stem simply from my having dared to reject my mother's values at a tender age while remaining emotionally deeply attached to her. It was rather that my having done it brought into question the whole value system of which we were a part. It threw the whole universe into question for me. Why did I retreat into a more or less schizophrenic state? For one thing it seems to me that I couldn't accept the discrepancies between stated belief and actual practice that I seem to see and feel, not only in my mother, but on every side. In fact it has always been difficult, or impossible, for me to dissemble and it seems that this is a serious 'failing' in a woman. Although I loved my mother desperately, I could never change myself to please her, or pretend to a feeling or opinion that I did not have. So I adopted a frozen, immobile mask. People complained that I never smiled, that I was expressionless, that I looked afraid or alienated, that I was 'stuck-up'. This first began in the presence of my mother – I felt insubstantial, lethargic, dead almost. It was either that or expressing thoughts and feelings which I knew would be unacceptable.

Since becoming a mother myself it has seemed important to me to try and work out my relationship with my own mother. Mysteriously my daughter and my mother have had, from the start, a deep rapport. This pleases me emotionally, but frightens me in other ways. So the conflict remains. It's a bit like the mind/body split in sex. I have not been able to work either of them out yet.

I would like to try and say more about why and how I came to have Emma and what my experience of motherhood has been.

It often happens in families that the father is alienated. It often happens that the world views of the parents are rejected by the children. I believe that particularities of personal circumstances are so much raw material given to each of us – *how* we shape it, what it leads us to, is up to each of us, is *chosen* by each of us. Nevertheless, when I survey the history of my sexual life it presents a pretty gruesome spectacle. (I once had to take Emma to visit a speech therapist. She asked me certain questions about my life which I answered as well as I could, as I found her unusually sympathetic. When I had finished, she said 'Well, you've certainly had a good stir of the pot haven't you?' I felt rather pleased at this, but not convinced that it had really been that.)

Although I rejected my mother's political views, and many of her attitudes to people outside the family (she had an unswerving allegiance to everyone within it), I was not able to make the connections which I now see existed between her ideas in different spheres. So it came about that I *did* accept her views on sexual morality, and sought to please her there at least. She instilled the concepts of private property and commodity value as they are applied to women into us with remarkable stringency. 'No man likes soiled goods' she would tell us with complete conviction. 'Never make yourselves cheap' – in fact her message was 'Make yourselves as dear as possible'.

The idea that men only respected women who 'saved themselves' for marriage, seemed the more appealing to me in that the teenage 'necking' parties that I attended were utterly repellent – people groping each other wordlessly in the dark. When I was seventeen, I acquired a regular boyfriend, really out of curiosity to know what my girlfriends were all so excited about. He was quite experienced sexually but respected me 'for being a virgin'. He said it was very difficult to find 'a nice girlfriend'. He gave me my first climax manually. (I had no idea what it was at the time and thought I had had an experience unique in the history of 'mankind'.) We mutually masturbated for several years (it was quite exciting really but I felt guilty about it), until my marriage to someone else – a fellow art student who seemed brilliant and attractive and surprised me by his proposal of marriage. He, also, was impressed by the fact of my being a virgin. It appealed to the Romantic strain in him, he said. By this time I was both petrified by the prospect of actual penetration – having put it off for so long – but also tremendously excited with expectations out of all proportion. I was in such a state that it was not until some time after the 'wedding night' that my husband succeeded in the act of consummation. I was so grossly insensitive as to say 'is *that* all it is?' I had no intention of wounding him when I said this – it was simply ignorance and amazement. I was just as amazed to find that, although we were both art students doing precisely the same course, he expected me to do all the cooking, washing and housework. It appeared that because I was a virgin he had expected me to turn out to be a 'perfect wife'. In some ways my mother had brought me up to think like a man, in that she had waited on me hand and foot. Just like my husband, I was in search of someone to take over my mother's role.

It was not until some time after my divorce that I began to think in an abstract kind of way that I 'ought to have a child, if I was to fulfil myself as a woman, etc'. I allowed myself to become pregnant by an unusually nice man whom I very much liked and respected and got on well with in every way but sexually. Our sexual life was rudimentary and not very successful. Once pregnant, I was astonished to find myself overcome with repugnance for him. I couldn't 'bear the sight of him' and I felt I could not possibly have the baby. We were able to get an abortion and remained friends. But I felt appalled with myself. Not only the world outside, it seemed, but my own responses were totally arbitrary and unpredictable, beyond my control. (I speculate now that the reason for this sudden abhorrence was my unconscious fear of total commitment to another.)

The remarkable thing about Emma's father was that, for me, our sexual relationship was total and unmitigated bliss. This was really the first time that sex had seemed totally *right*. I really wanted to have the baby – in fact, another abortion was unthinkable. The father was unable and unwilling to live with me but he was not opposed to my having the baby. So I decided to go ahead positively.

I felt amazingly energetic all through my pregnancy. The

periodic depressions that I had had before it disappeared completely. For the first time in my life I felt warm – I didn't have to be always carrying jackets, cardigans and coats about. I felt mentally and physically warm. My pleasure in alcohol and nicotine completely disappeared. I didn't smoke and hardly drank all through the pregnancy. I believe that the actual experience of pregnancy changed me both mentally and physically, not only during it but ever since.

I had always thought of myself as a physical coward and felt terrified of the actual experience of birth. I managed to get booked into Queen Charlotte's Maternity Hospital, impressed by its reputation, and started to go to Natural Childbirth classes. As the pregnancy advanced, my fears evaporated until, when the time came, I felt none at all. Just excitement. The 'pains' began just as I had completed my final preparations. I had been at work in another city the day before – the last day before the period of agreed leave for the birth began. So it seemed fairly miraculous that the 'pains' began that very next morning. I drove myself to the ante-natal clinic and was sent straight to bed. I didn't feel any pain – only tremendous physical exertion. I had wanted a boy (this seems strange to me now) and I was a little crestfallen immediately after the birth. Emma's face was very squashed and cross-looking and I felt disappointed by her sex. But a few hours later her face opened out like a flower, and she seemed to be bathed in celestial light. A rapturous flood (very like the first instalment of being in love) swept over me. Again I felt astonished by myself, by my feelings. As usual, I felt them to be unique. In fact, I was simply discovering what most parents feel – as they bore their friends with their total absorption in what, to everybody else, seems a perfectly ordinary baby. I recognised this feeling in her father's face when he first saw her. I have never forgotten the remarkable intensity of those first few days. I brought the baby out of hospital in a blizzard. She was born deep in December. I motored through driving snow with my sister, who had helped me so much during my pregnancy and was almost as excited as I was, to my mother's cottage in Suffolk. The dark landscape with the falling snow, the baby wrapped up warmly and snugly in the back of the car — everything seemed so strange and exciting it was almost as though *I* was newly born.

My mother was very diplomatic. She refrained from asking questions or expressing opinions about the birth because she was afraid of driving me away. She confined her attention to the baby — her first grandchild. Her delight in the baby pleased me, warmed me. Right from the start, I felt that having the baby was rather like having a piece of myself adrift in the world in that every nuance of every response that people make to her, *I* am aware of, and affected by. This is an enormous extension of myself, in a sense, as well as being very taxing and painful at times.

Before I left the hospital I was asked to see a Welfare Officer or Social Worker of some kind. She asked me what arrangements I had made for the baby. I explained that I would be returning to work after three weeks and that a friend would look after my baby for the first three months and that then I had found a babyminder who was a trained nurse to look after the baby with her own three children. I had not been able to get more than three weeks (unpaid) leave because I was still in the probationary year of a full-time teaching post. I also had not been given the usual maternity benefit because I had had various part-time jobs in the past and there were complications about the tax. I had felt too embarrassed to make any sort of stand about these things at that time (1970). I felt that if I pushed anything, the huge weight of disapproval which I sensed on every side, would cascade down on my head. So I used my savings. On this occasion, however, I felt baffled and hurt by the icy disapproval this woman met me with. She said nothing, but made some marks on a form and then dismissed me. I had not expected this as I had imagined that her function was to advise, encourage and support.

I was living in a house in London with two women friends, one of whom had a baby a little after me, and one of whom already had a son. It was the latter of these friends who looked after my baby for the first three months. I very much liked living in this way, close to other women. I only had to be in my place of work for three days in the week, I was able to work at home on the others. However, there was a serious flaw in my arrangements – and that was that my home and all my arrangements for the baby were in one city and my job was in another. This meant that those days when I was away were very long and tiring.

That part of my life which had to do with exams and degrees, and interviews and jobs and making money, seemed to have carried on in the same miraculous way as in my schooldays. Although I love my subject, and get a great deal of pleasure from it, I was beset by all sorts of inhibitions and found teaching a great strain in many ways in those days.

Because of being so involved in surviving and getting by, I was rather late in coming to know about and understand the significance of the resurgence of the women's movement. But over the last few years this factor has made an incalculable difference to me. It has transformed my way of seeing myself and the world, the way I tackle my job and my situation. It has enabled me to become more positive on all fronts.

To return to the difficulty of living in two cities. It was finally solved for me by my own body which developed glandular fever. This meant that I was forced to realise that I had to choose between leaving my beloved London or giving up a very good job. I chose to move to the provincial city. I have not seriously regretted it. I enjoy London and my friends in a very intense and concentrated way when I return, which I can do often, fortunately. And it is marvellous to be able to take Emma to the sea and into the country without any hassle. I've been able to afford a house with plenty of space – which I couldn't have done in London – and I've made new friends. The move meant that I no longer saw Emma's father regularly. At that time I was still very emotionally involved with him and though the break was painful it was also an immense relief.

I've met with a great deal of kindness and sympathy during the eight years of Emma's life, and I have made contact with a much wider cross-section of people than I should otherwise have done. Through meeting the parents of her friends at school, I have made friendships which I treasure. But, also, I've had experiences which still make my blood boil when I think of them, especially with male doctors. I will give just one conspicuous example.

Before I left London, Emma had just begun to go to a play-group. Wilma (the babyminder) took her there in the afternoons. The supervisor felt that her behaviour was 'withdrawn'. There *was* cause for concern here. My attitude had been that as long as Emma was well cared for and given plenty of stimulation, she would be fine if she only saw me for short but regular and intense periods of time. I'm sorry to say that I even drew an analogy with the upper classes with their system of having children raised by nannies and I thought to myself, it seems to have done them no harm. However, at this time I was *not* giving Emma enough of my time and attention as I felt too tired and ill. The school suggested that I take Emma to see a paediatrician. As it happened it was a man who is now a famous pundit giving 'advice' in books and broadcasts, as well as in person. His line is that everything that is wrong with the baby is the mother's fault.

At the time of the visit I was already suffering from glandular fever, although it had not been diagnosed. I felt extremely ill all the time, I was worried about my job which I was too tired to do properly, and worried about Emma who wasn't getting enough of my attention. After the usual wait we were shown into the office of a whey-faced bespectacled middle-aged man who was deeply sunk in the perusal of some document. I waited in silent polite-ness for some five minutes while Emma played on the floor. Then he raised his head and asked 'What does your husband do?' I replied, rather taken aback as I had assumed that he might have some information about me already among all that documenta-tion, that I had no husband. He made no comment but turned his attention to Emma. He asked her a series of questions. Emma had spent most of her life surrounded by women and this may have accounted for her completely ignoring him except for an indifferent stare. After a few minutes of this he said that it was clear to him that both of us were deeply disturbed, that he was not qualified to help us, but that we should see a psychiatrist as soon as possible, that he knew a good one and would try to get us an appointment but unfortunately this man (his friend) was terribly busy. He then dismissed us. I never heard from him again.

If only he had asked me a few questions about my actual life, he may have been able to see and point out to me that I was attempting the impossible and that I should move nearer my work. If he had asked me about my health, he might have realised that I was ill. As it was, when I pressed him to tell me how he had arrived at his conclusion as to my deep disturbance he was forced to say that he could tell from 'the expression on my face'.

It was my general practitioner who finally diagnosed glandular fever. I was forced to rest, and then we made the move to Portsmouth and both became much better.

Emma was always a remarkably 'good' baby. She never cried all night, she was never ill. I enjoyed feeding, bathing and changing her but of course I was not with her all the time. If she had been a 'difficult' baby, I don't know how I could have coped. I suppose I would have had to stop working and to go on to Social Security. I have observed with other women I have known who have had babies on their own that the births have been good and that their babies have been healthy and no trouble. I conclude that when women are tied to their babies all round the clock, those complicated problems which so often preoccupy them (as to feeding, teething and so on) have time and space to develop. Although I had the balance wrong for some of the time, I still believe that it is better (for mother and child) if the care of the baby is shared among several people. If it devolves entirely on the mother a bond of unhealthy mutual dependence is likely to develop, in my view.

I have often wondered what it would have been like if I hadn't found Emma beautiful, physically. As it is I never tire of watching her, of wanting to touch her. This was an all-important element in my relationship with her father. And in that relationship there was a strong element of narcissism. In a way he looked rather like me. People sometimes said we looked like brother and sister. I realise now that I envied him a lot. I envied his life style. I longed to *be* him, in a way, I think. I tried to merge with him, to lose myself in him, to *become* him – and all these things were clearly impossible for me. Perhaps being 'in love' in this sense is an impossible state to sustain. I haven't been able to come to any conclusion about these things.

There *have* been periods in my life (the longest was about two years) when I've lived quite happily à deux and some of those times were *very* happy. But there have been those other times when I've lived with someone *unhappily*, and they have been so painful, so gruesome as to make solitude seem infinitely preferable.

I've never lived intimately with an (adult) woman, but I feel I should like to.

My constant and, at the same time, growing and developing relationship has been with Emma. I can sometimes feel guilty about perhaps not enabling her to have enough contact with others, but on the whole I do my best to ensure that she is never lonely and relates to a variety of people. However, the argument that children should 'have a father' doesn't move me. From what I have experienced of the relationships between fathers and their children the reality is often very far from what propaganda for the family claims it to be. Fathers are very often alienated from their families, through no fault of their own, and because of the resentment they feel their effects on their children are often destructive. They are distanced from the process of childrearing.

The question of why I find myself living alone with a child is one that has preoccupied me a great deal, as I said at the start. The overriding need in the first twenty-five years of my life to protect my own individuality in order to preserve it, meant that it was virtually incarcerated where no one could get at it, deep inside me. It was in danger of being suffocated to death for some time but enough sustenance got to it to keep it going. There are times when I feel very alive and powerful now and a certain freedom of thought and action which I feel I have maintained fills me with euphoria. The bad times are when I get overtired and suddenly find myself alone and lonely – usually when Emma has finally gone to bed and when I have planned to do some of my own work. Careful organisation can prevent this happening – but it *does* happen. Then I feel sorry for myself and long to have someone to share everything with. Yet, I know that too much of the company of another or others would be very difficult for me to tolerate. I would lose that sense of myself which seems to be so crucial to me. However, I feel stronger now than ever before and more able to trust myself to others, to reach out to them – far less afraid to express my own thoughts and feelings. I feel I have a lot to thank Emma for. Sometimes I feel that we are learning together, through each other, how to live, and this is very exciting. I hope that I might find another or others to come closer to us for rather more of the time than happens now. Yet as things are, I feel there are good things about our situation *as it is* which I must develop as much as possible.

I used to feel both before and after Emma's birth, in some part of me, that our being alone meant that I was an abysmal failure and that no one could stand me, although I seldom admitted this, even to myself. Some men have been disarmingly honest about their responses to me. A journalist who once came to interview me for an article he was doing on people who live alone, suggested that the cause might be that I am 'socially inefficient'. I think there is something to be said for that – I sometimes feel that I am on a wavelength all my own and find it very difficult to tune in to other people. Another man said, although he liked me, it was clear to him that I would never 'look after him' (true), and another (Emma's father) said that he and I could never live together because I want to *know* about everything. I'm afraid that's true too.

Generally, as a Single Parent, I would say that the most crucial problem is *time*. The great challenge is how to organise time in order to fulfil the demands made upon me by the situation I have got myself into. This is exciting and challenging – it is also very hard. There are the demands of the Job (which are not at all coincidental with the demands of the Subject), there is the Subject in itself, there is Emma, there are my friends, there is my house and the students I share it with (at varying degrees of distance), and there is the garden – in theory if not in practice. Is it really the garden that suffers most?

To manage to be able to give one's whole and undivided attention to something for as long as it takes, without interruption – that is what I miss most, together, I suspect, with countless other women. Things are often arranged for men so that the way is cleared for them to be able to get down to work. Up to now it has been the role of women to perform this clearing of the way by their servicing activities.

I often think of a character in Dickens (I think she's in *Our Mutual Friend*). She is a Mother who has a Cause. She longs to help the starving children of some island in the South Seas. Dickens is very hard on her. She spends all her time furiously writing pamphlets and letters to help these far-away children while her own offspring suffer from neglect and keep nearly falling into the fire, etc. They are rescued, of course, by one of Dickens's impossibly self-sacrificing heroines.

DAVID TRIESMAN

Michelene Wandor is a socialist feminist, a poet and a playwright.
She compiled *The Body Politic* (Stage One, 1972), had plays
published in *Sink Songs* (Playbooks, 1975); co-edited, with Michèle
Roberts, *Cutlasses & Earrings* (Playbooks, 1977). She also contributed
to *Tales I Tell My Mother* (Journeyman Press, 1978) and is a regular
contributor to *Spare Rib* and, since 1971, Poetry Editor of *Time Out*
and also theatre reviewer. Her plays for radio, television and theatre
include *Whores d'Oeuvres*, about prostitution, and a dramatisation of
Elizabeth Barrett Browning's *Aurora Leigh*.

Michelene Wandor

The question of whether to have children hits people differently at different points in their lives. The way I made my decision was fundamentally different from the way in which many of my friends are now making theirs – women friends who have all through their twenties asserted their right to choose a childless independence, are now, in their early thirties, realising they have a limited number of years during which they may safely choose motherhood. The painful dilemma this need to choose can raise would have made no sense to me when I married and had my two sons in the early 1960s, since I assumed that all women were like me and simply wanted children. The question was 'how soon', not 'whether' and certainly never 'why'. I suppose I was in the middle of that decade of the 'graduate wife', when desires for a career were often seen as something which would conflict with motherhood, rather than provide one of the vital options for women. At the time I also gave little thought to what it meant for a man to want children – I don't mean the simple desire to be a *paterfamilias*, but the sort of emotional need and curiosity which some men feel about having children and taking equal responsibility for their care.

I am, of course, talking PF – post-feminism. My rationale BF – before feminism – was breathtakingly simple and, as I look back now, it fitted sweetly into the dominant ideology: I was female, liked babies, was frightened at the big wide world, fell in love . . . I *had* wanted to become an actress after university, but I was worried about the prospect of disappearing into obscure repertory. When I tried other jobs and prospective employers suggested I should take a shorthand-typing course – that clinched it. With hindsight and the trauma of a marriage break-up and divorce a certain note of cynicism always creeps into my account of this period in my life; but the fact is that on the whole at that time middle-class women worked despite motherhood not alongside it, and in the face of a cold and hostile world of work, love, marriage, building a home and family were exciting and potentially fulfilling prospects.

In effect I went from one family to another – with only the three years of university in between. I wish I could have avoided that. Compared to many other women (and compared to almost all men) I missed out on those vital few years of coping with an adult life among adults, earning my living as a non-mother. Since I didn't start earning and writing seriously until I was nearly thirty, I reckon I have lost about eight years. It's no good being told that the experiences I have had 'compensate' for those years. Of course at some level my life and work now must be affected by the insights and experiences I had during that time – but it is very hard to work out what the real relationship is. Motherhood is so intense and *private*, so individually experienced, so extraordinary, that I have no real grasp of how it affects the rest of my view of the world – except at occasional moments when symptoms erupt: I get impatient at the 'childish' way a friend is behaving and 'tell her off', or someone sneezes and I offer them a tissue from the store of things I keep in my bag 'just in case'. During the years when my children were small, my handbags seemed to get bigger and bigger. Now that my sons are teenagers (Adam, born 1964, and Ivan, born 1966) my handbags are getting smaller again.

134

However, despite my 'lost' years, I have never once wished I had not had my children. To wish that would be like wishing they were not alive, and that carries the weight of a kind of blasphemy. I have very often wished I could have suspended their material beings, magically rolled them up and carried them in my head, whole and complex as they concretely are – and then given re-birth to them six or seven years later than I actually did. That way I could have had the best of both worlds – had my work and my children, and we would all have lived happily ever after . . . I forgot: happily ever after is a BF (before feminism) concept.

There were a number of other BF concepts which took me through some of the more difficult times of motherhood – or rather, they were rationales which gently but inevitably bit the dust. First, there was the rationale that having two children was no more work than having one; second, that once both children were at school, life would be miraculously simple; third, that once they no longer needed babysitters, my time would be my own. Two children are, of course, at least twice as much work as one. It is not only the different material and physical demands, but the different emotional needs that literally make motherhood a twenty-four-hour occupation. (They were, of course, often twice as wonderful.) Once the children were at school other challenges appeared: combining work and domestic responsibilities was (and still is) a great strain – even for a relatively privileged working mother such as myself, who can do a large proportion of her work at home. It has been relatively easy for me to cope with ill children, compared with other single mothers who work a nine-to-five equivalent and have no one to call on. The third rationale (what would happen when the children no longer needed babysitters) has also worked out rather differently from how I imagined. It's as though I'm going through a faded second adolescence. I still occasionally feel a thrill of excitement when I stay out until midnight or later, no longer restricted by the costs of babysitters. I find myself looking at my watch as the evening wears on (the curfew conditioning dies hard) and every time I get home I have a sense of relief that the house hasn't burned down. It is amusing to think that as my children live through their adolescence, discovering the adult world properly for the first time, I am rediscovering it for the second time. I have in one sense more time for my work, but I now have the challenge of how to organise a home life with two boys in a way that doesn't make me into a super-heroine – doing all the housework like a 'good Mum' should and producing young males who will always expect women to follow suit. I think, actually, there's no fear that they will remember me as anything like a super-heroine; I am ratty enough about trying to share housework to have scotched that particular myth. My current rationale is that when both sons have left home we will be mature, familiar friends. Perhaps this one is going to be the exception that proves the rule.

The rationales came into being as a kind of compensation for the fact that motherhood wasn't what I had expected – unadulterated wonder. The shock of the isolation and much of the sheer slog and boredom were exacerbated by the fact that I felt I wasn't supposed to feel dissatisfied. One of the liberating discoveries feminism brought me in 1969/70 was that it was all right to complain, to be bitter, frustrated, angry; subterranean discontents, previously only spoken about collusively, half-jokingly to other mothers, suddenly erupted. The discovery that one could develop a critique of the family, the proud defence by many women of their independence, were sources of immense support to me; but ironically, these two elements of feminism also collided. I remember having fierce and supportive discussions with other feminist mothers about how society (that is, other people) should care for and about children. I certainly had a tremendous sense of excitement at the prospect that the transformation of 'the family' was just around the corner. Of course it wasn't; a woman's choice not to be a mother is as intense as a woman's choice to have a child. I had arguments with childless feminists who didn't see why they should 'give up' their time to babysit for others. I wrote a poem out of frustration and anger, which was published in *Spare Rib*, Britain's monthly women's liberation magazine. It earned me some gleeful sympathy from mothers and terse hostility from non-mothers.

I had come slap up against one of the basic contradictions which all socialists face, and women face in particular ways: that which exists between individuals who are able to seize the moment for their liberation, and individuals who are not; between collective action and individual choice, between social and individual transformation. It is the area in which questions of a socialist/feminist ethic appear, to which there are no easy answers. The structure of a woman's life as a mother radically affects the degree to which she can participate in political activity. The fact that feminist as well as left-wing politics tend to be dominated by non-mothers is a reflection of the very real material and emotional gap that exists.

My own attitude is now equally selfish. Whereas when my children were small I was happy to look after other people's kids in return for similar services, now that my children are almost grown-up, I guard my childless moments jealously. I am far from the ideal feminist I searched for years ago: unless it is for a very close friend and a special occasion, there's no way I am going to fit babysitting for others into my life ... that may change, of course.

After my outburst of resentment at not being immediately liberated from the more oppressive aspects of domestica, I went through a phase of rediscovery of the pleasures of being with my children. I've never been the kind of mother (guilt, guilt) who took her children on exciting and educative trips, or who spent hours playing games and reading to them. But I have a great sense of pleasure in the quite ordinary, domestic minutiae of the harmonious moments of living with other people – and children. The very private, intimate moments (when you're not dog-tired) of feeding a tiny baby in the middle of a very still night are unrepeatable. Similarly, when my children were still at primary school many evenings were cosy, intimate and special times; early supper, eaten together in front of the television, then sitting on the couch, a child on either side of me, my arms round them – the warmth of the closeness to other human beings is a very special aspect of parenthood, also unrepeatable.

The privacy and intensity of such moments is very difficult to retain or remember. Each stage of the children's lives feels as though it is the only stage. There is no past and no future. An erratically kept photograph album reminds me of how their faces, now developing an adult bone structure, were once soft and malleable. Other photos show grinning or sulky babies, bony heads covered with soft hair; they remind me of times just after breast-feeding, holding a tiny baby up on my shoulder to wind him, his face towards my neck, his nose breathing soft warm air against my skin, indicating his contentment. Another photo reminds me of a two-year-old, asleep, floppy and relaxed in my arms in the back seat of the car, his trust and warmth entirely compensating for the fact that he has been cantankerous all day.

The photos are fixed moments; they remind me of the good times, flashes of experience which cloud and recede as soon as the album is closed. Today's experiences will soon join them.

The present: 1

The petrol pump in my car packs up. I take the tube home. The Automobile Association is permanently engaged, my local garage too busy to look at the car. It is now mid-afternoon. The garage suggests ways in which I can try and start the car and in the course of the next three hours I make three trips back to try. Futile. Meanwhile the kids are home, flopped after school. Failure and the world flood over me. I collapse into tears. I am useless, there is no supper and how will I ever catch up on all the years I've missed. The television is on and I'm sobbing.

Ivan: Why are you crying?

Me (*sob*): Because I'm tired and horrible and useless.

Adam: Don't be silly. You're fine, you've got a busy life and you're earning a good living.

Me: But the car's broken down, I'm tired and I haven't got you any supper, and I've got to go out tonight. (*Self-pity sets in.*)

Ivan: We'll have take-away for supper.

Adam: Take a taxi if you're going to be late.

Me (*more tears*): But what about the vitamins and the proteins and the carbohydrates?

Ivan: We *like* take-away, and anyway I'm going to see Spurs play their last match of the season because I'm a loyal fan, so we'll all be busy.

Me: I'm a terrible mother.

Adam: Bullshit. (*Turns the television up louder.*)

I sniff and dry my eyes, consoled. I look up. There is Ivan, his face red, tears pouring down his cheeks; Adam is sitting on the couch holding a cushion up to his face.

Me (*surprised*): What's wrong?

Ivan: If I see you cry it makes me cry.

Adam (*muffled*): I'm not crying, I haven't cried for years.

I hug Ivan, kiss away the salt on his warm face, laugh at Adam and we all sit there crying and laughing and nobody would believe how corny and amazing the whole scene is. I love them. We are all extraordinary.

The present: 2

It is Saturday morning. I am exhausted, having spent two weeks in rehearsal of a play of mine. Being a writer is a double-edged thing, producing curious and occasional reverberations with motherhood. Both involve long periods of isolation and tedium; both involve periods spent very intensely with other people, which can be emotionally exhausting.

Quick breakfast, I wince at the mess in the house, and go off to the supermarket for the week's food. Stagger home, to find Ivan watching television. 'At ten o'clock in the bloody morning?' I switch if off; resentful howls, his bedroom door slams shut. I go off for my weekly visit to my parents, telling both kids that I want their rooms cleaned, the living room tidied and the washing-up done by the time I get home. We have a rota for basic housework jobs, with Mum doing the lioness's share, so I reckon that today they can do a bit more than usual. Feminist principles on paper are one thing; application in real life quite another. Do them good.

I arrive home at one-thirty, having bought Cornish pasties for lunch. The living-room now has cereal plates and milk-stained glasses placed at tasteful random. Ivan is lying on the floor, watching a sports programme, Adam is lying on the couch complaining of a backache from his paper round. The kitchen sink is full of plates, empty milk bottles, the waste bin is over-flowing. I sweep into the living-room, switch the bloody television off *again*, appeal to their reason, my full and busy life, their laziness, flipping choice four-letter words into the tirade.

Ivan: But it's not natural for a kid to want to do housework.

Me (screams): It's not natural for people *not* to want to do housework. (*warning*) You'll be male chauvinists when you grow up.

Ivan (sweet reason): But everyone is male chauvinist.

Me: That's the trouble with everybody; the whole world is unnatural.

Adam has gone silent and by now is in the kitchen, wearing rubber gloves, washing up a glass. He puts it on the draining board. I feel the water. It is cold. I put the glass back in to the sink. He washes it again and puts it back on the draining board. The water is still cold. We repeat the tense silent dance once more, by which time the water is getting lukewarm. I leave him to it.

When he has finished washing up I return to the attack.

Me: You both want me to be your bloody servant.

Adam: Don't worry. I'll leave home soon and then I won't have to think about anyone but me.

Me: Oh yes? Well, you'll find that life isn't bloody like that.

He pulls off the rubber gloves and flings them into the sink so that the insides get wet.

Me: And you haven't taken the empty milk bottles out.

He takes his jacket.

Adam: I'm going out. You may see me tomorrow.

Front door slams. Bloody kids. Bloody hell.

The present: coda

I am working at home. I stop when the kids get back from school and go off to do the shopping. When I get back, the children's eyes light up. They pounce on the bags and packets, dumping them on every available kitchen surface, inspecting goodies for instant gratification and turning over the prospect of the next few days' meals. I am a wonderful mother.

That evening Adam announces he's going out. I suggest he shouldn't be back late. He says he'll do what he wants and reminds me that he doesn't need me to tell him when he's tired, cold, wet or hungry any more. Next morning, as I yawn over breakfast, he tells me I shouldn't have so many late nights. *Touché*.

The only people I can say I love with any sense of confidence are my children. I can say that because I feel more secure about my feelings for, and obligations to them than I do about anyone else. The fundamental doubts and confusions which exist in adult relationships are absent. That is both reassuring and frightening, since I know that in a few years they will be gone, living their own lives, forgetting my birthday and feeling guilty, going through all the convolutions that mothers and children go through as they decide whether as adults they can develop friendship, or whether they will be stuck in the emotional traps which dog so many mother/child relationships which haven't grown up.

In one sense, of course, I will always be a mother: but I hope that will mean a deep sense of attachment that can span anywhere they go and (almost) anything they do. Certainly the next few years are going to be interesting, as certain changes already herald a negotiation between us into some sort of adult relationship. The cuddly sensuality of the early years has virtually gone. Now I am hardly allowed to touch them, and that's okay, since it isn't 'them' I want to touch; it is the earlier, more dependent stages which I somehow think I can recall by contact with these two large almost-adults. Adam is already taller than me, Ivan not far behind. The move into adolescence requires a rejection of all the old childlike intimacies, except in times of crisis, and except as a sub-text to our daily lives: somewhere deep inside them they still want good old Mum to provide all the creature comforts, and somewhere deep inside me I still (occasionally) like doing just that. I've had a go at up-dating intimacy – squeezing adolescent blackheads (I hope my children won't be too angry at these revelations) but that isn't really the same thing, so I think I'll drop it.

Now and again I have a pang of regret that I didn't have a daughter, just to see what it's like. I worry that my family will follow the pattern of many others – children reacting against parents, and that my attempts to convey the lessons of feminism to the next (male) generation may come to very little. I also worry about losing a very important skill that I have developed and refined: a neat line in baby and toddler-talk. I haven't yet tried this skill on many adults – and I would be sad to think it might turn rusty with non-use. While in many ways I am proud of the fact that I have so far managed to see two other human beings along their way, I wonder now whether I will always continue to have my learned maternal reflexes called up. Recently on holiday I saw a group of teenagers camping on a French beach. One of them appeared to have sunstroke and/or bronchitis. I had to restrain myself from going up to him, telling him off and giving him some helpful advice. I'm convinced still that I'm somehow responsible for his subsequent suffering if he really was ill. Until a few years ago I would stiffen with concern whenever I heard an anonymous cry of 'Mummy' in the street. 'Mummy' was me, and somehow I was responsible for that child's happiness. It could be that once a mother, always a mother. Or it could be that when my children have fully grown up, I will be able to hold on to a healthy but detached interest in other people's welfare without the guilt trip. Perhaps as my children 'grow up' from childhood, I will 'grow up' from motherhood. Or perhaps 'growing up' is itself another rationale . . .

Judith Barrington

Like many other women, I arrived at raising children without ever making a clear decision to do it. Unlike many
of those women, I am neither the biological mother of the
children I am raising, nor did I marry their parent and become
a step-mother. I am a lesbian, living with my lover and sharing
the raising of two children with her.

In order to understand some of the issues that affect my
particular situation as a parent, a few historical facts are necessary. Harriet, my lover, cannot conceive and when she was
married she adopted four children – two girls and two boys.
Her reasons for choosing motherhood are very different from
mine, and I will include them in the form of a short interview
later. After being married for ten years, Harriet and her
husband were divorced and she decided to live as a lesbian.
After a short period when she lived alone with all four children
and then with one daughter and one son, the custody of the
children was settled: both daughters live with Harriet (and now
with me too) and both sons live with their father. I came to this

Judith Barrington was born in Sussex in 1944. She was active in the women's liberation movement in London before moving to Portland, Oregon in 1976. There she continues to work for women's liberation as a campaigner, teacher, poet and parent.

situation from a background of mostly lesbian relationships, although for about seven years I was unable to accept that part of me, and tried also to have relationships with men. I had been married, too, for a little over a year. Naema, the oldest of the four children that Harriet adopted, is fifteen. She is racially mixed (black and white), goes to a public high school, and has difficulty in dealing with her home not being a traditional nuclear family. Anyika is nearly nine and is black. She has attended an alternative school for two years. The four of us have lived together for more than two and a half years as I write this, during which time Harriet and I bought a house in north-east Portland, a primarily black neighbourhood in the city. I mention the racial differences because the children experience a real sense of difference from many families they know, not only because the two parents they live with are women, but also because we are both white.

I hear voices. All women do — although they may not call them that. Recently, the writings of Susan Griffin have helped me to understand this question of voices and it has been very helpful for me to give a voice to those attitudes and expectations of the patriarchy which, one way or another, put pressure on all of us women — even though we may not all experience the pressure literally in the form of a 'voice'. By giving the patriarchy a voice that also reflects a part of myself, and by recording the actual words of that voice, I can more easily separate patriarchal attitudes from my own beliefs as a woman. This, in turn, gives me the power to choose whether or not to listen.

All my life I carried in my head the voice of the patriarchy, mostly without being aware of it. The course that it advocated for me was in conflict with almost everything that was good for me as a woman and a human being. In the past I called this voice 'guilt' and accepted that it was mine, and a part of me. Now that I have started calling it 'the voice of the patriarchy' it has become theirs: something imposed on me that does not have to be a part of me. It is something I notice, fight against, and name for what it is.

I was better than some at keeping the patriarchal voice at bay —

at least as far as letting it influence my choices was concerned. I do not remember, as a child, ever imagining myself as a mother and I think, in some dim way, I grasped the essential destructiveness of making important decisions on the basis of other people's expectations. Also I was stubborn. And, more than that, I was always mystified by my mother's position in the family since it was absolutely clear to me from the earliest time I can remember that my mother was a superior being; she was certainly superior to my father. When children are supposed to stop thinking that, and transfer their reverence to their fathers, I failed to do so. Psychology would say that I was defective. It occurs to me, however, that it is equally possible that my father was defective – or that psychology is defective. What about mothers who actually are superior to fathers? Anyway, it continued to amaze me that my mother deferred to my father and treated him as if he were more clever, more wise, more important. I had a sense of conspiracy that I did not understand and my fury about it was usually misdirected at my mother, until finally, as a teenager, I managed to show some of how I despised my father, mostly by refusing to speak to him at all.

And the voices said *how petty to resent his power; your mother accepts it, she is a better person than you; you need to grow up; when you are mature enough you will be able to love him and accept his authority; if you don't – you are simply infantile.*

I grew up wanting to free my mother from injustice, but not wanting her to free herself. Once or twice when she could not stand my feuds with my father, she announced that she would have to leave, and I was seized with terror. If she could actually step outside her place in the family, where would that leave me? If she took power, I would have to take even more, in order to keep her with me. Most of this was not consciously thought out, but by the time I was eleven, my dreams and waking fantasies were of rescuing women from a variety of perilous situations that involved such things as killing lions, calming rabid dogs, or riding a horse for help through an electric storm at night. The idea of my becoming a mother had no place in my dreams, nor in any thoughts I had for my future.

And because the voices couldn't change what I did, or what I thought, they started to work on what I was. *You're different; your friends have different dreams; you don't fit in; you're different . . .*

My brother and sister are both much older than I am. Once when I was around six and my brother was twenty-one, he was mistaken for my father. I grew used to being the youngest everywhere and a daughter to many people. At school I was the youngest in my class for eleven years. My mother believed in raising independent children, so I was not at all 'babied' or protected, even though I was somewhat spoiled with possessions. The role to which I aspired was that of the 'successful daughter' of whom my parents could be proud, not a daughter who was a burden or needed anything. I had to stand on my own feet, but retain approval. I was a teenager when my brother and sister started having their own children and I liked the babies well enough but was not moved to any maternal feelings of my own. I could not see myself as a daughter and as a mother at the same time. *You're different, you're not normal; you'll never be like them; you can't do what you're supposed to; you're different.*

I often wonder just what it was that pushed me to act out my lesbianism. The mystery is not that I was attracted to women, as I am sure almost all of us are at some time, but rather that I, who was so conventional, should have allowed my emotions such freedom, when everything I knew intellectually condemned such a step. The voices had a field day during the period following my first affair with a woman.

You're sick; perverted; there's something wrong with your hormones; nobody must find out, they'll recoil from you, be horrified; you're sick, perverted; nobody must know . . .

I was always very stubborn about getting what I wanted, and there was no doubt that while I was in love with a woman I wanted a complete relationship, including sex. The patriarchal voice, which I did not yet recognise for what it was, weighed me down with guilt. For several years I did not look my close friends straight in the eye, as I became adept at living a double life: one heterosexual, the other lesbian. Meanwhile, my friends were getting married and having children.

I did not know how to relate to children; couldn't talk to them and felt awkward and embarrassed trying to play with them. This was no particular surprise to me: *Only Real Women know how to be with children; that's part of being a Real Woman; you don't belong around children; in fact if your friends really knew, they wouldn't let you near their children; you're not a Real Woman.* Once in a while, the way a child looked would hit me in some romantic spot. Usually it was a blond little boy, and a momentary sweep of the eyelashes would trigger a place in me that I kept well buried most of the time, so that I would not succumb to a lifestyle that I instinctively felt would be bad for me. *Time is running out; how long can you go on being an exception; can't you see all your friends marrying, settling down, having children? What makes you immune? You think you are different, you have a career, everyone is proud of you and you think you're so wonderful because you're not just a housewife; but sooner or later . . . your time is running out; this is just a bonus, a little extra time; sooner or later you will have to become a Real Woman . . .*

I continued being a daughter. I had a passionate affair with a woman who had a daughter almost my own age. My lack of 'legitimacy' both as a lover (which I was) and a daughter (which I pretended to be, to explain our closeness) nearly drove me insane. I continued to fabricate a heterosexual life, believing in it myself, since I had no basis for knowing that a lesbian life could exist. I had never heard of such a thing, and had only read negative accounts of such people. I could not imagine ever knowing a woman who accepted herself as a lesbian, so finally I let in the voices, gave up on my romantic dreams of living with a woman lover in some isolated place, and married a man I liked.

Before we decided to be married, I got pregnant and it was a terrible shock to me. I knew immediately what it was, even when the doctor insisted that I had hepatitis to explain my daily vomiting. By the time I managed to produce a positive pregnancy test and find out how to have an abortion, I was eighteen weeks pregnant and the operation was painful and frightening. At the time, I never considered having the baby, since motherhood was so far removed from my consciousness and I was still just struggling to accept marriage as a real option. I was also too proud to run the risk of having Colin marry me because of the baby, thinking that if I were to be married at least I wanted to know he was making some kind of choice about me. While I was pregnant I had no feelings at all about the baby. The voices, if they were there, remained at a great distance, assisted by the large amounts of alcohol I was drinking at the time. More than a year later they got through to me: *How old would your baby be now? A year old — just like that little baby there. I wonder what he would look like* — (the voices always spoke about a boy child). *If you had had that child, you would have someone of your own now; someone who needed you. He would have been beautiful and clever . . . I wonder what his name would have been; he wouldn't leave you; you could have been proud of him; you could cuddle him and know he would always love you . . .*

And I started to notice little children.

It wasn't until I had left my husband, abandoned my career as a company director, and become involved in radical feminist politics that I started to accept myself as a lesbian. In spite of the overwhelming evidence of my passions over the previous seven years, I did not think of lesbianism as a viable option until I met other women who accepted it. Feminists helped me to understand some of the political reasons why homosexuality is such a taboo. I felt a profound shock of recognition when I finally understood that society relies on the nuclear family and the dependence of women on men to maintain the division of labour. Many things fell into place, as I grasped the significance of feminism and saw the lengths to which white men would go to maintain their position of privilege and power. I saw why I had hated myself as a lesbian and why that hatred had always seemed so much in conflict with the love and respect I found within lesbian relationships: there was really nothing wrong with me after all! I was just not doing what the patriarchy requires women to do.

The question of children now took on other dimensions, and I began to think about it politically, as a feminist. Women I knew who were mothers talked with me about the oppressive nature of motherhood. Women's groups I was involved with talked vaguely about shared responsibility for children and the women's liberation movement demanded better childcare facilities, but very few women with small children were active. The women who spoke of shared responsibility were women I respected and I assumed that I ought to take part in it, but I didn't know how. Nobody asked me to do anything concrete, and the voices were beginning to confuse me with conflicting messages. *What can you do? Why are you thinking about being with children? You are just a lesbian; children won't like you; you don't have any right to step in and deal with someone else's child; who do you think you are? You're not the kind of woman who can do that; you know nothing about children and you never will; you are not that kind of woman . . .*

I was in a double bind. As if this voice was not enough, there was a second voice pushing me in a different direction, and confusing me with whispers of 'freedom' when I knew quite well I wasn't free at all: *What right do you have to be free? You are free, compared to those women with children; they have to be home, can't go to meetings without a babysitter; they worry about their children; you, too, should have to worry; what right have you got to be free; who do you think you are? Lesbians are so selfish; it's just another way of caring only about yourself; how can anything change if you don't share the tasks that women have to do; what kind of feminist are you? All talk, but when it comes to doing . . .*

Sometimes this patriarchal voice and the voices of angry, frustrated mothers became confused in my mind. Mothers and non-mothers each resorted to patriarchal attitudes, as we put each other down, having no real idea of how to start a dialogue, much less a sharing process. I had considerable experience of this struggle, since I became romantically involved several times with women who had children. The attraction was not that I wanted to be around children particularly, but was more concerned with my 'daughter' image and how that fitted in with the 'mother' in my lover. Since the voices were telling me that I ought to be a mother, and would be when I finally 'grew up', I assumed that mothers were good and I was bad. However, I had somehow avoided marriage and motherhood out of a stubborn sense of self-protection and of my own potential. The part of me that had done this and was immune to the voices was also a part of me that had little respect for the 'mother' in the women I loved. I did not believe they were choosing the role, as indeed they often were not, and I could not understand why they had succumbed to the voices, since somehow I had struggled not to. I began to hate the mother role, and gradually to separate out from the role the nurturing qualities of women, whether or not they were mothers, and value those qualities for what they were. Once I separated mothering qualities from the institution of motherhood, I saw that I could adopt those qualities myself and value them in other women. I could give and receive nurturing without having to reproduce a mother/daughter power dynamic. I felt as if I was really growing.

The responsibility for children continued to be a political question that I thought about. There were women who had made deliberate decisions not to have children, and who wanted nothing to do with shared responsibility. I understood their feelings. There were also single mothers who had borne children because of ignorance, the desire to please, failure of birth control, violent men, or a genuine desire to do the one thing they were allowed to do well without interference. Some of these women now wanted to move away from the limitations of single motherhood. I understood their position too. But where did I fit in? I had never really decided not to have children: in fact, whenever I managed to think about it without pressure or guilt, I rather liked the idea of teaching a child about the world and watching her grow. I knew that I did not want to raise a child alone, as a single mother; the isolation experienced by some of my friends, and their anger, warned me. I nursed fantasies of collective households that included children, but none of the women I was living with seemed to be thinking about it seriously and I was still too unsure of what I thought about collective responsibility for children to risk more disapproval by raising the subject. It seemed that I had never really had a chance to make up my mind about my own connection with children because of the constant pressure: to conform; to be a wife and mother; to share responsibility for children; to have my own child and gain a little security; to prove myself a normal woman. My solution was to volunteer as a helper in a daycare centre. I thought that by being around children I would find out if I really liked them and how much of my awkwardness was simply unfamiliarity.

All the other volunteers were mothers of children who were in the centre and they viewed me with suspicion, thinking – quite rightly – that I knew nothing about children. The first day, with one other worker, I took some twenty-five three- and four-year-olds to the nearby park. I was terrified that I would lose some of the children, and would not know which ones I had lost since I did not know any of their names yet. I did not know how to talk to them; I was afraid to take control when necessary; I knew they would not want to play with me; and generally I felt as if I had no right at all to be there. I felt so inadequate that it took me weeks to learn the names of the children, even after I had developed favourites and was familiar with all of them.

I was sure that the mothers who worked at the centre were prejudiced against me because I was not a mother and, even worse, a lesbian. I did not look like them and my life was entirely different from theirs. The children knew I was different too, and in a few cases had a problem figuring out if I was a woman or a man, because I rode a motorcycle and did not look like their mothers. Even though it was an 'alternative' centre, run by a collective of parents and started by a women's group, the children had very rigid ideas of sex roles that left me unclassifiable and embarrassed. Many of the problems I encountered were due to my lesbianism. The voices rattled on: *Children belong in families with mothers and fathers; if they don't have that, at least they know about it and want it; you can never be a part of that world; what are you doing around these children? Do you have bad motives? Maybe you secretly want to molest them . . . at least their mothers probably think so. You're not a Real Woman; you don't have a 'way with children'; you don't belong here; anyway, it's not fair to think you can learn on these children; you shouldn't have to learn at all; if you can't do it instinctively, you just don't have what it takes. Real Women are not afraid of children.*

I was horrified that at the age of three and four these children were displaying sexist attitudes to one another. It seemed to me that I could play a part in breaking down the stereotypes they already had fixed in their minds, since I was a strong independent woman who was not trying to act like a man, but didn't fit the traditional female role either. If I could only laugh off their questions and mistakes without embarrassment, feeling good about the person I was, I was sure I could have some influence on them, and on their mothers too. This goal became another voice in my head that, for a while, I thought was a rational one – my own female voice. Later I began to distrust it, seeing it as a more subtle way for the patriarchy to push me towards motherhood. *The best way for you, as a woman, to influence the world is through children. How can you work for any kind of revolution that does not educate the next generation? What women can do that is really important is raise children with different attitudes.* I questioned this, in some confusion, suspecting a trap in the idea that revolution requires our individual efforts towards individual children. It seemed like the same kind of thinking as the idea that revolution lies in the way we each separately lead our personal life. Children *need* to be influenced. But what can we, as single mothers or groups of parents, hope to do while the children are raised in the same patriarchal system, with the same schools, the same teachers, the same textbooks, the same television programmes and the same fathers? Once we have children, there are ways we can work to counteract the sexism of these institutions, but having children in itself does not seem to be the answer to the problem. We are just not strong enough to fight the institutions that ultimately control how our children are raised. Like so many of the reasons women give for choosing motherhood, it may be just another version of what Adrienne Rich calls 'filling the void', or obscuring the futility of our own lives and struggles. Back then, I became convinced of the political sense of child-raising just when I was beginning to realise that my passionate commitment to feminist politics was unlikely to have any serious effect on the patriarchy. It was appealing to think that I could educate another generation to my views: although not easy, it seemed more possible than fighting the whole system.

Even though I had already begun to think quite seriously about somehow living with children, the reason I live with them now is because I fell in love with Harriet, and they came with her. This may sound a little callous, but it is accurate; I tried, at first, to rationalise it in other ways – to believe I would have chosen to live with these children anyway. It was easy to believe this about Anyika, who was younger, more trusting, and easier to love. But the fact is that I had to work hard at developing relationships with the children, since I had fallen in love with their mother, not with them. Many traditional step-parent problems arose: I was tested, struggled against; I inspired jealousy. For my part, I resented feeling like an outsider – particularly when we moved into our new home, which I felt should mark the beginning of our equal 'belonging' in the group. The patriarchal voice started telling me exactly what I should become: *Mothers are selfless; you have no right to expect the children to go away when you need to work; they are always the priority; it is heartless to resent their existence; you should always meet their needs; they will be terribly damaged if you cannot give them unconditional love; how can you possibly expect them to understand your needs; you are not supposed to have needs; you are an adult, they are children; mothers never act selfishly; it is selfish to want to do anything without them; put their needs first; always be available . . .*

But the same mechanism that had protected me earlier in my life still operated. I did make demands, I did insist on being a person, and I tried to treat the children like people too. Anyika, who had been having a lot of behaviour problems in school, seemed to thrive on my expectations. It was a struggle, but we all adapted slowly. Probably the most difficult part was working it out with Harriet, since we loved each other, and differences between us were painful. The process of learning how to share parenting was long and difficult, and is still going on. At the beginning, I did not realise how difficult it was for Harriet to trust me to make my own decisions around the children – even though she wanted me to, and hated it when I asked her to act on my behalf. She could not stand being an intermediary between me and the children, but part of her wanted to retain control – since she was sure that she loved the kids, and for a while wasn't sure that I did. As for me, I wanted to be trusted and to be responsible. I was hurt when the children ignored me and went to Harriet, and when, since she was so used to being a single mother, she did not notice.

Now we have moved a long way beyond that, although at the moment I do more parenting around Anyika and Harriet does more with Naema. This is partly due to the age difference and the fact that Naema will never completely transfer her love and trust to me at this stage of her life, and partly because I am noticeably lacking in the patience that seems to be required in parenting a rebellious teenager. Since I do not have Harriet's long history of love and commitment to Naema, I am often unable to summon up the time and energy that Naema demands. I participate in major decisions, but I cannot always produce the depths of understanding that are called for.

Although Naema is old enough not to need me as a parent, Anyika has completely accepted me in that role, which has made me vulnerable in new ways: there are real dangers, and the voices echo the dangers: *You have no legitimate connection to this child; you are nothing; you are not really a parent; you are not a legal guardian; what claim could you ever have to credibility? What rights do you have? If you do not stay with Harriet, you will have no relationship with the child; she will be taken away, no matter how much you love her; you cannot claim any parental rights; two years of parenting does not make you anything. Who are you anyway? Her father is the one who has the rights – he is her father after all; nothing can change that; even though he lived with her for less time than you have, and it was long ago; even though he knows her less, sees her rarely; he is legitimate; you are nothing; you have no rights; you are nothing; be prepared; you will lose her if . . .*

Harriet's different approach to some of the issues we deal with comes from her history as a woman, a lesbian and a mother. Rather than trying to interpret Harriet in this account, I decided to interview her.

Judith: When did you decide to have children and why?

Harriet: I always knew I wanted to have children; that was a very important part of my growing up. It was part of my image – I bought the whole 'wife and mother' bit, hook, line and sinker! When I was eighteen and found out I couldn't have children, it was devastating, so when I met Don I told him that I wanted to adopt them. I wanted them – it wasn't something I had to decide – I just always accepted that that was what I would do.

J: Have you any way of knowing how much your decision was tied up with the traditional female role and how much was to do with the kind of person you are outside that – if you can separate them?

H: Well, it would be hard to separate those. I mean – now I can do it, but then I couldn't. It was very tied up with how I saw myself. For a long time I thought I wasn't a complete person – I wasn't a real woman – because I couldn't have children, and I'm sure that adopting four kids was part of that – I mean I really did like the babies, but I think there was a lot of trying to prove myself by society's standards of what a woman should be. I was all hung up on being creative; I had a very brief therapy session before I got married and I remember making the connection between not being able to have kids and being a creative person. I was working in the theatre and it was very important to me to be a creative person; it was like a substitute for being a mother. I couldn't create babies, and in a way being a costume designer was a substitute for that.

J: Did you feel that adopting and raising children would satisfy the same creative urge as actually bearing children?

H: Well, when I adopted children, I didn't say to myself 'now I am going to be creative' – I just wanted children; I love children and always have. My mother loved children, we always had kids around, I babysat, I work with children now. I love watching them grow and develop and I think the future is in their hands and it's important to me to be part of that developing process. And I really love babies, so each time one started growing up [laughter] I went to the baby store! We had arbitrarily set a figure of four kids from the beginning and we didn't question that a whole lot. I don't regret adopting the kids.

J: Do you ever regret the limitations that four children have put on your life?

H: Oh sure. I would like to have options of being independent; wanting to go off by myself without feeling guilty because it means that you have to watch the children. I'd like to be able to say 'I need some space; I'm going off into the woods for a couple of days.' It has been hard to do that in my life. Now it has implications for you and means that you have to watch the kids, and I don't do it. I've never been alone — never lived alone — not completely. I had a roommate and she moved out when Don moved in. And then there were the kids; Don and I split up but the kids were there, so I've never been alone. I want to be with you now, but it's one of those things that everyone has in a little corner of themselves — a little wish. I don't regret it though. I would never not have done it, and if I had it to do over again, I'd do it again.

J: Do you have any ideas about how it could be different, so you could have had the children — as you say you would do over again — without having so many limitations put on your life?

H: Well, kibbutzim are a wonderful idea. I think children should be raised collectively. I think they should not be dependent on one figure to meet their needs. I think if I lived in a communal setting, there would be a children's house, and there would be our house, and a big communal house and . . .

J: Do you think it's possible to do that within this society?

H: Well, you could do it on the outskirts of this society. Any kind of communal living is not within this society, really. When one is living in cities, or within the structure of society, there is pressure to be nuclear.

J: Do you ever feel guilty about how being an open lesbian affects the children?

H: Occasionally, but not a whole lot. I do in the sense that I wish the kids grew up the way I grew up with lots of aunts and uncles and cousins and an extended family. I feel really good about the way I grew up even though I was poor. I don't think the kids have enough adults to relate to. You know, when you're actually related to somebody they don't go away and stay away. I always said that women friends could provide that – you know I thought that way about M— and T—, but they're not there any more so I feel it doesn't work. I wish the kids had more adults so that when they're having trouble with us they could go and talk to someone where they felt welcome, or if they needed space they could spend a couple of days or – for that matter – if we did, we could too.

J: Did you deliberately choose to adopt children of colour, and how do you feel now about their situation, growing up black or mixed with white parents?

H: We did not deliberately adopt black children or mixed race children. We went to the adoption agency to adopt Naema and the woman asked us if we would accept a mixed-race or a black child and we said that we would. We decided then that the race of the child mattered less than that the child was an infant, and at that time that kind of an answer ensured that we would get a mixed-race child, because they had a much harder time placing mixed-race children than white children or all-black children. So we adopted Naema and less than a year later the agency called and asked us if we would take another one – this time a boy, and we agreed. Then we decided to get another child and to try and get a child with a different race involved – I guess we were committed to mixed-race or black children by then. It felt as if it would be a put-down of the children we already had if we adopted white children – like saying 'There's something wrong with you, now we have to get a white child.' So – we didn't set out to save the world or show the world that everyone can live in harmony, like some people I knew, who thought they could solve problems by having this multi-cultural melting pot in their own homes. We belonged to something called the 'Open door for adoptable children' and there were several families with women who could have children of their own, who adopted an oriental child and a black child, or something like that, who seemed much more crusading than we were. At the time we adopted they were having a hard time placing mixed-race children, and we wanted children, so we adopted them.

We anticipated that when the children were in their teens there might be some identity problems, but we felt we could handle them. We also knew that adopting them would affect what kind of environment we lived in – we couldn't live in an ultra-conservative community. I didn't anticipate being divorced and becoming a lesbian; I anticipated living in a fairly liberal, academic environment, being married to a professor. We made a conscious decision to live in a black or mixed neighbourhood when we moved to Portland; we thought it was important for the children to become familiar with and associate with black people and not feel alienated from black people. Sometimes I think maybe it made them feel more alienated because we were definitely different: they were the only black kids around who had white parents. Still, even now, Naema's friends say 'Is *that* your mother?' when they see me.

J: What do you think are the advantages and disadvantages of sharing the responsibility for children with another woman?

H: Well, the advantages of course are that there are two people to share the responsibilities, two people to solve the problems, two people for the kids to come home to, so that one isn't always overloaded with being there. If one is late for dinner, there's someone else, you know. Two different points of view. Kids are people – they don't always get along with other people, even their mothers . . . there's another person the kids can go to and say 'I can't stand what she did. I don't think she was fair.' Plus, there's all that support – emotional support. The disadvantages are [laughter] you can't do it all your own way! You have to hassle it out, you have to agree, you have to say 'I didn't like what you did' or 'I think you weren't fair' or 'I don't like it when you interfere'. You think one way and I think another, so I can't just come home from work and think to myself 'to hell with what I was going to do, I'll do something different with the kids' – I have to consult you.

J: Do you think it's possible really to share the ultimate responsibility, so you don't feel as if the other person can always walk off?

H: Yes, I do. I feel, with us, that it's easier to share that level of responsibility for Anyika with you than to share Naema, because I feel that with Anyika you have a much more real relationship. There's a lot more involvement, a lot more love on both parts, and at this point in my life I would think very seriously about how my not being with you would affect her and where she would live. I don't automatically assume that she would go with me if we were not together. I do with Naema because your living with her is much more 'being involved with Harriet's daughter' or being involved with somebody who lives in your house. You parent her, but you do it in a much different way than with Anyika, and that's because Naema is much harder to get involved with since she's fifteen. A lot of her self is more formed — you had more involvement with the development of Anyika, and you can see your influence. Naema won't let you do that. I think it's possible to share that basic responsibility, but I think it's crucial at what age the person who is not the parent becomes involved with the child. I think it's also crucial how the mother feels about herself as a mother, at the time — I have been working through a lot of things about being a mother, probably due to your influence, and it has been a good thing to see myself as a person first and a mother as part of that — but not so consuming a part as before. I am capable of sharing it now, when there's somebody who wants to share it.

J: I wonder if there's any difference between sharing with a woman than if, say, you had got married again and the children had a step-father?

H: I think in some ways it's harder with two women, because there are no models. You have to work it all out yourself — I mean, whatever you think, roles have functions. It can be comfortable when you know what's expected of you. A lot of women are very threatened by getting away from female roles because they don't know what they're supposed to do. I mean, if there's something you're supposed to do and you do it well, you're a good person. Now, if you take that away, you have to find another set of things for how to describe yourself as a good person. You know — we have roles: I do most of the shopping and cooking; you do the baking of the bread; you mow the lawn

160

and I do the weeding. I know that's not traditional roles, but we do have roles. Sometimes they're preferences, but sometimes I resent them.

J: How does having children affect your relationship with me?

H: It takes too much damn time, that's what it does! Having kids doesn't give you a whole lot of space to keep a relationship alive and exciting. We really have to work at it much harder than if there weren't kids around. There are so many things that get in the way: you can't follow the natural warm feelings that happen: you have to make dinner if the kids are hungry; you can't keep them waiting for things as much as you would keep yourself waiting, if you decided something else was more important. We have to keep meal times and bed times and coming home times and being with the kids times, in a much more regular way, and that eats away at spontaneity and time to keep a relationship growing and alive. We've had to work hard to overcome that.

J: How do you feel about the children leaving home, and how your life will be without them?

H: I look forward to it, and yet I know I'm having a hard time letting Anyika grow up, because I want to be able to hold her on my lap and cuddle her when I want to. I don't think she'll be like Naema though, who won't let me do that. I think probably Anyika will be different when she's fifteen. There's also an element of . . . when they're gone I can do what I want, and that's scary. I've got this cop-out: I can't be whoever I want to be now, because of the children. I have this fantasy of us, doing interesting work and being free; toodling around the country in a camper; doing exciting things. Everything changes. Right now, I live with kids and some time I won't. I can't say if it will be better or worse. It'll just be different. There are rewards from raising kids and also from not . . . I wouldn't like to think they'll always be living with me [laughter] – but I'm glad they are now.

At the beginning of this essay I said that the children experience a sense of being 'different', partly because they are either black or mixed and live with two white women. Naema has, at different times in her life, identified very strongly as white and as black. Right now, she wants to be black, and is strongly involved with black culture, black music and black friends. Anyika often used to say she wished she were white, and envied kids, who had long straight hair. Last year, she called herself 'brown' and felt hurt if anyone said she was black, in spite of efforts at home and at school to give positive value to her being black. She seems to have less of a problem with it now, possibly because her sister is so obviously selecting black people in her life.

Although I have lived with Naema and Anyika for nearly three years, and have recognised that they are confused about their racial identities, I have only very recently started to question some of the things I originally took for granted. Because Harriet felt that they should be able to identify with black culture, we bought a house in a predominantly black neighbourhood. Some of the kids on our street added to our children's sense of being different by questioning them and teasing them about their white family. I had assumed it was in their best interests to live where we chose, but now I am not so sure. I also assumed it was in their best interests to make friends with black children and their families. I still do, but I now recognise that it is hard for them to feel part of the black community while Harriet and I are tolerated as liberal whites, and while socially we associate almost exclusively with white women in the women's community.

When Naema started having problems about six months ago, we sent her to a counsellor, but never realised at the time that she probably needed to talk to someone black. Only in the extremity of Naema's recent unhappiness have I understood that we, alone, cannot help the children through the racial identity crisis. It is not enough to reiterate that they are good people – that their different colour from ours does not matter, because it *does* matter to *them*. Nothing that I can say to them can be separated from the fact that I am white: that I have the power that goes with that. Even though I am saying, and genuinely believing, that it doesn't make any difference within our family, the children know somewhere within themselves that I could, if I chose, define our relative values any way I wanted. This is not because they don't trust me, but simply because I am not only an adult but I am also white, and I have to accept that additional aspect of the power imbalance.

I am only just beginning to think about what we all need to do, in order to maintain mutual respect and support across the racial differences. I worry that by the time I have any sort of understanding that goes beyond the glib liberal line, it will be too late. I also worry that some of the things I see as important are simply not there: black families who share our concern, accept our situation and are friends to the children; black women in our community who can show the children that the women's community is relevant to them as well as to us. I know that it is not enough to learn how to braid hair with beads and take African records out of the Children's Library, but I have not yet looked hard enough for the right kind of support.

The political implications of childraising continue to worry me. As a parent I do have certain power, which I want to use both to give the children I live with more power in their own lives, and to expose them to attitudes which will counterbalance the patriarchal stereotypes they see all around them. However I am constantly aware of all the other influences they are exposed to. Possibly my inability to sit back and accept the inevitable is connected to my past reluctance to become a mother. Pessimistic as it may seem, I continue to think that it is very difficult to parent in a way that equips the children to avoid the limitations of a heterosexist, misogynist and racist society. There are many frustrations and contradictions.

Every day I watch a teenage girl play out many aspects of the oppressive female role, since at this point in her life peer pressure is stronger than anything else. Far from finding any advantages in a home where pro-female values exist, Naema needs all the support she can get from Harriet and me just to survive the difficulties inherent in being 'different'. She cannot adopt our values and our feminism, because she would have to explain them to her friends and that is too great a risk for her to take. Although I feel that our belief in feminism will be a positive thing for her later on, right now she has to reject who I am, as a lesbian, and my political beliefs. The situation is even harder for Harriet than for me, since she could easily feel guilty for 'imposing' her values on the children. This guilt, another product of the patriarchal voice, is one of the ways we are inhibited from passing on what we have learned to our children, especially if what we have learned means that we live outside traditional society, and we ask our children to do that too. It is one thing for a woman to make sacrifices or take risks for her beliefs, but quite another for her to see her children suffer because of them.

Now that we are all living together, I hear the voices more clearly than ever, maybe because I am watching out for them.

What is wrong with this household? Listen to the sounds; where are the sounds of happy children — laughter — friends coming in and out? Where is the cheerful, independent group of kids? Kids that ask advice when they have a problem? Fun-loving, polite children? Where are they? Listen to the sounds; there are fights; listen; listen; there is bad temper; they sound as if they don't like each other; they are unhappy; you are failing; where is the sunshine? The comfortable home? The idyllic years of growing children? You are failing; you are failing; the sounds are wrong; you are wrong; weekends and vacations are not what they are supposed to be; you know — you've seen it on tele-vision — those families all hand-in-hand and smiling; you're not like that; you are failing. Maybe it's because you don't love them enough; you are not a nice person; you're intolerant; you're selfish; listen to the sounds; listen; listen; you're failing . . .

I know this voice now, and I talk back. I'm not going to buy that myth any longer; I know you too well; you are the patriarchal voice and I know you now. I know that living in any kind of group is at best a struggle, given the way you have structured society. I hear your voice and I name it; it is the voice of the white male; I know you; your ego relies on the dependence of women and children, and so does the economic functioning of the world you have created.

My struggle with the patriarchal voice will go on — I cannot stop fighting it now. I hope that what I learn from it will be useful to the children, but if it is not I cannot stop anyway. One thing I know is that they, too, will hear voices telling them what to do. Setting them up to struggle, maybe setting them up for a hard life, but I want very much for them to carry on this fight. Feminism has saved my spirit and I believe it will save theirs too. When the voices speak to them, I hope they will answer back.

JILL POSENER

Kathy West was born in Oregon, USA, and grew up there and in California, Washington and Minnesota. She lived for two years in a small town in Tanzania, where she taught in a girls' secondary school and worked on a rural vaccination project.

Since 1969 she has lived in London, during most of that time working for the National Association for Mental Health (MIND). She is now employed by a housing association specialising in housing for single people.

Kathy West

I'd been on the pill for years, and then used the coil
and the cap and nothing had ever gone wrong. I was using the
cap carefully and just expected things to continue that way. All
those years with no problems must have lulled me into a false
sense of security for I certainly did know that the cap wasn't
perfectly dependable. Then one week my period seemed a bit
overdue. Then it seemed a bit more overdue and some vague
worries started. I felt like it would come any day, as I was
bloated and swollen the way I always am before a period.
Finally after three or four weeks I went for a pregnancy test.
The woman spent a very long time stirring the various solutions
together. Then she turned around, looked directly at me and
said I was pregnant and what was I going to do? I burst into
tears.

I'd been thinking about having children or not having them
for years. I'd had grave doubts about raising children myself
because I didn't much like what happened to either children or
mothers during my own childhood in the United States. Staying

at home for years to keep the house clean and cook and go to coffee parties seemed boring in the extreme. Then the kids I knew always seemed to be fighting with their parents, and certainly thought that they came from some different world. I didn't want to get into any set-up like that.

After university I went to teach in Tanzania for two years. The children there were almost universally delightful and different in many ways from their American counterparts. They were given important responsibilities at a very early age, yet they were playful and friendly among themselves and with others. You often saw three- and four-year-olds taking care of baby brothers and sisters, or helping with cooking and washing. Many children would be cared for for long periods by relatives if their parents were in difficulties or had to be away, and yet the children seemed happy and secure. My many observations of children in Tanzania encouraged me to start thinking that children could be raised differently from the way I had known. They could be given a lot more responsibility and not infantilised for so long. They could and should be close to a lot more people, and they didn't have to be considered so much as possessions. They could be encouraged to get along with other people rather than spending so much time competing. Later I visited several countries in the Far East, including China, and got more ideas about healthier child rearing, but I wasn't sure I was the person to be able to do it.

Now I was well into my thirties and I still wasn't ready to make a decision about having children. Whatever my years, I still felt too young. I liked being independent and doing what I wanted, when I wanted. I hadn't yet found any man with whom I actually wanted to settle down or with whom I believed I could share childcare equally. While a big part of me wanted children at some point, it was difficult to imagine ever making the sacrifices necessary to do it. And I also believed I could be quite happy without ever having them.

Now, all of a sudden, I was pregnant and some sort of decision was being forced upon me. There were only a few weeks in which to make it. Maybe the question was now or never? It didn't seem any longer as simple as 'abortion now,

168

maybe children later'. I *was* getting lots older and I very rarely met a man anymore whom I could imagine as the father of my child. The father of this one was okay at least, and as we had just completely broken up there wouldn't be any complications from him. I felt in a complete panic, and this surprised me as my theoretical approach to this problem had always seemed quite clear. What should I do? How could I come up with the right answer? Was there even a right answer to be found?

At this point I certainly thought there was a right answer, and if it didn't appear fairly immediately, then there ought to be one somewhere. I would just have to try really hard to find it, and I would have to move pretty fast. First I'd have to think through all the positive and negative reasons for either keeping this baby or having an abortion. I'd have to make lists of the reasons, and compare the priorities. I'd have to examine my feelings very carefully, starting with what might lie behind my current state of panic. Then I needed more medical information, to talk to other people who were parents (especially single ones), and to talk things over with friends who might challenge my assumptions. This was the approach to problems that had been successful in the past, particularly when I was feeling strong and competent. I wasn't feeling very strong now, but if it was a good method it ought to work reasonably well.

First, my living circumstances seemed rather unfavourable on the whole, but not impossible. I had a job working for a mental health charity which paid a living wage and would allow me maternity leave and my job back afterwards. I also had a car and some small savings. My main problem would be housing as I'd just moved a couple of weeks earlier to a room in a flat belonging to a friend's friend and it obviously wasn't the kind of place for a baby.

Next, my feelings were in chaos. There must have been many reasons for this. One was certainly my belief that having children cut your opportunities and tied you down. I'd been raised to be a typical, unassertive woman whose role in life was to please other people and be dependent on them. I was supposed to keep my needs for competence and achievement secondary. It had taken many years of experience and the encouragement of the women's movement to make me begin to believe I could survive on my own, that I had the right to be treated equally and that I had skills which were as good as anyone else's. It had been a long battle and I hadn't won yet. I still had periods of wanting someone to rescue me and tell me what to do. I still wanted to try different jobs and get more experience and training. After my teaching experience I'd gone into mental health education, and had got particularly interested in the mental health of women and children, in patterns of childrearing and in the effects of employment and housing on mental health. I wanted the opportunities to develop some of those interests in a more practical way, but I didn't yet know how I was going to do it. It was a time for something new, and I wanted to go on and develop the part of me that is able to survive in the ordinary working world, still mostly peopled by men. Could I ever do the things I was interested in trying, and have a baby too?

Thinking of the total dependency of children was frightening. I'd have a lot less money and a lot less time and a lot less sleep, at least for a while. I would be totally responsible for another human being; night and day; my time and energy wouldn't be my own. I'd have to plan for two rather than one, and it would be very difficult to be alone.

I also considered the possibility that I might not *like* the baby. I felt that if I actually went through with having it I would have to keep it whether I liked it or not, and the possibility of spending all that time and energy, combined with the hypocrisy of pretending to like someone was horrifying. Even more probable, the baby might be sick or generally unhealthy or have nightly colic for months. How could I work and how could I stay sane if I didn't get any sleep at night and devoted all my energy to a baby?

Then there were my own emotional needs. I liked the idea of children being around and of sharing affection and activities and the different ways in which children look at things. I liked the idea of physical closeness. People who had children around them often seemed more human and nicer. Spending time in this way seemed a good way of investing in the well-being of future generations, as well as in my own. I had a need to achieve in different spheres, and felt I could be a good parent. I'd done a lot of thinking about parenting and had lots of ideas about it. As I was always so keen to give advice, it would sound a lot more convincing if I'd done it myself.

Next, what about the fact that I was getting older. I'd be thirty-five before too long, and all the propaganda says you shouldn't wait too much past your middle thirties to have a first baby. There were certain health risks to older women, and an increase in the incidence of handicapped babies. Then, what about my fertility, which would decline with increasing age? Several of my friends had been trying for years to have babies and hadn't succeeded. And if I waited until I was forty and did get pregnant I might not have much energy left to take care of a new baby.

Happily, I wasn't under much pressure *not* to become a single mother. The moral climate in Britain has changed, so many people are positively encouraging. None of my friends or colleagues tried to talk me out of the idea on moral grounds. I was worried about my family, however, particularly my mother. She'd always seemed incredibly puritanical; she had never mentioned sex. I can remember once being told not to play too much with the girl next door, because her mother was divorced. Although my mother was in the United States I didn't relish the prospect of telling her.

I kept thinking about these kinds of things and many, many others as my pregnancy got more and more advanced. I was carrying on a full-time job, and I hadn't realised how absolutely exhausted early pregnancy can make you feel. I came home from work and collapsed on the bed for most of the evening. In the mornings when I got up I felt sick for several hours, and vomited at least two or three times every day. Moreover my flatmate didn't want a pregnant woman in the flat and asked me to leave before anything began to show. She couldn't understand why I didn't just make up my mind and get on with it.

My friends were wonderful and I got at least half a dozen offers of temporary accommodation. I moved when I was fourteen weeks pregnant, still unable to decide whether to have an abortion. While I felt supported by my friends, I also felt low about having to make the decision on my own (my ex-lover, although aware that I was pregnant, never bothered to know the outcome) and about the fact that no clear answer was emerging. All this time I was also trying to talk to as many single parents as possible, and to friends who would force me to examine my own reasons and needs more carefully. I also went off to visit the National Council for One-Parent Families for practical advice and talked to my doctor. I learned a lot about myself during this time but a decision became no clearer.

My dilemma got worse as the weeks went by, and I began to feel a bit crazy. One hour I would definitely want to keep the baby and the next I'd decide to have an abortion. Flip. Flip. Flip. This way, that way, this way, that way. My lists of reasons Why and Why Not kept getting longer and longer. The priorities on each list kept shifting and each shift affected things on the opposite list. And a lot of the logic was theoretical anyway. Things would change if I had one kind of baby or another, if a wonderful job came along either tomorrow or in a year's time, or if I suddenly got a wonderful house and lots of money.

My anxiety level reached an all-time high. At sixteen weeks of pregnancy I went to arrange an abortion for the following Monday. I couldn't wait any longer to decide or I wouldn't be allowed the abortion. It seemed that while I remained unsure, it was probably the right thing to do. The parting words of the gynaecologist who saw me were that I didn't seem to be very clear about what I wanted: if I ever were to have a child, I ought to have one now. He said I could change my mind even at the last minute.

By the morning of the operation I had worked myself into such a state that my stomach was in knots, my skin was in a cold sweat and I was shaking. I should make clear that I had no religious reasons for being in this state; nor did I at that point regard the foetus as a 'baby'. For whatever reasons, at the last minute I didn't go. After that I had to accept that I'd made a decision and get on with it. I began to realise that *there wasn't*

172

going to be a right decision or a wrong one for me. Whatever I did there would be costs and benefits, and it was up to me to work towards as many benefits as possible. I would simply never know how I would have felt had I gone through with the abortion. I could still work towards what I wanted in life. Some things would be harder and others easier and some would just be different.

My ambivalence continued throughout the pregnancy, although now it was clearer that my goal was to make the most of my 'decision'. I was finally able to move in permanently with a good friend about six weeks before the baby was due. I informed my employer that I wanted maternity leave, and my job back, and continued to work until two days before the baby was born because I was worried about money. Everyone at work was very supportive, and this made a tremendous difference. I also managed to get together plenty of baby equipment and find a helpful local GP. My friend Jude went to all my ante-natal classes with me.

Amy Susanna arrived on Christmas Eve 1977 in West London Hospital. I had a Caesarean section because of sudden high blood pressure and a narrow pelvis. I remember feeling great relief when Jude, who had waited outside the operating room, announced that I had a healthy baby girl. But I don't remember much else as I spent the next few hours coming out of the anaesthesia and feeling such incredible pain that it seemed it would be better to die. Finally I recovered enough to have some attention for my new baby. She was all there and very pretty and I was pleased. But I didn't feel full of the joys of motherhood or anything that appeared to be maternal instinct. It would have helped, for there was a tiny, totally helpless baby and I didn't know what to expect of her or how to hold her or feed her or change her. But I did have to get on with it because I was responsible.

I spent nine days after Amy's birth in a large ward full of new mothers and babies. The babies were supposed to be with you all the time, but on the first two nights a nurse came and took mine away so I could get a few hours sleep. That nurse, a West Indian, was an angel of mercy and I still have a vision of her looking like one. She knew I couldn't properly get to know my baby if I was feeling tired and miserable. The rest of the week all the babies were with us all of the time, wanting feeding or changing or cuddling every two or three hours it seemed. The minute mine dropped off the one in the next cot would start screaming, so it was almost impossible to get more than a couple of hours of sleep a night from then on. By the third day I had thrush, which almost drove me mad with itching, and cystitis as well. I felt the kind of total desperation and physical exhaustion that had brought me to tears a few other times in my life.

It didn't now take much to send me into fits of weeping. I could easily have smashed a couple of the nurses and doctors who said, 'Oh, its just your hormones'. It might well have been partly my hormones, but mainly it was exhaustion, thrush, cystitis, my cracked and incredibly painful nipples and the constant noise and crying on the ward – plus having to learn about a new baby. No special efforts were made to do anything about these problems. It took me almost a day to get an antibiotic for my thrush.

Meanwhile, there was Amy. She was a small baby with straight dark hair and big blue eyes. She cried too often because she was hungry too often! She dirtied her nappies regularly and burped up milk so that you had to change both her clothes and her nappies several times a day. She seemed to work perfectly, but with the constant attention she demanded and with my other problems and worries there wasn't much time or energy left to think about whether I liked her or not. I tried to hold and cuddle her as much as possible and to take her into bed with me much of the time in order to help her feel secure. This was as much because of feeling I ought to as because of wanting to. I had read articles by trendy psychologists on early bonding and believed them enough to try to be as close to Amy as I could manage. I did keep waiting for this feeling of strong warmth and attraction to happen – something that felt like a bond. While I was often fascinated or protective or proud or totally pissed off when she wouldn't stop crying, there wasn't, at this stage, anything that felt like love or being bonded.

The next few months were difficult and it took a long time for my affection and attachment to develop. Amy seemed a lot more appealing when she began to sleep through the night and I was less tired. She also seemed a lot nicer when she began to smile and become more interested in what was going on. Things also improved when I went back to work after four months at home, and could do something totally different from taking care of the baby. I'd been offered a place for Amy in a very good local council day nursery, and I've been able to leave her there knowing she is both happy and well cared for, and that we're both glad to see each other in the evening. I got really depressed being at home taking care of Amy all day, and now know I'm not the kind of person to make childcare a full-time career. Happily, I believe a job and motherhood can mix, and to the benefit of all concerned.

As I did spend lots of time with Amy, in the beginning all day and later on evenings and weekends, it was possible to learn more what babies were like, and how they reacted and what they needed. I also met lots of other mothers and other children and began to find out what their lives were like. Just the ordinary practical difficulties of having a child require real management skill, and I've developed a tremendous admiration for the ways in which many mothers cope and their children survive and grow. My growing knowledge about children is very satisfying and it also means that being a mother has become much easier to organise and more predictable. This means I have more time and space for pleasure and enjoyment.

Amy is now nineteen months old and my feelings about having children are still mixed. Some things are very much more difficult than I ever imagined and others are more rewarding. I used to think you could get little babies to go to sleep at about seven in the evening in order to have some peace. Now I know there are babies that just won't sleep that much, and mine is one of them. I also hadn't realised just how much energy and attention is required to keep tabs on an active toddler. It doesn't leave much time or energy to get out in the evenings and keep up a social life, so at this point at least I'm much more of a recluse than I had anticipated. It's really easy to see why mothers often spend so much time talking about children and things around the home: there isn't time or opportunity to keep in contact with much else.

On the positive side, I've found Amy a lot more fun than I ever expected. She has a real sense of humour and often makes me laugh when the minute before life seemed not at all funny. She's also, like other young children, incredibly curious and when I've been exploring things with her I've found all kinds of new and exciting things to be interested in. And there are surprises. All of a sudden there will be a big crash and I'll rush out to find Amy on a table top or in the middle of a terrible mess, staring angelically at me with her big blue eyes and halo of (now) blond hair. It is wonderful to watch someone whose spirit and character haven't been beaten out of her. She will try anything, climb on anything, crawl into anything and express any emotion she's feeling immediately. She's also affectionate and friendly to dogs, cats and complete strangers. So I'm forced to meet a lot of people and animals I wouldn't have otherwise, often with very pleasant results.

I find myself liking and loving Amy most of the time and disliking or hating or resenting her some of the time. I manage a lot better when I admit to these varied feelings, even though I feel society 'expects' mothers to love their children all the time. I've also found that the list of things I would never do to my child has shortened considerably. I now know that I don't like small babies all that much. I know that I have come close to battering my child on the long nights when she wouldn't stop crying. My ideas of how I was going to dress and feed her and the amount of time I was going to take to play with her have often taken second place to convenience and expediency, as have many of my efforts towards discipline. I may give Amy a bath only once or twice a week and she often eats tinned food or beans on toast. Instead of always taking the time to persuade her not to do something or to distract her with something interesting, it's often just NO in a very firm voice. The practical demands of living in fairly cramped surroundings, without a washing machine, with little play space and with few babysitters and a full-time job have sent my idealistic ideas to flight.

I still have the challenge of trying to break some of the old patterns of rearing girls and relating to daughters which I have always disliked. Already I get a secret thrill when the day nursery staff keep commenting that 'she should have been a boy'. What they really mean is that she is outgoing and daring and will stand up for herself. It's unfortunate that the staff don't see this as a common and healthy attribute of children of either sex.

I try very hard to let Amy get close to as many people as possible. She loves Clare, my flatmate, and adores our upstairs neighbours, Lil and Ron and their two sons. When Amy sees any of them she will run and throw herself into their arms. She will stay with these people, and several others, for quite a long time, and so she doesn't have to depend on me for all of her care and affection. I can happily go off and do things on my own without worrying about her. If I'm really going to do much for Amy I have to have time to do a lot for me. People, and particularly women, learn to be self-sacrificing by being around people who always put other people's needs first. If Amy is going to grow up to be competent and independent, she's got to grow up among people who are competent and independent, and so I have to be that way as much as I can manage.

It's hard to know exactly what I will do in the future to encourage Amy's development. I don't want to encourage sexist patterns, but at the same time I want her to get on with other people. I encourage her to play with cars and lorries and hammers and brooms and teasets. They'll all be necessary one day, and both sexes should know how to use them. I also encourage her to stand up for herself, in the hope that she'll get a firm foundation in 'self-defence'. Now she can hold her own, but later on I'm afraid people will try to push her to be more 'feminine'. I also try to relax when she gets especially daring, so she'll be encouraged to be physical, to make mistakes and to try again. It's a bit nervewracking at times, but she definitely seems to enjoy life and to have character and guts. The more things she gets to try the better.

Although I do have periods of anger and despair and depression I wouldn't go back on my decision. I can still see many ways of building a life that either includes children or doesn't. Many things would have been possible had I waited to have children or decided not to have them, but many things are still possible and new ones have opened up. If I'd chosen to wait I also would have had to wait to learn some of the valuable lessons that having a child has brought. One bonus of having a child is that my political and feminist consciousness has changed tremendously. I used to be extremely idealistic and quickly got impatient when women didn't get organised to fight many of the problems that were oppressing them. Now that I have a better understanding of the pressures on women's lives my admiration has swelled and my goals and strategies have become more realistic. And I'm even angrier at a society which is so organised that most women can't or don't play an effective political and economic part.

For myself, I still have similar needs for identity, achievement and friendship. These needs are now definitely harder to satisfy. Being a mother hasn't solved anything for me apart from satisfying the part of me that wanted children. Being a mother, a single mother especially, is a hell of a lot of work, and sometimes life seems a lot less fun. But I have learned to plan better, to be more efficient and enjoy what I *can* do more. So amongst the pressures and responsibilities there have been bonuses.

Since becoming a mother I've talked to many other women for whom the positives and negatives of having children were fairly evenly matched. Some of those who will never have children also wonder sometimes if they made the 'right' decision. I've attended various group discussions on motherhood, and ambivalence seemed to be one of the major themes. I'm convinced that for a great many women a real choice, or the 'right' decision, isn't a genuine possibility. Birth control isn't good enough and career education and opportunities aren't widely enough available; neither are easy, free abortion or good childcare. When women grow up in a culture where marriage and children are expected and when it's not easy to combine the options of children and a career, a 'free' choice is pretty nearly impossible. The real decisions seem to be about how we cope with our ambivalence about having children – whether or not we really choose them – in a way that allows mothers and fathers and friends and children and employers and people in general to come out sane and respecting of each other and themselves. For me there were so many contradictions that the only thing I could be was ambivalent. Once I realised this I was free from the guilt of worrying about a 'wrong' decision and could get on with taking constructive steps for dealing with change.

I hope other women who have similar experiences will be able to free themselves from feeling guilty about not making a clear choice. We've got a *right* to be ambivalent about such a complicated decision as this.

EILEEN WILLENBORG

Jane Melnick is a photo-journalist and fiction writer. She has been
active in anti-war and feminist politics throughout the last decade
and has worked on the news publications *In These Times* and,
currently, *Seven Days*. She is now living in Brooklyn, New York, and
working on a book about women's culture, to be published by South
End Press, Boston.

Jane Melnick

The moment I decided to keep 'the kid' I was standing in front of some Chagall stained-glass windows in a museum in New York in 1961. All I can remember now about the windows is that they had wonderfully strong reds and blues. 'The kid' already had an identity to me (my roommate had named it Fig Newton). I sensed Fig Newton wanted to hang on a lot and was an interesting character. I had fantasised a lot about smuggling her/him through a minefield of obstacles, sensing that in the near future parenting would be done according to no cookbook I'd ever heard of. But there were no models I'd seen of women raising children on their own and not being treated like terrible victims or pariahs.

Half-heartedly, I'd gone through the motions of getting an abortion. Castor-oil, scalding hot showers and an enema all at once was a doctor friend's prescription to bleed enough to get into a hospital for a D & C. There were also abortionists. I didn't try hard at any of it, especially the enema. I'd become pregnant by a fluke: a combination of very bad luck – in terms of what were supposed to be the fertile times of my cycle – and the foolish fact that I'd thrown away my diaphragm when I wanted to throw out all traces of the lover who had paid for it a few months earlier.

I had strong feelings which told me I could turn my bad luck on its head. There were many ways in which I wanted to have and raise a child. It felt like the best thing I could do at the time with my energy to do work – maybe not creative work (whatever that would come to mean for me) – but just plain day-after-day devotion and effort.

A friend, whom I'll call Steve, had offered to marry me, just to help, on the condition he would not have to support me. I'd said no, but it was right then, in front of those windows with the sun flooding through the colours, that I realised, why not? He was one of the few people I'd met at college or anywhere else who cared as much about literature and art as I did; he knew a lot about politics and Marxism. I wanted to learn from him and teach him about feelings. He had implied I might be good in that dubious role and I, I'm sure, was flattered.

The biological father – whom I hardly knew – was with me, having wanted to help me go around to doctors' offices. The night before I'd talked him into marrying me only to decide that morning there was no way I'd marry someone I'd talked into it, and who thought – as he explained at length – I was a 'threat' to him because I was smart and not subservient. The double standards around education and sexual infidelity among many liberal-radical men were as infuriating to me then as they are now: *they* could have these things, 'their' women were not supposed to.

We had met on my twenty-first birthday and commiserated over not being accepted in an élite, advanced creative writing seminar: many had come, few (virtually all men) were chosen in a hurry by a tired old grey eminence. It was a fitting way for us to meet. Both of us were energetic, ambitious, conflicted. Both had been somewhat battered, driven children (emotionally battered, in his case – physically, at times, in mine), even if also respected and loved. We both had strong ambivalence and confusion about many things, particularly around the definitions of success and love given us by our families. We knew, even then, we'd be an explosive disaster as a married couple, romantic in some ways, maybe, but not compatible.

We also both wanted to have the child, even while we knew how corny and how un-smart of me the 'smart sets' we'd moved in and out of at college would find it. Some of us had been zealously building the vanguard of the sexual revolution. No doubt a desire to thumb our noses at them was a minor part of our wanting to have the child. For a few days I'd played with the idea of doing it unmarried. But I feared that that would be rough on the child, and on me, too. I was glad this man felt that positive about his genes. Actually *I* felt positive about them; the Chagall window reminded me of them. It was the way he was with me that I was not so positive about.

In those days, of course, unless you were working-class black, you got sent away or married if you got pregnant in the United States and couldn't swing the cost or risk of illegal abortion. (Working-class non-whites are still the only group that regularly gives single mothers shelter and support.)

If I had come home pregnant and asked my parents to help me figure out what to do, they would have thought I was a creature from outer space asking for help in an unknown language. My father had been outraged that fall when I'd worn sandals home; we had been writing angry letters back and forth about whether partially bare feet were 'beneath the bounds of decency'. My mother and I would always have long, vague talks about feelings. Yet I could never talk to her about the years of confusion I'd already gone through. My parents still believed – I now see – that women could get Ruined.

So there I was one summer morning, three weeks after graduating from college (I skipped the ceremony), sitting up in a hospital bed, nursing a squirming, wirey dark-haired infant that Steve and I had named Ben. We had been married six months earlier at a small home ceremony I'd gamely called, to the few friends I invited, my Shotgun Wedding. A nurse's aide had just helped me start Ben nursing, after my expensive doctor (on whom I'd spent all my wedding money) had shown no interest or expertise.

In my first few hours with Ben, I'd just held him and stared in amazement, as I waited for lactation to begin. He was twenty-one inches long and his head was no bigger than an orange. He made soft gurgling noises and loud cries, a hundred refinements on the sigh and the groan.

With matter-of-fact nonchalance, he took his first swallow of milk. Then another, and another. I was amazed at the concentration that came from such a small, helpless-seeming creature. His eyes were so bright and eager and new; he could focus all his bodily energy on this gentle, but determined sucking. I was both dumbfounded and happy, and experienced little of the post-partum blues – that was to come later, in more subtle forms. It seemed impossible that the world would do anything but welcome us with open arms.

No doubt having a child in this way was a form of escape from the various futures open to me as an honours graduate of a prestigious women's college. Publishing (which I'd tried out the summer before in New York) had interesting people, but precious few openings for women other than secretarial. I'd also turned down a few prospects for Real Marriage: marriage to someone else's career did not look that appetising either. All I knew was that I wanted to write fiction – I'd already won two prizes for it – get into Real Life, get far away, see what I could do for and with the kid. I had never travelled more than two hundred miles away before the age of eighteen. I wanted to roam all over the place, taking the kid with me.

Why is it hard to describe the story of mother and child On the Road? For one thing, so much of the most important work as well as happenings were as invisible and mysterious as growth. Motherhood for me has been nothing as much as a long term routine of nurturance: allowing the growth of another at the same time as trying to make room for one's own growth. It has meant – above all – keeping in constant communication and providing meals (over one thousand a year). Yet out of the whirl some pictures emerge, some caught at turning points, others at our best and worst times.

One soap-opera scene I've never forgotten took place a year after Ben was born. The two of us are arriving on the doorstep of a crowded tourist convent in Rome with five small suitcases, a folding high chair and baby bed.

Steve had grown impatient with the paraphernalia of parenthood. I had grown impatient with the need to go where he wanted to go. His year on a Fulbright scholarship had included the luxury of slightly irrelevent graduate study in France; mine had centred on poverty-level home economics, European style, circa 1962: rinsing boiled diapers out in cold water, scouring pots, beating rugs, grinding up vegetables with potatoes so as not to have to buy the expensive baby foods. Doctor Spock was almost the only book I'd had time to read; I'd had to fight to salvage an hour a day to pursue my dream of writing fiction. I definitely looked downtrodden in a way I hadn't the year before. Yet I was proud of having had Ben and of having made it through his first year.

Ben was cute and lively; I'd put my best energy into making sure his first year went as well as possible. My mother had convinced me that some very simple things were the most important, lots of hugging and making faces at each other, eating, playing, making friends with people on trains, sleeping, learning how to survive falls (say 'boom' and get right up).

I explained to the shrewd-looking old nun who opened the door that I'd just split up with my husband and that it was the baby's first birthday (I was off by only a day); I knew she wouldn't turn us away.

That night I wrote my parents and told them that Steve wanted and needed his freedom and that he wasn't Ben's father. I'd felt a great amount of anxiety at Steve's need to keep up the lie to our families; my father had always insisted vehemently on honesty. I asked for financial support for a year to help me get on my feet in the same way they'd been willing to help Steve to do the previous year.

I'd feared my father might not go for it – though he was then wealthy he was also very rigid – but I didn't anticipate the degree of his negativity, or the pain it was to give me. In a few days, I got a letter from him that said little else besides 'Get on back!'

I'd hoped for more support from my father. He'd rebelled

against his parents in many ways to tune into the realities of his generation. Yet he continued to talk in letters as if I were 'no better than a prostitute', and had 'damn well better hurry up and find another father for Ben'. I pretended to myself that it didn't hurt and waited in vain for effective support from my mother, even though I knew from her vague responses that she felt at a distance from my father's position.

While we negotiated back and forth in letters, I pushed Ben over the ancient pavements of Rome in a stroller. I learned street Italian from the barber's family we'd found to stay with. Ben took his first steps on the parquet floor of a museum.

My father finally agreed grudgingly to provide minimal financial support for another few months if I'd return to the United States. Returning then to the New York area, a few hundred miles away from my father, I began the long process of extricating myself from dependency on him.

I recall a scene a year and a half later. I have just burst angrily out of the small house we're renting in a Connecticut suburb. It's early March, with lots of wet dirty snow around. Ben toddles out behind me, his dark blue snow pants down at his knees. He trips on them, falls, cries louder. I'm late for the train to a job in the international department of a publishing company. 'Mama, wait . . .' he cries and I'm wrenched to a halt, only then realising he has fallen. I rush back, pick him up, then feel a slow wave of despair come over me.

After all, why hurry to a job where you type labels all day to Japanese and Australian bookstores? 'Mama, we go see the red kites?' he asks suddenly, abruptly replacing his tearful mood with a more hopeful one. The Sunday before we had gone to watch some kite flying. I say no, but walk much more slowly towards my old car. Why hurry to that job so I can leave him with a babysitter he obviously doesn't like? And go out to lunch with men friends from college who turn pitying and pompous as their careers flower and their salaries swell to more than six times mine. I was then making around $4,000 a year. I've definitely missed the train; I call in sick. When the sky clears, and the March wind comes up, we go fly our kite.

Another picture, two years later: we are parked somewhere in the Southwest in our 'new' car, a seven-year-old Rambler station wagon filled to window level with bags and furniture. The car has just boiled over again but I am gazing off at the desert, marvelling at its beautiful tan bleakness as I wait for the radiator to cool. Ben, sitting beside me, looks worried for a minute, then starts driving a small, model sportscar up and down my pant leg. He wears a cape and a silk scarf I'd worn at college and sings the theme from Batman. I have discovered that television is the only free babysitter around; we both watch shows like Batman every night together.

I've just given up a fellowship at the University of California in Berkeley and am feeling mostly pleased at having successfully avoided the only other real career besides publishing that was open to me: teaching English literature and composition to people who didn't like either one. (I was soon to add Avon door-to-door saleslady to the lengthy list of odd jobs I tried between the ages of fourteen and twenty-eight.) I'd been drawn to graduate school at Berkeley because of the Free Speech Movement, but was shocked at how little kindness and respect many of the brave young radicals had for mothers and children.

We are on our way, in the boiling-over Rambler, to rejoin Steve, who is working for a postgraduate degree in New Orleans; he has said he misses us and wants to help again. In my growing loneliness – there is too little money and time to squander on much socialising – his offer of love and shelter seems welcome. Though I feel none of my father's urgency about Ben needing a father, I am concerned with the question of shared parenthood. I am beginning to believe there is something unhealthy, at least for me, about one person raising a child alone, and having that child as her most constant companion.

A happier picture, almost straight out of *The Sound of Music*: Ben, five, walks on an alpine hillside, slowly and carefully picking a bouquet of flowers. Steve and I are teaching at an American college that has easy admissions policies, high tuition and low salaries. Ben walks a mile down to the village each day to school and back again, bringing one of us a carefully thought-out bouquet of wild flowers each day.

A year and a half later, we were back in the States, without Steve, in Cambridge, about an hour away from my parents' home. Steve and I had made a game try. We had done well as friends and lovers, but badly in our attempts to be husband and wife. Also, his response to the mounting frenzy of the Vietnam war had been to want to remain an expatriate; I was anxious to get back and be part of the protest.

We returned in the middle of the year; I had to teach Ben how to read English. We were both sad and subdued after the split-up with Steve, but determined not to get bogged down.

The next picture is from 1970. With three of my students from a junior business college in Boston, I am running down Massachusetts Avenue through some thin clouds of tear gas. One of the students is carrying Ben. It is the week of Kent State and the Cambodia bombing. Ben has looked up through the clouded twilight to see a vision that strikes him with terror: a wedge of nightstick-wielding blue-helmetted cops moving relentlessly towards us. I've promised Ben we won't get hurt; I didn't think they'd hit anyone with a seven-year-old kid. But Ben doesn't seem convinced and from descriptions I was to hear the next day, his instincts are right.

It is also the week I've been laid off from my job, the first decently paid one I have had. I have engineered, with these same students, a strike that three-quarters of the student body have honoured. All three women in the humanities department have been laid off, although we are all more experienced or more respected than most of the men they are keeping.

The strike at the college was an exhilarating end to what had promised to be one more foolish venture into the infuriating world of women's careers. I was also coming to wonder more and more why I got no credit for what had clearly been my real career to date: motherhood.

One month after this street scene, I joined the heaviest

political collective I could find. Though I was occasionally to question the sanity of this act in subsequent months, it turned out to have been one of the best things I've ever done.

Joining the collective was not only a way for me to do the political work I'd found I had a knack for, but also a way to have some of the support I had dreamed of from a family. The group was called the Panther Defense Committee and in its first months we worked to raise money for the numerous Panther trials.

The Panthers are known for their talk of gun possession, the constitutional right guaranteed to all, but assured only for whites; they are less known for their great respect for children. They spent a lot more time doing good things for children than they did possessing guns.

Several things had fed my susceptibility to depression and anger, all relating to my growing outrage at the situation of women. Among them was anger at my boyfriend of that year — simply because I realised he would probably never have total responsibility for a child. One day I added up how much money it cost me in babysitting to conduct our relationship for nine months and was dazed as the figure approached the thousand dollar mark.

Contributing to my mood at the time was the failure of my parents' marriage. My mother had thrown my father out two years earlier after he had been violent one time too many. With her children now grown up, she had nothing clear to do, no training for a job. That year she drifted into a nervous breakdown. It infuriated me that she was labelled the crazy one.

It felt necessary to my survival to get out of myself, out of my futile anger for my mother, and into the streets. I sold newspapers, talked to people about the war and the Panthers, pulled together a slide show on repression of the Panthers, helped organise demonstrations that culminated in the huge May Day demonstration in 1971. A few people in the collective took a lot of sustained responsibility for Ben during the entire next year. There is a published report of what he experienced in his own words. It appeared in our underground paper, *Juché*: 'There was a cat who was raised with one mother and she got moved into the collective and got pretty freaked out. It was the same way for me at first. It was just like everybody stepping on top of you because there's so many of them. But then I got used to it. The people started liking me and I started liking them. I wanted to sell papers and pass out leaflets and it made me feel more like talking to people. It's very hard because you have to struggle [i.e. wage idealogical discussion, à la Mao!] a lot and dish out your own food.'

The years around 1970 were a critical turning point for us. The world considered our concerns utopian; I considered them inevitable and necessary.

After the police busted the collective, Ben and I moved with a group of them to Vermont in 1971. We ended up at a commune in a town outside the small city of Burlington. Many of the people there were political activists with children. I initiated a very ambitious multi-media show about Vermont economics and Ben, after six months of running wild in a noble experiment we called The Kids' Collective, entered the fourth grade at Charlotte, Vermont. He was to stay in that school for three years. It felt critical to me that we stay in one place for a while. I got a grant for the slide show, then organised people to help me get it done. It took a lot of time and energy as did two very important, successive relationships I had with women. Ben felt neglected at times, and I worried that I was not being a good mother any more. A scene comes into focus out of the happier whirl of those years which brought this home to me.

Ben, eleven, scraggly, bratty and smart-ass, is swinging somehow from the top of a door in the middle of a long collective meeting. He is parroting verbatim some long-winded phrases being intoned by one of our articulate, but wordy male leaders. We all crack up.

Ben had gained a sense of his own power to protest from the few months of The Kids' Collective; it had reinforced his sense of responsibility for his own life. The kids had meetings every day. At one point Ben and another kid organised a successful protest against powdered skimmed milk in favour of whole milk. Now he was telling me, more and more, that something was not right with his situation. He was the oldest kid in the commune. The little kids, demanding and lovable, got most of the attention. Ben marched bravely off to school every day, the first in the school to wear long hair. Two years later he had become a popular leader who got good grades, was on the student council, was co-editor of a humorous mimeographed newspaper, and put on plays with his best friend about a dumb superman character named Mr Big. (His long-standing lack of enthusiasm for male macho was encouraged by the gentler men in the commune.)

As I helped him down off the door and went off with him to his room – we lived in a huge, beat-up old hotel – I sensed that another change was at hand. I let myself look at a buried concern, that communal living was estranging us from the real world, not to mention each other. I felt a sense of desperation – that he needed more nurturing, also that I couldn't give him as much as he wanted. Yet I could, I let myself realise, give him more if we lived alone, and I wanted to do this, at least for a while.

The next snapshot is a real one. Ben, thirteen, is standing in the woods in the snow beside his dog. He has a sled at his feet on which he has just sailed over a two-foot jump. He looks very happy. Thanks to three part-time jobs and a small amount of family money, I'd been able to get a mortgage on a cramped two-family house. Ben and I developed our building skills enlarging it and our gardening skills trying to raise a few vegetables. Another single mother who had been in the commune lived downstairs. I was spending most of my free time with women. Ben's life centred around his friends and his dog. He had never been able to work out having a pet successfully in the communes. This dog, a sweet-natured labrador, was his constant companion. He taught her to heel, sit, fetch. She got up with him at five to go with him on his paper route.

After a while, however, the effort of paying off a mortgage with too little income got me. As did the lack of decently paid jobs. Ben was increasingly dissatisfied with the school options, too. Once again we moved. Ben went first to a progressive-type co-ed boarding school, where he revelled in the concerned, careful teaching, if not the lonely, élitist kids. I finally decided that sending him to any school would always feel like throwing him to the lions.

I had gone with my recent lover to a job on a new socialist newspaper in Chicago. I'd correctly anticipated both vital involvement and impermanence. When Ben's biological father suddenly offered to have Ben live with him in California, we were both very glad. His father promised he would keep him through Ben's high school years which would allow him to spend those crucial years in one place, something all of us thought was important.

Ben had visited his father for a month each summer since he was ten. I had stayed in touch with him over the years and we shared some basic outlooks, even though we had different styles and situations. He had undergone a painful divorce and his wife and two other sons had moved across town. If Ben had been any younger, I'd have been uneasy about this arrangement. But Ben's father was — and is — very willing to try to be a good father to him. And Ben has been very glad to get to know his father, and to have discovered his two half-brothers with whom he is very close. One of the amazing things in his life is how his brothers and father took him on so completely. He has been with them two years.

Now a major concern of mine is to figure out a way to spend more time with Ben before he gets much older. He has now had time to get away from our former over-dependence and to find another person upon whom he can count for certain things, to be there if anything bad happens. But we both feel that we did not spend all that time together only to end up on opposite coasts.

What is Ben like now? I will pull out one final picture, and also let him speak for himself. The picture comes from a few months ago, from a basement pizza bar in California. I am there with my new lover; Ben's girlfriend and his half-brother are sitting nearby. We're all waiting for his pop group to appear at the open mike. They finally saunter out, Ben leading, nodding and smiling. As I sit back in amazement and somewhat unexpected pleasure at the quality of their fine voices and rich harmonies, I can't help marvelling, just like all mothers, at the process of growth. How had the small, bright-eyed infant I held in my arms sixteen years ago turned into this five-foot-nine teenager with a gentle bass voice, shyly moderating before each song for this 'anti-heavy-metal' group?

The other day I telephoned him so that he could help me end this article. I know he is as reluctant to draw conclusions about his upbringing as I am. I tell him that it's better that he do it with me than that I do it by myself, and finally he clears his throat. I urge him to be as honest as he can, while I attempt to be an 'objective' reporter.

'Has it been hard not having a nuclear family?'

'People shouldn't feel they have to have an exact nuclear family in order not to be loonies. I mean . . . in a traditional nuclear family with the father away at work and the mother at home, the mother ends up dealing with everything. She's not given respect for it. So this means she doesn't feel she's accomplishing anything.'

'Do you want a nuclear family some day yourself?'

'Probably yes, but . . . well, I definitely think the nuclear family is overemphasised. It depends on the personalities of the people, what happens in the family I mean. The main reason I want a nuclear family is that I want to raise children and I don't want to get separated from the mother.'

'Was it hard having a mother who has been living with women since you were nine?'

'It's weird but it's okay. It's something you have to keep secret from some people, which is a drag . . . but it never stopped me from doing anything. I've told all my good friends.'

'Has it helped you?'

'Yeah. To understand women, given all the women who were around. A lot of boys my age have no idea how girls feel about things.'

'How do you relate to girls?'

'I have friends who are girls and a very nice girlfriend. I'm very monogamous; she has lots of energy — we never get dejected or bummed out.'

'What about the way I didn't exactly put the emphasis on placing three meals a day in front of you at exactly regular times?'

'You brought me up to be independent . . . everyone says I'm very capable for someone my age, and I guess it's true.'

'They say that?'

'Yeah.'

'Was it hard on you, moving so much?'

'It was hard, but it had its advantages. I missed the security at times, but I learned to meet people, develop my own security, carry it with me I guess you could say . . . Besides, I can always write term papers about the sixties!'

Later, I ask him, 'What do you think is the worst thing about the way I brought you up?'

'Oh, come on, Ma . . . '

'Just get it out; it'll do us both good . . . '

'All right . . . ' I hear him swallow and then say, 'The single parent thing . . . The way you would space out because I was your only companion. It made me feel you didn't want to listen . . . '

I say, weakly, anticipating a half day at least of strong guilt, 'Yeah, I think it was the worst thing, too . . . ' and then try to make light of it. 'Well, at least I like to listen now . . . ' I flash on the long minutes of inattention over the years, listening to endless recitals of entire movie plots and, later, all the funny things that led up to the really funny thing that happened that day in class. And how I sometimes tried to make my mind jump out of its track and into his world and could not.

Then he tells me that the next worst thing was that there weren't any men around and that he thinks this is related to some problems he has getting along with his father. I say, somewhat defensively, but what about the men in the commune. They weren't really around, he says. But one of the biggest problems he has with his father is that he doesn't like to take orders from him. I think to myself that this is not the worst problem in the world.

How can you wrap up the responsibility for nurturing another into life into a neat written package? Neither of us is sure exactly how to describe it all.

I had advantages that helped make single motherhood easier for me that it is for many — even though I chose not to accept many of the material advantages around which my parents had centred their lives. Yet there were pain and loose ends and there still are. Nothing will get me to assert glibly that it's easy for one woman to raise children on her own. I see many women doing it by choice now, and see them receive much more support than I did. Yet even they say, as I've heard myself say often, that it's harder than you ever thought it would be. It's an irrevocable responsibility; irrevocable is a foreign word in the country that created disposable diapers, that would like to make everything disposable, that wants people to focus most clearly on 'selfhood'.

For a long time, I did feel weighed down by my responsibility. I had realised that I'd missed a lot of things related to my own development in my total absorption in Ben during his first six years. I was 'not there' in the middle years as much as many traditional mothers think they are 'supposed to be', yet I continue to think that it would have been worse for him if I'd sacrificed my life for his.

Ben has problems, but he *is* well-prepared for the uncertain future we all face. He is practical, bright, adaptable and warm. I feel vindicated at my unorthodox method of childrearing, as well as amazed, sometimes, at how well it has worked out. Living the life of the questing, nomadic radical, we never did get wedged into the numerous stuck places this society creates. There is no pension, alarm clock or final grading period for parenthood. Furthermore, you are certain to do some things wrong, no matter how determined you are. In the end, so be it.

Paula Weideger is the author of *Menstruation and Menopause*
published in the US by Alfred A. Knopf, Inc. and in paperback by
Delta, New York, and Penguin, Australia. In the British edition,
published by The Women's Press, the book is called *Female Cycles*.
She is currently writing a book called *Is There Love After Liberation?*
which will be published by Simon and Schuster in the United States.

Paula Weideger

I am a writer. I am a woman on her own. I do not have children. I was raised to believe that a woman must have children and that a woman with serious ambition for her art will be a rotten mother. And I came to believe that having children defeats the serious ambition of the artist who bears them. I was raised to believe that a woman must have children and I grew up wanting to be an artist – a woman who cannot have children.

These facts of my life are not like a stand of cool pines nor do they resemble a litter of cozy kittens that frolic when they are not busy nuzzling. These facts of my life, no matter how many tap dancing lessons I have dragged them to, go right on refusing to perform as an ensemble.

Also. I have certain gifts for the creation of emotional opera, and am given to longings for spiritual detachment and temperamental grace. I spend some of my time making up plots about how to get rid of the man's world – and when.

And so. The facts of my life are, sometimes, explosive. How

on the subject of motherhood, womanhood and work can it be any other way? For me. For a woman of my ambition and of my time. How damn it, can it be any other way? For me. For a woman of my temperament, my ambition and my time?

An example. At breakfast this morning a poet my age who three years ago 'went back' to writing poems, said: I wouldn't trade one of my children for any book in the world. That, I said into my orange juice, is why I did not have children. And toots, I added without saying a word, you do not have a book to trade.

I was being huffy all right. Not because it was early in the morning or because I naturally drift toward the snotty rejoinder. Either explanation might be correct but, as it happens, neither is. I was in a huff because the woman seemed so smooth, so pleased with herself, so sure it would all work out – in her favour. She was so awfully content. And what if she were right . . . My God, what if she were right?

In the company of women who are writers and mothers I feel diminished. I get provoked. I feel competitive. If it really is possible to be such a superlady then I want to be one too. Right away I am defensive. Depending on the emotional weather I go all gluey with vulnerability or prickle with contentiousness. It isn't dignified. And it isn't fun, either. Not for long.

The poet's remark was stupid, but she isn't dumb. She knows that you can't compare children and books. We agree that you can't equate them either. Two books don't equal one curly headed tyke, and a set of triplets do not a *War and Peace* make. And I knew that the poet was being defensive, too. After all, she has the children – I have the books. But comparison and equation are not where the trouble comes from. Not for me. The big trouble rolls when the subject is rivalry. As in: either children or books.

It is not possible to have both. History reveals that as a rule to which there are precious few exceptions. Too few. Women writers of the first rank do not have children. Hardly ever. But a female, to be a woman, must have children.

My mother is a lapsed artist. And happily so, she says. She was not a stage mother at all. On the contrary. My mother's design for my happiness was that I should grow up and get married. I should have children. That would make me happy. I thought that would make me bored and boring.

I myself had a busy childhood. There were lots of things I wanted to do – and lots of things I was able to do. I was bright and verbal. I made up stories and was a passionate reader. I painted and I drew. Though born a child of the working class, by the time I started school I was a child of the upper middle class. In other words, along with feeling lonely most of the time, I was lively with talents and the pleasures thereof and I was blessed with opportunities.

As far as I could tell my mother's life was much more boring. Apart from such obvious pleasures as gardening and having me around (the latter not sufficiently enjoyed by her – in my opinion), there wasn't much in her life to keep a person interestingly occupied. I didn't understand how she could enjoy herself but I didn't want to dwell on that. After all, one of those domestic lives was in my future. All girls grew up to have one.

Work and family life. In my very own childhood home confusion, ambition and rebellion sent out their hairy, determined shoots. And how else? Not even fairy tales give a child useful guidance on growing up a woman, a mother and an artist.

I grew up wanting to be a painter. A writer. A world traveller. Which should I be? I didn't have a calling and my faith in myself was fragile. Still, I was stubborn on my mother's side and resolute on my father's so I knew that eventually I would find out what it was I meant to do, and then I'd do it and I would be it.

I wanted to enjoy my gifts. I wanted to explore, to have adventures, to come upon my work and get strong inside it. And I also wanted to love and be loved and be a mother and be nice and be liked. That is, I also wanted to be a normal woman.

I did not want to make sacrifices and I did not want to be sacrificed. I wanted neither a failed adulthood nor a failed womanhood. I refused to choose between children and art. I would not. So I concocted what I thought of as a smart way around it.

I would do everything – but I would do it backwards. I would go back to fertility later in life, very much as the poet at the breakfast table went back to creativity. I would get married and have children. I certainly, definitely, would. But later.

This *is* the later in my life and I have not done it. I do not want to have a child now. I look forward to the next few years of writing and the next few years are all the time left if I am going to have a child. On my good days I am enthusiastic about the choice I have made and the future for me is not the negative of some maternal positive.

Work is not the negative of maternity. But questions about maternity and its permanent rejection are not swiftly or neatly settled by the doing of work, either. The letting go of motherhood is not easily accepted and if accepted at all it does not go unmourned. Not in my case.

I really do believe that birth is a miracle. And that conviction only increases as I get older. When I was young, after all, I only thought that birth was magical. And isn't having a child like making an umbilical cord that is connection with the whole human race? Can a person be really nourished without it?

Is a woman who does not have a child sentenced to exile? Is she doomed to inhabit outlying districts where the walls are decorated only in the latest fashion and the touch of flesh is on the surface — always? I have been afraid so.

These are not benign thoughts.

There is still time. I cannot think about having children as a woman of twenty might think about it. Or as a woman of sixty would look back over it. Nor do I think about it the way a woman in love might be thinking right now. And I don't think about it the same way I would if I already had a child. I am thirty-nine years old and I am thinking about having a child.

I think that I will not have a child now. And if not now, when. I probably will not have a child ever. This *is* the later in my life.

The subject will not stay closed. It doesn't want to stay quiet and settle down. And I have refused to bury it deep or seal it up in a tomb. Time is so damned short. I do not want to arrive at the other side of fertility without knowing something more about my desires and my needs than I know right now. I do not want to betray myself with evasions and thorns or with promises of jewels I can have instead. I do not want to make myself blind. Not if I can help it.

If I know something more about why I did not have a child maybe I will have learned enough to decide about having one. Now. Or a little later on. Maybe. Or not at all. And what I learn might be usable for someone else. I don't know of course. Not on any of these counts. But on all of them I hope so.

Like the apprentice in a fortune cookie factory I manufacture an old familiar message: She who wishes to go forward might well start out by going backward first.

How come I did not have a child? Why, between the age of seventeen when I put it off for a while and the age of thirty-nine when I consider putting it off altogether, didn't I produce a child or two. Now that there are only fifteen minutes or two years left, I want to know.

Not for me the fatalistic: Because it was meant to be. I am a terrific reason-maker-upper and finder-outer. And I like to work fast. I want to rush in and say, 'Why do you think I didn't have a kid, dummy . . . I didn't have one because I didn't want one.'

Saying I didn't have a baby because I didn't want one is like saying I didn't conceive because my moon dawdled in Taurus. It just won't do. It doesn't say anything and besides it is not true.

I always wanted to have a child. It never occurred to me not to want one and it never occurred to me — not for years and years anyway, that I would not have one. Having a child was inevitable. It was only that I didn't want one right away. Later on, after I was working well. Then I would have one.

Well. Why didn't I?

In I go. Tumbling, bumbling and shouting. Circumstances and seaweed. Dreams and lies. Wiggling up nearest my eyes are the memories of being in love and wanting a child. There was even a time when I tried to have one.

I tried to have a child because the wife of the man I was in love with could not. Or so he said, hinted and alleged. I was young and so naïve in my jaded-looking fashion that I believed him when he told me that his wife, so help me, did not understand him.

Happily I did not succeed. I *was* happy when my attempt to conceive failed. I was heartbroken, too. My love for him — or was it his for me — had, I discovered, suffered a failure too.

In my attempt to get pregnant and in the fact that I did not, I found out that I didn't want my married lover's child. Not because he was already married. The moral issues — having such a serious affair with a man who was already married, having a child 'out of wedlock' — didn't concern me. Not very much. And anyway I was sure — whether right or wrong — that he would marry me if I conceived. I didn't want my lover's child because it would have been his. That, for me, was no small lesson.

I didn't want to have *his* child. I didn't want to be his wife. I would have to be in service. To him, to his children, to his pursuit of the goddamned Nobel Prize. I loved him but I didn't want that. But *that* was who he was. An owner. A possessor. I didn't want him.

I was ambitious. I had a lot of ambition even though I didn't know in what place to put it. But I had always known it would be in some work and not in a man. And from this pregnancy that didn't happen, I had learned something more. I was not to be a voyeur — I would not be content to satisfy my ambition vicariously, living through the success of 'my husband'.

I was in love many more times after the married man. I wanted to be in love. I meant to have a child. I wanted to find a way. But being in love and wanting a child were never together long enough, surely enough, or mutually enough, for me to have one.

I continued to be sure that I would have a child. Women have children. That was the catechism on which I was raised. It was the natural order. It was inevitable. It was ordained.

If there was no god of gender there certainly was a god of hormones.

A friend of mine has accurately observed, I believe, that women who have not had this 'inevitable' maternity when young usually lurch in that direction sometime during their thirtieth year.

I had such a clockwork seizure. It happened while I was spending a summer in the country. There were children everywhere. Infants, toddlers, kindergarten refugees. They all looked beautiful. They didn't even seem to make much noise.

Children were in my dreams. Every night I dreamt about babies. I got scared. This child stuff was getting out of hand. Never mind how babies are supposed to be made, I was sure that I'd get pregnant if I kept on having those damned dreams.

As a present to myself on my thirtieth birthday I went out and bought a dog. A puppy. After all hadn't I always wanted one? What better time than while spending a summer in the country? It might be all right to have a small but constant responsibility to another living thing.

A puppy is no substitute for a baby. It does not compare. I know that. Certainly I do. What I don't understand so well is just what language hormones talk or listen in. I merely report that I brought home a puppy and stopped dreaming about babies.

On the subject of childbirth my mind, like my hormones, went into temporary retirement. In fact, for one or two years I don't think the subject once came into my mind. But when my consciousness finally snapped awake again it was in what I thought was the least likely though seemingly most appropriate place. I was in the midst of teaching a class on the psychology of women.

I was telling the students something like 'Helene Deutsch asserts that girls have menstrual cramps because they are afraid of having children.' I, who had not had a menstrual cramp in adult life and who thought Deutsch too dependent on Freud to provide her own illuminating power, was filled with the positive knowledge that I had always been afraid of having a child. Childbirth had terrified me. Always.

It was a lovely afternoon. The students and I were sitting on the grass. The autumn was chilly and colourful around us. Nature was congenial indeed on that particular day. Magnanimously I forgave myself for being afraid. And why not? I had been ashamed of that fear long enough. I'd been so ashamed of it, in fact, I had almost succeeded in repressing it completely. But why shouldn't I have been afraid? Why shouldn't I still be afraid? What was there I was supposed to be so brave about anyway?

I grew up when nobody talked about pregnancy or how childbirth actually feels. Never. Not in the presence of a child, anyway. Not in the presence of a young woman.

My friends, when I got older, were supposed to be more open and more bold than the ladies of my childhood. And on lots of issues they were. But the only difference between the way my bohemian forthright friends approached their pregnancies and the way in which my more conventional relatives did was, of all things and as far as I could tell, in the way that they dressed. My friends went in for billowing ethnological creations, for bright colours and declarative Mexican stripes. The relatives, meantime, were suited up in mass-produced maternity wear, stuff that was supposed to be tasteful because it was supposed to be camouflage.

Childbirth was hush-hush but was it ever orchestrated. In absentia, so to speak. Not only was 'it' a good, it was also a sacred duty. It was fulfillment, the realisation of one's sex. Babies, one was supposed to sense, slid into sight all wrapped in satiny pastel ribbons while their mothers sweated pearls on the delivery tables of the world. So much for packaging. I was not taken in.

Without knowing anything I knew that childbirth was — well shall I say otherwise than as presented . . . I knew that childbirth was red with blood and blue black with pain and a person could die from it. Women did. Infants did. I might.

Women, I knew, were supposed to birth as mares foal — without self-consciousness and just because. In childbirth woman was like the beast of burden and the lily of the field. For the occasion only she was turned into a saddhu living in the hand of god. How nice for the men who came to worship her. And how awfully nice for *Woman*. For me, of course, it was terrorising.

I was ashamed of myself. That was the penalty for my fear. I was self-conscious and anxious about having a baby. Therefore I was unnatural. I was some kind of witch. A freak. That's how I felt inside and there were no romantic overtones or associations around it. I was sure that I was irreparably flawed. Well perhaps not irreparably. But almost.

As time passed and I did not have a child I was more and

more given to the feeling of shame and to the conviction that I must be unnatural because I was not a mother. The inevitable was not happening to me. Something was surely very wrong. With me.

My ambitions had not quieted down. All this time I went on with my work. I would from time to time become immersed in my work. My concentration finely tuned, my exhilaration mounting, a feeling of momentum building. Whoooeee. Whooooaaaa. Wait up. I would never have a child if I went on like this.

I could never have a child if I paid real attention to my work. How could I? I was much too selfish. Much too self-absorbed . . . If my work was going well that was proof that I was unnatural. Further proof. That was all I needed. Still more reason to think something was wrong with me – as a woman. I'd lose momentum in my work and not feel good about myself as a woman either. What a terrific arrangement.

Enter the women's movement. Thank goodness. I took to it and from it as fast as I could. I built a stronger commitment to my work. That was help for sure. But on the subject of mothering it was not a sensational help. Not for me.

Motherhood is a matter with ambiguity built right in at the beginning. Even before the beginning. But the women's movement has yet to be very good about ambiguity. I suppose movements of every kind find ambiguity altogether unwieldy. So it happened that on this matter of whether to have a child or not, the feminists nearest to me came upon dismissal as the quickest solution. Before the liberating idea 'We do not have to have children' could make much of a breakthrough, it was railroaded into 'To hell with mothering'.

'To hell with mothering' as politics or rhetoric was not really useful help on the subject of maternity. Not for me. But I was not awfully troubled by this particular failure of feminism. I hadn't expected much more so early on. It would take time. ⁓

During the liberation of maternity I acquired some new embellishments for my fear. I learned, for instance, about the transition stage of labour during which a woman could expect to lose her mind. Temporarily only I am relieved to add. Before the women's movement I hadn't even known there was a transition stage in labour.

I also learned about the biggest orgasm of all. During childbirth was the biggest — or was it the best? — they said. I didn't care which superlative was attached. In my opinion it was not sufficient compensation. Which is only to say that, for all I know, for all anybody knows, the orgasm that takes place as a person jiggles at the end of the hangman's rope might be the truest, biggest, most stupendous that life — or death — has to deliver. I would rather pass. You be the one to find out.

I am a feminist and the women's movement zipped right by me on the subject of having a child. I still wanted one, of course. I still thought I was unnatural because I didn't have one. I went on being defensive around women who had them and did their work as well. I thought I was a lousy person for not wishing them all the best. I felt ashamed of myself on that account, too. According to the women's movement rhetoric, and no matter how dopey I found it I was still affected by it, I was not liberated enough. According to me I was a sinner and also not a very nice person, either. I was a freak. I was not normal. Living within fortifications that offered splendid — or was it dreadful? — isolation... No this was not the loving maternal life I had been putting off until later.

I needed liberating all right. And I looked for it where women traditionally were supposed to look for it. I was going to do something the right way. I looked for liberation in a man.

Prince Charming was created for just such circumstances. Somewhere in the forest, on a lily pad, beyond the other side of the mountain, in Emerald City at the end of the yellow brick road, there lurked or sauntered or snoozed a Prince Charming. The man who would save me. And Prince Charming, whatever he looked like when he galumphed into view, would have to have pretty good eyesight. X-ray vision in fact. I wasn't going to tell him a thing and there was an awful lot a Prince had to know.

The royal fellow would figure out that I wanted a baby. He would also figure out that I did not want motherhood. He would understand and he would offer absolution. This done he would figure out how the two of us could raise the kid. Because, of course, we would have one.

The Prince would figure out how I would be able to give love to a child and energy to my work. Then he would make me understand too, and we would all live happily ever after. In a manner and a style to which I was not accustomed. Not only wasn't I used to such a life, I couldn't even conjure it up in my dreams. I couldn't imagine it all. Even wide awake.

A snapshot taken in 1943

A roly-poly little girl is standing on a wooden chair. She's standing on the chair so that she is tall enough to reach the sink. There she stands bent over the washboard which is sunk into the hot and soapy water. Her black curls are tied up in a red polka dotted scarf and her navy blue guimpe is covered with a white and green striped apron — so the soap suds don't get all over it. Her cheeks are of high colour — the steam is blasting on to her face. And her blue eyes shine like Velvet's at the Grand National. The wash is almost done!

Rub a dub dub . . . socks and underwear in thè tub. Rub a dub dub . . . sheets and towels are nearly done.

In what is called reality this picture is of an event that never took place. But it is just the sort of thing that happened many times over in the little girl's mind's eye. The little girl who was me did her own laundry and her brother's, too. In fantasy. She had to be prepared for when she might have to take over. Mother was worried that if something happened to her — well what would happen to little me and to my brother. So I practised. In case. I suppose my brother practised too. How to bring home the dough.

My father was very much alive and well enough. My mother was in perfect health herself. And no one had problems with laundry. There was my mother's fear of course. Something would happen and the children would be thrown out — on their own. They must be ready so that they could survive.

By the time I was seven I thought my friends were babies if they had to ask permission to do anything. I was already independent. I could make decisions. Not to worry Ma.

I grew up to be terrible at cleaning house but I was wonderful at the independence performance. I kept it up all the time. But right underneath my expert rendition was a pool of dependence — it was deep and cobalt. Whenever I thought I was around some Prince who could take care of me I'd stop the performance. Right away I'd start to drown in the dark and radioactive liquid that was the inside of myself.

I set about trying to raise myself again. To make the inside of me solid, again. To find a spot where it was not so all or nothing, so brave or so helpless. I started to search for the way to be a grown-up without being a false adult — or a drowning pool. Other women chose to have children to do their childhoods over again. I chose to do my childhood over again, too. But I chose to do it over with myself as mother and myself as child. I spent a child's lifetime being a mother to myself.

More or less I can take care of myself now. In something of a more gentle way. Without being so scared of falling in. And without a non-existing Prince Charming as intermediary, either.

Now that I am not looking for Prince Charming any more, now that I am not so terrified that I only pretend to survive without him, now that I am not so afraid of taking help any more, now I wonder where it has been all the time. Where has the man been who would at least offer to help me? Not to figure it all out for me, but to offer and try to help and find it? Where has one of them been?

I am full with impatience, anger, fury, disgust. I am filled up with it and angry besides that I am not above all this rage and repulsion. I long to coast off on the plane of golden, snowy detachment. Meanwhile I sit and stew and seethe in muddy attachment. Ha!

Where were my helpers? Where were my mates? Where were the men who tried to serve me as I tried to serve my work? Where were the men to accept me as I was, confused as I was, to work it out as it was and might be? Where were *they*? After all hadn't I been trained to accept them, to serve them? And though I hadn't served them I had loved them and imperfectly in my fashion even sometimes tried to aid and to help them. Where were they? For me?

For every man I've heard about who went to work too early on in his career, who jeopardised his art because he had to feed his wife and child, I have seen three or a dozen men with wives who were muse, momma, agent, promoter, domestic, peacemaker and brow-mopper.

I am furious all right. And at having to hear that women cannot be great artists. To hell with you all. And to hear the crap about the divinity of the bearer of the child. The mother goddess no matter what. To hell with you all, too.

Women go on thinking that they should and can do it all and be it all. First for a man, of course. Then for the children. It is ordained. And finally, if there's time left and energy and belief, then for themselves. After all they once did have a life — there is something to go back to. Isn't there?

From the age of seventeen until I was twenty-five I was a painter. That was not my hobby. That was my work. I had part-time jobs so I'd have the time and money to paint. And I painted.

From the age of twenty-five until I was thirty I was a student and teacher and researcher in the field of psychology. I had fellowships so that I could do my work. And I worked.

From then until now I have been writing. In the beginning I had some help to start and since then my work has paid for me to do my work. And I know how to get along without very much money though I don't plan to do it any more, not if I can help it. And I do my work. And I love it. On good days — and even, sometimes, on crummy ones.

I have had three careers. I have supported them financially and emotionally — because I wanted to. About that I have never felt a martyr. And all the time I have fought inside about what was happening to me as a woman — on the way to being an artist. It's been a long time coming and about that sometimes I have felt the martyr. And I know nobody asked me to be an artist.

I don't have writing to go back to the way the poet at the breakfast table does. I was not a closet writer, or a teenage writer. I was a child writer but there are no prodigies in this particular line.

There isn't time for me to put my work aside for a while so that I can have a child. I don't have time to fit it in, here and there and in-between. Besides I am terrible at sharing my attentions. It isn't possible at all.

Or is it?

A suspicion as delicate as clematis is creeping along the walls of this fortress. Maybe I don't have to be quite so fierce any more . . . Maybe I don't have to be such a cockamamie version of a Samurai warrior . . . Not any more. Maybe . . .

I persist in lauding ambiguity while also looking up and down everywhere for a neat arrangement. I want to look inside and see dresser drawers where scarves however multicoloured are carefully folded and put neatly next to the socks. Some perfumed sachet wouldn't be a bad addition either. But there is nothing in my past apart from habitual yearning to indicate a drift in that direction. Neat and tidy resolution is not my style.

Oh, do I yearn to have a resolution for this business of being a woman, an artist, a mother. I mean, I am thirty-nine years old. It wouldn't exactly be premature.

Well, I haven't come up with a resolution. The best I have located is the gentle vine with the violet flower, the suspicion. Maybe something is possible. Maybe I could have a child. Or maybe I could have more surety that I don't want one.

Waiting

My body knows it will never bear children.
What can I say to my body now,
this used violin?
Every night it cried out desolately
from its secret cave.

Old body, old friend,
why are you so unforgiving?

Why are you so stiff and resistant
clenched around empty space?
An instrument is not a box.

But suppose you are an empty box?
Suppose you are like that famous wooden music
   hall in Troy, New York,
Waiting to be torn down
where the orchestras love to play?

Let compassion breathe in and out of you
filling you with poems.[1]

Will I learn that compassion? Will I learn it with a child and
without one? Will I come to my fiftieth birthday far less angry
than I am now? Or will I come to my fiftieth birthday ringing
still more changes on the anger I have nurtured since so early
on? And maybe will I come to fifty and be a mother to a child? I
hope that I will have compassion. I don't know. Not yet. It still
has to wait until later on.

[1]Jane Cooper, 1971. In *Maps & Windows* by Jane Cooper,
Collier Books, Macmillan Publishing Company, 1974.

Anna Wileman was born in 1947 in London, and went to school there. She took a degree in English at Sussex University and afterwards worked at a variety of jobs, including advertising, local radio and teaching, before becoming a mother of four. This article is part of a longer account, written in moments snatched from childcare when the triplets were barely two. They are, as this book goes to press, three and a half, and Anna is still writing.

Anna Wileman

I've got triplets of two years (two boys and a girl) and an older daughter who is nearly seven. I am absolutely surrounded by children and it takes me nearly all my time to feed, clothe and keep them clean. The physical demands on me are enormous, and the mental demands leave my head spinning by evening.

Why did I do it? How did I manage to land myself in this impossible position? Was I conditioned to want children? Certainly, I played a lot with dolls. I had a particular favourite called Betty, whom I dressed each morning and undressed to lay down in her cardboard box bed each night. I loved her passionately. I recall one day when my elder sister tore her from my arms and smashed her down on the ground, screaming and raging with irritation at my stupid devotions.

In primary school I was given the part of mother hen in *The Little Half Chick*. They told me I was the motherly sort, and I was rather proud to be so described; after all, my own mother was the person I loved most, and to be like her was surely a compliment. Maybe it was at that moment that I began to regard my life as being inevitably filled with children.

For years I don't think I thought much about babies. I'm sure I wasn't a teenager who thought constantly about getting married and having a family. Real babies always seemed a bit revolting to me. But I did have a desire to do work that involved looking after people. I saw myself as a nurse. Everyone said I would make a good nurse. But then I did so well in my O- and A-levels that they decided it would be a waste. One person only ventured to suggest being a doctor. I was overwhelmed. I honestly didn't think I was clever enough. I honestly thought only men could do that sort of thing.

In my teens I used to make my friends laugh by talking about my plans for the future and adding 'but I must find time to have my babies'. I imagined myself as some marvellously creative eccentric: painting, sculpting, living in a garret surrounded by illegitimate offspring.

Imagine my anxiety when, as a student, I began to have periods less and less regularly. I felt as if both my womanhood and my future were being taken away from me. However, the university doctor told me I was just being neurotic and that my cycle would re-establish itself once the strain of finals was over. So, I waited patiently.

I lived with someone for a while, as people usually do, and then we thought we might as well get married. By that time I was having about one period a year, and if I thought at all about children in the process of making the decision to be wed, then it was to tell myself that the marriage would no doubt be childless. But we were young and didn't want children then, so the question didn't arise much. I think I sort of believed that something could be done if I ever got very broody. I was too emotionally tied up with the man to worry about his babies.

Ironically, I was pregnant within a few months. It seemed a bit of a disaster. We were not altogether happy about the way our future looked. The whole business of being smiled upon by our respective relatives, of being encouraged to collect household possessions and start saving for a house, made us feel uncomfortable. Added to this we had moved to a new town and had nobody but each other. Were we to end up as Mr and Mrs Average?

We both hated our jobs too. I was meant to be a personal assistant in local radio, but I was just at the beck and call of a few big-headed young men. I was terribly bored and listless. I don't think my husband felt much better about his marketing job in industry.

When I got used to the idea, I began to relax and enjoy the physical side of the pregnancy. It had a remarkable effect on me. I found that my appetite became keener, and that food tasted better. I gained weight in all the right places and I found myself more sexually aware. It was, in fact, in the early stages of the pregnancy that I experienced my first orgasm and I never found any difficulty in achieving this satisfaction time and time again. I had waited a long time for this, and I can truly say that I was happy as never before.

By the time it finally happened, I was quite calm. It wasn't easy to relax when the pains got really bad, but somehow I managed to drift and transcend the sensations. I was taken over. The baby knew what to do. I just lay and let my body open up like a strange flower, heavy with fruit. I can feel it now as I write, that sensation almost like orgasm, the massive shape descending through me and falling between my legs, warm and bloody. I was dizzy with it. Sweet Matilda. A gift.

We had a terrible time with the baby to start with. We were both so ignorant, and now I look back I can see that we did not always handle her wisely. But the whole thing was a challenge to me, and I did at least feel that I knew exactly how I wanted her to be brought up. At last I was my own boss; with Robin at work all day until late, I could assert my own personality in the flat, adorning it as I chose, reading, finding out about childcare, learning to cook and exploring all the possibilities of domestic life.

As time went by though, I became lonely. I found myself living a bit like a hermit, especially as the only mothers I came across seemed to me, in my arrogance, to be stupid and trivial people who only wanted to talk about babies and recipes. I thought I was above that sort of thing. I was terribly wrong.

I became more and more of a martyr to the home. Because of babysitting problems, I let Robin become my go-between with the outside world. After some months I gradually became aware that I was in danger of becoming a boring cabbage.

It sounds ridiculous in view of what I have just said, but in spite of all these doubts, I was filled with a mental and physical longing for a second child. I felt that Matilda needed a playmate. I longed to be pregnant again to relive that marvellous feeling of well-being. I also felt that another child would somehow fill the loneliness that Matilda and I had as just two. I still felt really intoxicated with the whole experience of childbirth because it was just about the only meaningful thing that I had done successfully. Anybody would have thought I had invented it. I cannot fully explain this obsession, but my inability to conceive a second time was a terrible cross for me to bear.

I finally found a part-time job teaching. Matilda went to a nursery and by the time she was three years old I was in a full-time job. I enjoyed it. It was difficult at first, but the staff room was full of interesting people who became my friends, and I could have lovely conversations that had nothing to do with the children. I began to feel more like my old self.

But I could not contemplate a life devoted to my job. It always remained secondary to my home life and my private life with its growing number of interests. It seemed as if I was being restricted, not by a baby this time, but by the necessity of putting in so much time towards a job that seemed of such doubtful value to society. The kids certainly weren't interested in the things I was supposed to be teaching them. I seemed to be doing a sort of cover-job for the real problems festering in society.

When Matilda was about three, I began to wonder about adopting another child. I knew it would probably have to be a toddler or a mixed-race baby, but I didn't mind. Robin got quite keen on the idea, and adoption became a sort of hobby: we would spend our evenings writing off letters to different societies, filling in forms and reading books about it all.

It was because of the adoption thing that I had to go to a doctor and get a medical check-up. She asked why I couldn't have a baby of my own and I told her that I had no periods. She seemed amazed that I hadn't done anything about it before. Didn't I want it investigated? I supposed I did. So off I went to the Chelsea Hospital for Women with an introductory letter in my hand.

I was embarking upon a series of medical investigations that were to become almost a new way of life. I was also undergoing cross-questioning from the adoption agencies. They were more interested in my soul than my body.

In fact, the contrast between the two baby-producing establishments never ceased to amaze me. Whereas the adoption people left no stone unturned in their desire to make sure that we would make conscientious and loving parents, the hospital gave not a single thought to how fit we were to care for the babies they were trying to give us. Just because the children were to emerge from our own genitals, we seemed to be exonerated from all responsibilities. We could have been raving psychotics for all they seemed to care.

In about August 1975 our adoption application was finally accepted, and we were called almost at once to meet a little boy of about six months, born to an Indian schoolgirl. During the same month, Chelsea Hospital announced that they had decided on the one and only treatment for my infertility. It would involve a short stay in hospital and regular injections of a drug, Pergonal. The drug was very expensive and not extensively used, but they felt sure that the treatment would be successful.

We were doubtful about the hospital business. We tried to delay our decision; they kept pushing me to say whether I wanted to be booked in. But the Indian baby was flesh and blood. We made a series of visits to him at his 'Home'.

It wasn't until we had been to see him on about four occasions that we finally looked each other squarely in the eyes and realised that it was no good. Even now, I find it hard to explain the reasons for our decision.

Maybe I was haunted by the thought of what Chelsea Hospital had to offer. But I don't honestly think I could have gone ahead even if the possibilities of ever conceiving had been totally wiped out. What I wanted was to relive the experience of having Matilda and to achieve another product from Robin and myself. I wanted all the physical side of it, the animalness of conception and pregnancy and birth and nurturing a new baby. It wasn't that I just wanted a helpless creature, that I was a frustrated housewife, that I had a strong social conscience that made me want to protect these little orphans. I'm afraid I was just a healthy, selfish woman. A foolish woman in many ways, thinking she could find fulfillment by having another baby, just like everyone else.

The lure was too much for me, the flesh succumbed. I telephoned and secured a hospital bed for late September. I muttered something at school about check-ups, packed a small bag and left Rob and Matilda with a larder full of goodies. The first night I cried myself to sleep.

At first, my hormone count was almost totally unresponsive to the Pergonal. After a week I became thoroughly tired of the whole thing. I asked if I could back out and go home. My own doctor, who seemed to be raging keen to crack my particular nut, refused to let me give up yet, although he conceded that to go on taking doses for too many days might be dangerous. He allowed me to go home and have a district nurse complete the course, provided I continued to wee into bottles and bring the dirty great steaming containers into the hospital with me every day.

This I did. There followed a hilarious period when I had to smuggle jugs, funnels and plastic bottles into the school where I was teaching, conceal them under a pile of rubbish in the ladies and sneak out during lessons to perform the strange ritual of collecting every drop I passed. I have always been a big drinker and I could hardly lug the containers on and off the train to get the stuff up to Chelsea. I had to get up especially early to make this pilgrimage before 9 o'clock when school began. I must have been mad.

The first course of injections came to an end. The following Monday I had a panic phone call from my doctor. My hormone count had hit the jackpot while he had been away for the weekend, and his colleagues had failed to contact me to give me the injection that would send the egg tumbling on its way. We had missed the once-in-a-lifetime boat! You can guess that this whiz kid would not let it rest at that though. Once again I found myself bleary eyed on the early uptown train with my strange parcels.

When the time came for a pregnancy test, I wandered into the ward to chat to some of my (by now) many acquaintances. Suddenly, the doctor burst in the door. He rushed over to me and embraced me. I was taken aback by this sudden affection. He had hardly seemed to remember my name up to now. But then I realised. He had succeeded. I was pregnant.

Of course, as I came to my senses, I became more cheerful. I had a baby. I ran from ward to ward to tell my friends. We laughed and chattered wildly about the baby, trying to convince ourselves that this little protégé of modern science would one day be a person.

There seemed to be rather a lot of people hanging around to see the outcome of my first ultrasound. My belly was greased, the nozzle descended on to it, and the doctors crowded around the television screen. I crossed my fingers and shut my eyes. They found a baby and almost at once they found another. They continued to search. I prayed there would be no more.

'There you are,' they said, 'the mother of twins. Is that all right?'

I was overjoyed. Twins would be fun. I left the hospital and caught a train home to Richmond where we were living. I felt so lucky as I sat on the platform. I had gambled, but it seemed to have paid off, so long as I did not now lose the babies.

My fear of losing the babies was actually to grow over the next few weeks. I experienced such a lot of weird sensations, things I had never had with Matilda. The morning sickness that I had found unpleasant with her reached such proportions that I was completely immobilised. However I was fortunate in that instead of morning sickness, I had evening sickness. I was still teaching, and arrived home at about five just in time to do a bit of cooking before the nausea began to creep up on me. Although I felt so sick, I had a craving for meaty food. Our shopping bills must have increased enormously.

At the same time, I was experiencing cramps around the region of my back and my belly similar to the aches and pains of a woman approaching full term. After a couple of months my waist had thickened so much and my torso had become so clumsy that energetic movements were difficult and uncomfortable. Quite early on, also, I developed piles. But it was undoubtedly my legs that suffered most. The varicose veins that had cleared up after Matilda's birth re-emerged almost at once. The weight pulling down on my belly and on the muscles between my legs were causing terrible swelling of the flesh around my fanny, and it became impossible to stand for any length of time.

From all these details you can see that the pregnancy soon took over my normal life. I was forced to leave work even before the Easter holidays. I was teaching some quite demanding kids in a comprehensive school in Greenford. They needed someone literally on her toes, and I could only teach from a chair. I already found the business of looking after Matilda and myself and the ordinary household stuff quite demanding. Things I had done standing on my head now took me ages and left me exhausted.

Now that Matilda was at playschool I was happy to have the afternoons with her and, to start with, it was fun to sit in the house and read and play puzzles and do all the things I was usually too busy or impatient to do. But after a while even this became too tiring because all I wanted to do was sleep after lunch, and I would actually nod off while talking to her and find myself coming to again with her calling my name. I couldn't understand why I was so tired. Twins, I thought, are certainly difficult to carry.

I had not had an internal exam since before the pregnancy was confirmed, as the doctors thought it might be enough to induce spontaneous abortion. One day in early May a doctor cautiously inserted a finger, withdrew it hastily and told me that I had the rest of the day to get myself sorted out and be back in the hospital. There was a baby lying with its head forcing open the neck of my womb.

My first reaction was to sit down and weep. The twins weren't due until the end of July (although there was some doubt as to the exact date). Matilda comforted me as we trailed home on the underground.

The weeks went by and, although the rest was doing me good, some of my symptoms got worse. As we entered June, the nurses and doctors began to agree that in view of my size and discomfort, it wouldn't be such a bad thing if I went into labour rather early. Some people thought the babies were due in mid-July, others said the end of June.

On the eighth of June the sister came to tell me that they had decided to take an x-ray of my womb to establish once and for all the position of my babies, in preparation for the delivery.

After I returned to the ward, one of the nurses who had become quite a friend came into the ward to tell me that my x-ray had come down for sister to see. I followed her into sister's office. We hooked the x-ray up on the illuminated viewer. I felt a sense of great anticipation. 'There they are,' said the nurse. And there they were. She pointed out for me the two dark rounded patches low down in my pelvis and rising up into my stomach stretched two spines, faint and feathery like two herring bones.

Almost at once, though, I noticed something that made me feel quite strange and then quite afraid. I saw another herring bone. This one was fainter than the other two and curled up on itself right up high under my heart. I knew what it must be at once. It certainly wasn't the kipper I had had for breakfast.

'It's another one!' I said.

'No it isn't.'

'It is!'

I went back to bed, and before I could lay my head on the pillow the tears began to flow. I remember saying, 'But how can I love three babies. I won't even be able to hold them. I only have two arms.' What worried me more than anything in these first hours was that I would not be able to 'fall in love' three times over. This seemed a bit like promiscuity.

But I cheered up after I talked to Robin. 'Three,' he said, after a pause. 'Oh well, what's one more?' My stomach loosened its grip on me. We laughed together. Suddenly it was all a farce. Triplets! Pergonal had let us down! So what! So what! So what!

One thing was for sure. I would never be the same again.

The doctors were concerned for the safety of the baby high up inside me, so a Caesarean was performed the following day. I was in hospital for three weeks after the babies were born, and during that time my spirits sometimes sank very low. I was still losing a lot of blood and was very anaemic.

The pleasure of returning home was soon marred by the growing anxiety over how I was going to pull myself together in time to cope with these three babies whose mother I suddenly found myself to be. I had imagined a situation in which I was a strong healthy woman. But whether it was the contraction of my womb to normal after the huge proportions it had stretched to, or whether it was the wound from the operation, or whether it was the bleeding from the three placental scars inside me, I have never been so drained by constant pain. I would return time and time again to the pain killers which at least took the edge off my discomfort. However, I don't believe that I had any real post-natal depression.

What I did have was two weeks at home without the babies (they had to remain in hospital until they reached six pounds), to contemplate the fact of their existence and chew over to myself the ways in which their arrival in the house was going to cause total chaos. I began to wonder what demon had possessed me to go in for the whole rotten idea. I felt I had dragged Robin and Matilda down a path that could lead to nothing but pain and poverty and enslavement. I felt so guilty that I could not even turn to them and confess my fears. I had to keep grinning and telling them what fun it was all going to be.

The burning broodiness that had filled my heart before the Pergonal experiment had completely gone. Pregnant women filled me with pity, not envy. I became terrified that my periods would return and I would by some bitter quirk of fate become fertile and pregnant by natural means. I even asked about sterilisation operations for Robin.

I have never been terribly keen on newborn babies and I

think the greatest satisfaction I got from mine that summer was to sit down in the evening, a glass of wine in hand, and reflect on how I had successfully steered them through another day. It was more the satisfaction of achieving the impossible than the satisfaction of loving a child. I liked them best asleep, and I would be the first to admit it.

Although I had been through this business before with Matilda, I had forgotten most of the details of how to care for a newborn baby. With three, the task was magnified beyond all belief. The nappies were never ending. I think we were washing about twenty-four a day. The bottles stood in rows on the draining board and we used to make them up in huge batches and store them in the fridge.

Our house was so tiny and the babies so numerous that we felt surrounded. They slept upstairs during the day and downstairs at night. We used to carry their little baskets about the house constantly. They were changed on the dining-room table and bathed in the kitchen washing-up bowl. I well remember one evening when I nearly suffered a cardiac arrest. I walked into the kitchen to see a small pink baby lying, head submerged, in a bowl of crystal clear water. My head spun and my insides did a leap. We had overlooked one. There were so many of them, it seemed well within the bounds of possibility. I rushed forward, calling Robin. It was Matilda's doll, a beautiful lifelike creature.

I often mistook this doll for a triplet. I was mechanically dealing with babies all day long, and the responsibility became such a part of me that I would leap to attention at the sound of any baby's cry, even if it came from the radio.

Meanwhile Robin had qualified as a solicitor and, just as we began to realise that the space problem could not be neglected for much longer, he applied for a job in Brighton and got it. We began to look for a house. You can almost imagine what we ended up with. It was very much the sort of house designed for a family with small children. But at the back of the house was a huge expanse of open land looking out to sea, easily accessible through the garden, which had ample room for vegetable growing. There was room inside for all of us and we felt we could build ourselves a little haven here to see us through the difficult pre-school years of the triplets. Here was some sort of retreat for our battered senses.

My life that winter was spent almost totally within the walls of the house or on the road between home and the school. The house itself was still in a rather dingy state, and the furniture was still not organised. Sometimes I felt as though I were living in a junk shop. Most things were decorated with little deposits of baby sick, which used to dry into a crusty white stuff that resembled pigeon excretion.

In the first few weeks of Matilda's school term, I was having to take the pram down to school and back in the afternoons as well as the mornings. Matilda's school was only a ten minute walk away, but at the foot of a hill so sheer that even without a pram it was well known for its treacherous descent, especially in winter. The snow that fell thick in January made the path so slippery that I had blisters on my hands from straining to keep the pram with its heavy load from dragging Matilda and me head first down the sharp incline.

Having left Matilda at the school, I was then confronted with the problem of how to get the pram back up the hill again. On the first day I decided that the only thing to do was to go on where the road gradually flattened out and ended in a small row of shops. It was possible to return home from these shops by a different route. It was four times as long, but the gradient was four times less steep, and this made it at least a possible journey.

Asking favours is an extremely difficult thing to do. It must be said that in emergencies, like terrible snowfalls, terrible head colds in the babies, acute exhaustion (more acute than usual), doctor appointments, etc., I did ask the neighbours in to help. They always came if they possibly could. Nobody ever told me to get lost. It is not easy to take on three babies when your own are off and forgotten. These ladies took mine on very bravely.

After some weeks of struggling on with this sort of precarious independence, I encountered a lady who really was to be my guardian angel. She became the backbone of my support team. She arranged to come in on various afternoons so that I could go alone to meet Matilda. She also came one morning and cared for the babies while I delivered Matilda to school and then went on to town for two heavenly hours.

I do not believe that one should wish one's life away, and I do appreciate that the baby years are magic, and never to be recaptured. However, that winter seemed long and hard, and the babies were still rather boring companions. I gave them all the love and joyful stimulation I could muster. But they were still too young to return the compliment. At the end of each day I felt not only physically, but emotionally drained. I felt a desperate need for someone or something that would recharge me with joie de vivre. The prospect of my weekly freedom of the town helped a lot.

Seeing how some of our footloose friends lived made us wonder how we ever came to want all these beastly children. I wondered, when with these friends, whether I could have managed, as they seemed to, without any contact with children, and came to the conclusion that in spite of the abundance of freedom and money that such a choice could have left me with, I would not have been happy. I decided this even though I was at this stage absolutely up to here with babies and was if anything less interested in the whole business than at any stage in my life before.

I have detected in most people the need to find something fixed and long-term in their lives, something that they could devote most of their energies to. It could be a job or an ideal. I suppose I have chosen people to devote my life to and that's how I have got lumbered in this ridiculous situation.

I expect our friends were all amazed by the way in which our household functioned. It was like a glorified nursery and it ran with the same clockwork precision. Up at a certain time, chairs out for breakfast! Three bowls, three spoons, three bottles, we did the whole thing automatically, complementing each other's work like a well-trained team. There were certain times for playing in the playroom, certain times when puzzles were produced and carefully tidied away out of reach so as not to lose the pieces. There were techniques for moving them round the house as the day wore on; we found that changing rooms could allay boredom.

We painted huge colourful murals on their bedroom walls, and stuck big pictures everywhere to help them learn a little speech. We found that speech was very slow coming, probably because they talked to each other so effectively with grunts and squeaks and probably, too, because I was usually too absorbed in my own thoughts to talk to them as much as I would have done with one baby. I really had to make the effort not to shut off when I was with them.

By the time they were two I was shortening their midday nap so that they still went to bed at six. We couldn't bear to give up the peace of our evenings. It was so important to us to follow our own interests and, when we had the energy, to get out and involve ourselves in a world that had nothing whatsoever to do with children.

Perhaps for this very reason, we found ourselves mixing more and more with childless people, both couples and singles. It was very refreshing, although often exhausting as we tried to keep their late hours and energetic habits as well as being on form for our domestic life.

On the whole we managed quite well, and it was well worth any problems created by babysitters or having to spend many evenings apart when one of us would attend events and leave the other in charge at home. It was particularly difficult for me to learn this sort of independence from Robin. I had always liked to have him with me, but this was now not always possible. It was very good for me to follow up my own interests alone and stand as an individual with needs that were often quite different and incompatible with his. I don't think this realisation weakened my love for him or my happiness in his company. I found in myself political and cultural interests that had never before flourished, restricted I believe by the female world I had been brought up in, even at university. I had always left that sort of involvement to men. Only difficult, aggressive women took an active part in social reform. Many things about the upbringing given to girls had not progressed much since the days of the suffragettes. I determined to give my own girls a different and more courageous attitude towards life and the role that women can play.

It is hard to say what bearing the babies had on these developments in my own personality. Probably very little. But they were there, and I was happy with them. I was always delighted to be greeted in the mornings by their distinctive little faces, even when I had only had a few hours sleep and too much to drink the night before. And there were times when I was positively relieved to sink into their world of innocence and simplicity after the complicated traumas that often cropped up in the sophisticated adult world of troubled marriages, broken love affairs, discordant communes and the like.

We have really had to work at bringing them up. I sometimes feel like the lion tamer at the zoo, struggling to keep on top against all reasonable odds. When we feel things aren't working out any more we have to sit down and figure out what we are doing that is wrong. There usually turns out to be some development in them that we haven't yet appreciated and adapted to. We aren't so much parents as time and motion consultants.

Sometimes, I feel so delighted with them. Today, we took them up to bath after their chaotic tea. Rolling and tumbling over each other, giggling and shrieking with joy as they clouted each other with the loofa, weeing ostentatiously into the air (or down her legs in Georgia's case), they seem to be having such a lot of fun, far more than Matilda ever had. No doubt there are things to be said for being a triplet. It will be interesting to hear what they have to say when they are my age.

And what about me?

I guess I've lost a bit of freedom. But freedom is a funny thing. It hasn't always made me happy to be able to do exactly what I want, when I want. In my amazingly irresponsible youth I used not to appreciate that freedom. I used to worry about silly things like the way I looked, the number of men who fancied me, whether I would do well in exams, things that now have proved to be of absolutely no importance.

I must say that I really fling myself into social events now. I don't stop to worry about the clothes I'm wearing or the impression I'm making. I just wallow in the adult companionship and the opportunity to forget all those tousled heads sleeping on all those dribbly pillows. The worst thing is to be introduced at a party as 'Anna, who's got triplets!'

Sometimes I think that so many kids is an almost insurmountable wedge between Robin and me. There is so much planning and organising that has to be gone through. Each morning when we open our sticky eyes our first thoughts are of washing and Weetabix, never of each other's warm and moist bodies. We take each other for granted and regard each other more as indispensable links in a chain of repetitions than as people with whom we live out of love and respect. There is certainly an element of that in it, anyway.

But Robin and I still talk a lot. We talk for hours and hours. I sometimes think that it is this fluency that keeps us together. I've never found him boring. I sometimes hate his guts, but I never find him boring.

I think the main problem with children is that they separate the men from the women. If only couples could really share the tasks, and ideally share a job, so that they can take it in turns to go out to work. Once a woman gives up outside work, she becomes the housewife and takes over all the domestic work, or at least most of it. Then the age-old pattern begins to develop.

Mind you, I've enjoyed my years out of paid work. I think everyone, male and female, should have a few in their lifetime. I've found all sorts of interests and had a chance to practise them just a little bit. I've learned a lot about people and even more about myself.

We struggle by. I try not to be the typical housewife and mother. I try to share it all with Robin. I try to teach Matilda to be liberal but not too liberal. I try not to be a domestic martyr, doing all the jobs and moaning about my hard life. It isn't hard. I chose it. I like it. But I shall like it even more when they're three years old and I can live for myself a little more than I can now. I've certainly learned my lesson the hard way.

I know that it often works out that you don't really realise that you are happy until after the event. Maybe this will turn out to be the happiest time of my life.

But I don't really believe that.

Lesley Saunders

Sometimes it hits me that these poems seem to be making a lot out of nothing very much — motherhood and childhood aren't new inventions, for god's sake. Except for every mother and child. The experience was a total shock to me, it wasn't like any of the books. On the whole, I'm pleased.

I definitely and consciously wanted a child, had done for a long time, before the circumstances in which this would be a good or even a possible thing unfolded themselves. I did not undertake the venture lightly or in blind ignorance. I now see I had not the faintest notion of what 'having a baby' meant. Part of what I've wanted to do in these poems is to say what it was like for me, the reality, not the image. I also wanted to be able to be a mother and a writer at the same time, a desire which has on occasions nearly torn me in half. There is no social encouragement for such a struggle, which after all is only one of the many fights in our daily lives to make the different bits of ourselves live somehow, anyhow, with each other.

The fighting necessarily leads to killing — clubbing to death

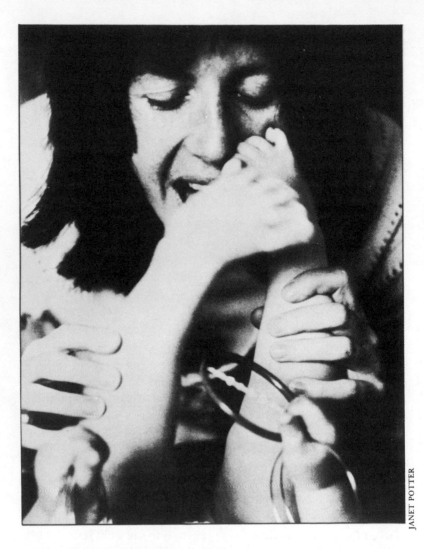

JANET POTTER

Lesley Saunders is a Classicist by education and disposition. She 'became a mother on 16 ix 1978 to a son. This fact is a meeting point for channels of the past, present and future in me, an almost impersonal knot of dilemmas and confrontations I am picking at out of personal necessity. I welcome the solitary nature of writing poetry but my context is some kind of emotional community, family, feminists, tradition. I should like to have more children.' The photograph and poems are part of a collection entitled *The Cradle and The Grave*.

of all those dreadful emotions like guilt and resentment that haunt us and sap our strength. I have not been able to rid myself of them and this shows in what I write, for better or worse. One false impression I cannot seem to do much about remains — it looks as if 'I' wrote the poems. But we know, especially if we're women, that all sorts of people and circumstances and arrangements are involved in whether a poem gets written or not. In one sense, these poems are anonymous, unattributable amalgams. And that sits well with motherhood too.

Birth 16 ix 78

The pod of my flesh
bulged, gaped, split
— dehiscent but unwilling
to let its contents go

A woman doctor shouted
at my lover and my friend
to get out: they stayed.
Tubes and catheters were inserted
a rubber mask put in my hand
the waters broken.
We all waited
we waited until
two days had gone by
and flat on my back
my feet in stirrups
draped in a green gown
all pain, all hurt
anaesthetised and banished
(but they threw my friend out)
I finally gave birth
two days had gone by
and finally
he was born

I cry now
for my pain then
for my body's anguish
and its scarring
which I think will never heal
 — the skin on my belly browned
and wrinkled with sudden age
my vulva stitched and raw
breasts swollen and dripping —
I cry for the man's tears
his fear for me
I cry for my fear of dying
I cry
for the child's terrible passage
and then lying in a metal cot
with a tube in his nose

I shall go on crying
until this birth is expiated

I can never go back
to the girl I was
I cry for my freedom gone —
whose is this child?
I cannot remember
who his mother is
who his father
as the child sucks at me
unerringly and without gratitude
as he pulls at my tender breast

I shall go on crying
until this birth
is expiated.

To the Authorities

You took my baby away
YOU TOOK MY BABY AWAY

when my baby needed me —

you ought to know, you're the doctors,
don't they teach you anything?
and it's *your fault* he had to be taken away
to have his lungs and stomach sucked clean,
three hours you made us wait
because the fucking registrar was asleep
and you didn't want to disturb him!
Three hours while my baby's head was stuck in my vagina,
he could have DIED! Or worse.

He needed me, I know he did,
warm & wet & close,
oh I needed you, I did, oh I did,
I want you, you're not here,
you should be here
you should have been here
warm & naked, just the thud of breath and blood
and the suck of milk between us,
not white gowns and sheets, metal beds, harsh lights,
loud noises and miles and miles of shiny corridor between
    us —

they should have *known*.

You shits, you stinking scum
you've taken my baby
it's like killing someone, do you know that,
it's like murder in cold blood,
it's like death, it's like losing my first baby,
oh my baby
I lost you, I want you back

I shan't let them have you
I shan't *let* you have him, *no*, NAOOO . . .

And I snatched him back,
I screamed and screamed and took him back,
I got him back, yes I did —

but not at the time,
not when it mattered;
a year later
it all came back

it was like death.

National Gallery

Beneath
towering panels
icons where each Madonna
magnificently
suckles her Child
in a rapture
                of lustrous gold
                glowing ultramarine and
                passionate rose
I dare not sit and
bare my breast
to feed *my* son.
So the housekeeper
                smiling
takes me to her room
where I rest on the day bed
nursing
and the blue and gold come
                        streaming
in through the window
and his eyes look blue into mine

as he lies
in his bright suit
curled and squirming
on my wide lap
wrapped in luxury, luxury.

Leon, riding in the Firmament eight months old

Leon
my lion my baby my son
torn from my vagina with metal spoons

bambino papoose piccaninny

who are you?

Now you play
at being a marsupial-beast
pulling yourself on to me
clutching and clinging to the front of my body
with your prehensile limbs
resting your face in my chest
making your yayaya sounds
with your thumb and all your fingers
stuck in your mouth

my baby

Often while you're sucking at my nipple
in apparent repose
a blue eye snaps open
that free arm comes waving up
and your hand, sure as dammit,
goes searching out the features on my face
without a by-your-leave
with no gentleness or compunction
trying to winkle out my eyeball

making a grab for my nostrils
prising open my lips
then returns to knead at my breast
impatient for more milk, faster

my lion

And now you arch your back
go rigid and screw up your eyes
you struggle, you have to get away
I put you down.
Crawling crabwise across the floor
crooning or smacking your lips
as I trundle you up the road
you're happy at being left
to yourself
to imagine a child
the spit of you
into being
to dream yourself
into the world

my son

As I dreamt you
inside me
riding in the firmament

my papoose my piccanin

Mother's Catalogue

I hate you for not leaving me be,
for crying even harder when I hit you,
I hate you for making me shake you,
for clinging to me and needing me —
your everlasting need —

236

when I don't want anything more to do with you.
I hate you for not doing what I want you to do,
for not going to sleep so I can have some time,
for not letting me sleep,
I hate you for stopping me doing
all the things I would do if you weren't here.
I hate you for having a will of your own.

And I hate *you* for making me a mother —
in other words, housewife —
and we don't even believe in marriage!
I hate you for refusing to see when I break into a million
    pieces
and silently scream myself to death,
invisible blood running down the kitchen walls.
I hate you for not doing things my way
and for just not doing things,
I hate you for being different from me.

I hate you for being better mothers than me,
for not being mothers,
for spending more time with your children, putting them
    first,
I hate you for spending less time with them than I do,
for putting yourselves first,
I hate you for having the energy to do more,
for being content to do less,
for teaching, for writing, for learning to dance,
for going on holiday, for having a better time,
for working things out better,
I hate you for having nicer births, children, places to live,
I hate you for not needing to push yourselves as much,
I hate you for making me compare myself with you.

I hate you most of all for inhabiting my skin
and not allowing me to be the things you make me want
    to be —

earth mother
zappy feminist (sisterhood is powerful)
storm-raising poet
rock-steady friend (always *there* in a crisis)
misunderstood genius (who'd have thought she had it in her?)
starry tempestuous lover
wise woman
magna martyr — it isn't FAIR!

Sometimes I am so consumed with hate
my entrails turn slack-green with it
and my eyes stand out on stalks
and I spit poison,
I stick pins in dolls and living hearts
and pull snakes out of my hair,
I clench my teeth and drive my fingernails into my palms
till I can't stand it any more
and I wear a black shroud, my witch's shawl,
and cover the house in it

then crouch in a corner and weep among the cobwebs
weep-weep, weep-weep
over the corpses of what I kill
a slobbering grimacing madwoman, a sad vampire

'Cross me palm, dearie,
with blood-money, with a silver nappy-pin,
with half your salary, with your life'

Sometimes I need my hate to help me stay alive.

A Salute

At nine months and one day precisely
you shut your mouth
against my breast
turned your head firmly away
and that was that

nine months of sucking
and now you're free

I'll wean you gradually
I thought
(as the books advise,
except for emergencies
like going into hospital —
they don't mention
the emergency
of growing up overnight
of being suddenly brave)
ignorant
that any weaning being done
was by you, of me.

You took me by surprise
you, child no longer infant,
I was ambushed —
breasts changed into
huge leaking stones
dripping white sap
on the kitchen floor
(your life source
I fondly imagined)
I sat with wet towels round me
had to hold myself in my hands
when I stood up
and walked bent double
dragged over by iron-hard and knotted udders,
my lovely breasts! and your father sucking the milk
and spitting it down the sink —
but you wouldn't have it,
not a drop —
except, you bugger, from a cup
(I refused to waste it all).

Nine months of suckling
and now I'm free;
thought I'd be sad
when the great day came,
had visions of nursing you
till you were two.

But you've a deal to teach me,
young man, my changeling,
your comfort comes from cuddles now,
not nipples
and your nourishment
from wherever you can get it;
and you've left me no excuse for slacking.

I salute you
you equal
young blood-brother
with your bird quick head
your quick bird eye
ever on the qui-vive;
your milk days are over
your milk teeth chew on a new world
your mild-as-milk complexion has caught the sun
and your forefinger wobbles my nipple
as if it had ever been
only a curious plaything.

Such forgetfulness
young man
such wanton complete oblivion
is why I'm making this,
a rejoinder to time
and the hurrying dark
in the years to come.

Weaning

Yes, in retrospect I loved it all,
all the unbuttoning and unlacing and uncovering, without
   respite
it seemed, how I loved
the drifting daze of it all, hardly knowing
where I ended and the babe (or the world) began,
and the settling down of bum and the hitching up of tit,
the nesting head in crook of arm
and the pull and tingle of him latching on, how many times,
drinking down the good draught from my benefic breasts:
I never quite tired of it.

I was in a state of grace
between bloodlettings, my offerings
to the great maw of fecundity;
suspended from normal duties
of bleeding and repairing, re-writing and scrapping
and trying again, spared from pondering
all my little ones, my unborn brood,
how they were faring.

To work again:
flushing out forgotten conduits,
clots of old gone-off matter,
dusting down unused equipment,
finding a former pattern,
trying old hats on for size,
knowing more this time, deciding to make good,
even though my legs feel unsteady
after such lapse of time and I'm still not sure
I want my unalloyed, my thin and singular pronoun back;
the new spate has run old circles
round me, drained the core. This is now the knot, the crux,
with what name I console the vacancy, what manner of
   creation
break the enclosing ring.

Karen Lindsey is a free-lance feminist poet and journalist. She has had two collections of poems published *Falling Off the Roof* (1975) and *A Company of Queens* (1977). Her articles have appeared in many journals including *Ms, Sojourner* and *Spare Rib*. She lives in Somerville, Massachusetts and is currently working on a biography of Anne Askew.

Karen Lindsey

When I first decided to get sterilised, at twenty-five, it seemed the natural outcome of a lifetime of not wanting children. I had no thoughts of the immorality of overpopulation, or of a woman's duty to define herself outside the traditional area of the home. I simply had never much enjoyed being around children, and saw no reason to spend a major part of my life with them.

How I escaped the conviction that as a woman I would naturally want children, I don't know. I was certainly well socialised into the other aspects of 'woman's role'. But I remember at the age of seven — we had just moved into a new neighbourhood — announcing to my new friends that I was going to be a trapeze artist when I grew up, and I wasn't going to get married and have babies. I had recently seen *The Greatest Show on Earth*, and despite the conventional love-story ending, I somehow realised that Betty Hutton wouldn't have been up there on a trapeze in her glittering turquoise costume joyfully flying through the air if she'd had to feed a houseful of kids. Or maybe it was just the disparity between that glittering fantasy figure and the banal reality of what being a mommy was in my world. While I soon outgrew Betty Hutton, I remained firm in my determination to achieve spinsterhood.

Meanwhile, in every other way, I was a conventionally girlish little girl. I giggled with my girlfriend Shelly and I loved pink dresses. And I dearly loved my dolls, who were very real people to me. I can vividly recall my feeling for Sally, the rubber doll with a hole in her arm I kept carefully bandaged, and the two nameless dolls who followed. I was very conscientious about not letting Sally be pushed aside for the newcomers, and about not letting the homelier of the two new ones know that I liked her prettier sister better. When I was separated from them for two weeks during one summer vacation, I couldn't sleep at night. And yet they were never my babies. They were my much-loved companions; they were my dolls. I never connected my love for them with some future life centred around children.

At the age of ten I read a Cherry Ames book (Cherry was the nurse version of Nancy Drew) and decided to be a nurse when I grew up. I also read *Little Women* and decided to be a tomboy. (The latter proved a rousing failure. I hated sports and couldn't climb trees. But I wore sloppy jeans and informed everyone I met that I was a tomboy.) But even after *Little Men*, when my beloved heroine Jo had two sons, I still didn't want babies. Jo could marry her professor – and I was romantic enough to share the universal depression over her rejection of Laurie – but *I* wasn't going to marry anyone, ever. I was going to be a . . . at twelve it was a lawyer. At thirteen I went to my first Broadway play and began a five-year monogamous passion for theatre. I went through four years of Catholic high school, accumulating graces and guilts, hearing with monotonous regularity that if I didn't have a religious vocation, my job was to be fruitful and multiply. It didn't work. They broke my spirit with Joycean thoroughness, but I held stubbornly to one tenet. I was going to be an old maid, and no one was going to stop me.

Meanwhile, my home life further persuaded me not to have children. When I was younger, my desire not to be a mommy had been patronisingly dismissed with a 'you'll change your mind when you grow up'. But I was left alone to outgrow my silliness. Then my mother decided to take in foster babies — twenty-four hours a day, short-term care for children who would eventually go back to their mothers or be placed in adoptive homes. The babies were cute, my mother enjoyed them, and I didn't mind helping out. And the grown-ups confidently waited for all my latent maternal instincts to blossom. They didn't. But my latent resentment blossomed beautifully. While my two brothers were sometimes expected to take the kids for walks or play with them, they never had to feed them or change diapers, I did. When I complained, both my parents told me it was good training for when I had my own babies. I couldn't believe it. Hadn't they been listening all these years? I wasn't going to have babies, I told them. Didn't it make more sense to train Keith and Warren for when they had kids and their wives were sick or in the hospital having more kids? It wasn't fair, my mother told me firmly, to expect boys to change diapers. Period. I changed diapers.

And, slowly, the grown-ups' attitude changed. It was no longer cute that I didn't want kids. I was getting to an age when girls start to think about getting married. When I met the right man, it was decided, I'd want his kids. Then I met Mark and for a year and a half I slept with him, pursued him, loved him, grew dependent on him, and dreamed of living with him forever. It never occurred to me to want his children, and when one of our friends mentioned the possibility, I was horrified. Children simply were not a part of either the fantasy or the reality of my love for Mark.

Eventually, and for other reasons, I went into analysis. The grown-ups (at twenty, I still thought of them as 'the grown-ups') heaved a sigh of relief. Now I'd get over this foolish, 'sick' notion of mine. When my father expressed, casually, the assumption that, as the night the day, analysis would lead to maternal yearnings, I started to tremble. I went to my analyst, in fury and terror, demanding to know if 'health' would mean wanting children. If I was going to be cured into domesticity, I'd keep my neurosis. My analyst, a good and wise woman, stared at me. 'How do I know what you'll want?' she asked, and explained, carefully, that there was no set lifestyle for a 'healthy' person, but rather an understanding of what her own, individual needs were.

With the advent of that tragic farce The Sexual Revolution, I found (so I thought) more acceptance of my disinterest in motherhood. My peers accepted what I did as part of the new tolerance we thought we'd developed; among the few straight people I dealt with I quickly slid into the role of Adorable Hippy Kook, and my not wanting kids fell into the same category as my miniskirts, SDS (Students for a Democratic Society) membership, and friendships with homosexual men. Unconventionality was acceptable if you were cute enough, and I developed the art of cuteness fully.

Meanwhile, my great fantasy developed. I would find myself daydreaming about being in a terrible car crash and waking up in the hospital with a handsome intern leaning over me, and saying, anxiously, 'Miss Lindsey, you'll live, but . . . you'll never have children.' And I would shout 'Hooray!' into his startled face. Of course, I would tell my friends, laughing, I'd never actually *get* sterilised. But the 'of course' seemed less and less valid as time went on. I had been on the pill three years when my twenty-four-year-old friend Sylvia had her stroke, which all the doctors attributed to the pill. I had heard bad reports of the IUD (intra-uterine device); three bright, sensible friends had abortions because they hadn't bothered with their diaphragms just once; and, though I deeply believed in the right of a woman to choose abortion, I was uncomfortable with the idea of personally stopping the life process in that way. It began to seem evident that, for me, the best solution was an operation that would stop the process from ever beginning. I soul-searched a bit, decided that, at twenty-five, I had been in love three times, had been in analysis, and that the desire not to be encumbered with children was an integral part of my character.

I went to my doctor, never doubting that it would be a simple process of announcing my intention and scheduling my operation. My doctor was understanding and sympathetic, but he assured me that no hospital in the country would sterilise an unmarried, childless woman. It was not a question of law: only two states have laws restricting sterilisation. It was AMA (American Medical Association)-run hospital boards, who also worked on an arbitrary 'parity' system: age times number of children must equal a hundred and twenty before a woman can be sterilised. My doctor told me of a thirty-nine-year-old patient with two children and a dangerous heart condition whom he could not sterilise because the AMA would rather give her a 'therapeutic abortion' (this happened *before* abortion was legalised in New York). I went to the Association for Voluntary Sterilisation. They wrote back that I *might* be able to get sterilised if a psychiatrist would certify that I was emotionally unstable and having a child would drive me over the edge. I was unwilling to go through the hassle and degradation this would entail, so I got a coil, crossed my fingers, and gave up. Once, I talked to some people from Zero Population Growth. They were simply uninterested in the rights of a childless woman to remain childless.

During the next two years, I would complain in conversations about my experience. And the reactions of young and old, 'hip' and 'straight' made me realise for the first time that this most personal of decisions was also totally, radically political. I expected negative reactions from the straight world – they'd *always* thought I was crazy. But young people who'd fucked around and had abortions and done acid and praised the Weathermen and even supported 'women's lib' were equally horrified. They acted as though I were proposing a terrible act of self-mutilation and – yes – a hideous betrayal of nature. Rarely did people respond as if I were making a purely personal choice: they were angry, hostile, threatened. At first, I simply didn't understand – even if I were making a tragic mistake, it would hurt me, not them. I developed a series of stock defensive answers: (1) Yes, it's an irrevocable decision. So is losing one's virginity. So is having a baby – with the added danger, in that case, of fucking up two lives instead of one; (2) If I change my mind I can always adopt. The world is full of unwanted children; (3) Shut up.

After a while, I started sticking with number 3. I got pretty tired of having to defend myself.

Finally, early this past summer, I read a Female Liberation newsletter in which a woman wrote of her laparoscopy (a simple operation involving only one day in the hospital) with a doctor who was willing to sterilise childless women. I made an appointment with him, and went in prepared for the usual hassles. He turned out to be the least oppressive male doctor I've ever dealt with. He talked to me long enough to determine that I did in fact know what I wanted and that I knew the operation was irreversible, and then scheduled me for surgery the following month. I was sterilised in August.

I still sometimes get the flack I used to get. I was at a party recently, and met an acquaintance I hadn't seen in a year. After a moment of party chat, he suddenly asked, in a lowered voice, 'Did you do what you were threatening to do?' For a moment I wondered if I'd made some kind of remark about bombing the Pentagon or assassinating Howard Hughes. Then it occurred to me what he meant. 'You mean my sterilisation? Yes, I did.' 'Well,' he said sadly, 'it's too late to say anything now.' 'Yes,' I beamed, 'it certainly is.'

I keep meeting more and more childless women who've tried to get sterilised and have had experiences nearly identical to mine. And, suddenly, people who once called abortion murder are eager for these women to take a chance on pregnancy and then go to New York for an abortion. I am convinced that as more women seek sterilisation, the right-to-life crowd will focus less on the increasingly more respectable alternative of abortion and zero in on women like me. Abortion and other forms of contraception still allow room for the myth of woman's destiny: 'I don't want children *yet*'. Sterilisation says, firmly, that for the woman seeking it, the question is not birth control but birth prevention, and childless women who opt for sterilisation are making it clear that they, and not society, will determine their 'roles'.

It seems wonderfully ironic to me now, after years of involvement in radical politics, that twenty-one years ago, at the age of seven, sitting on my girlfriend's stoop, I made the most revolutionary commitment of my life. Long before the days of the new feminist consciousness, I accepted as a given the right to control my own body. Looking back, it amazes me that for twenty years, not knowing what I was fighting for, or even that I was fighting, I held on to that right. And there is nothing in my life that I am prouder of than that first feminist decision, made under the spell of Betty Hutton's glittering turquoise costume and the exultant freedom of her dance through the air.

MICHAEL YOUNG

Sara Ruddick teaches philosophy in the Seminar College of the New School for Social Research. She is co-editor, with Pamela Daniels, of *Working It Out: 23 Women Writers, Artists, Scientists & Scholars Talk About Their Lives and Work* (Pantheon, 1977). She is now working on a book tentatively titled, 'Human Nature/Women's Culture/Maternal Thought'. She lives in New York City.

Sara Ruddick

Soon in the hot midday when the bees hum around the hollyhocks my lover will come. He will stand under the cedar tree. To his one word I shall answer my one word. What has formed in me I shall give him. I shall have children.

My children will carry on; their teething, their crying, their going to school and coming back will be like the waves of the sea under me. No day will be without its movement. I shall be lifted higher than any of you on the backs of the seasons. I shall possess more than Jinny, more than Rhoda by the time I die. But on the other hand, where you are various and dimple many times to the ideas and laughter of others, I shall be sullen, storm-tinted and all one purple. I shall be debased and hidebound by the bestial and beautiful passion of maternity. I shall push the fortunes of my children unscrupulously. I shall hate those who see their faults. I shall lie basely to help them. I shall let them wall me away from you, from you, and from you.

Virginia Woolf, *The Waves*

Only the act of giving birth seemed interesting, I knew, to the intelligent, independent young women facing me. Once that dramatic moment of creation was over, however, the image of motherhood took on, in their minds, hues of greying diapers and red-and-white gingham; they thought of unattractive housedresses, disorderly homes, interrupted careers, diminishing sexuality – with these miserable consequences wrapped in the most unobjective, uncritical, sentimental and enervating kind of love. They thought of lives which were uninteresting, conventional, over. And so did I.

Jane Lazarre, The Mother Knot

There is, I believe, a Freudian story that runs something like this: As young children, girls feel bereft (more violently, castrated') when they discover that they do not have a penis. Without this anatomical equipment they can neither consummate their love for their mothers nor gain the attention and powers the world-of-the-parents bestows on penis possessors. To the extent that girls accept the irreversability of their loss, they naturally look for recompense. Trying to make the most of what their own bodies might offer, they early invest in their capacity to produce a penis-substitute – a baby. This baby will be a present to their mother whose love they may recapture as they identify with her life and replicate her work. It will be a gift both from and to a brother-father who will be grateful for the provision of a child he could not produce on his own. Most important, this penis-baby will complete and justify the girl's own body by giving her belated power – over others in virtue of her baby, over her baby in virtue of her strength and its needs.

I can recover only the dimmest conscious memories of a desire for a penis. On the other hand, it seems that all my life I have so spontaneously and ineluctably desired children that they might well have symbolised for me the completion of my incomplete body. From earliest times I actually produced children – real dolls and fantasy families, siblings who were named, cared for, sent to school, who fought and made up, who got sick and were nursed back to health, who loved me, their mother. If I had a 'husband', if they had a 'father', I don't remember him. My sister, two years younger, was my only occasional mate – an early experiment with women-raised children.

About the time that dolls and fantasy children became

slightly embarrassing, my mother preserved my maternal life by having a real baby. My play training now proved useful in earnest. With one heavy turn of the psychological screw, I was able to transfer my maternal fantasies to a real child and in this transference deal with the confused, intensely ambivalent reactions the real birth engendered. I became passionately devoted to this baby boy, catered to him and planned and dreamed for him — all without the responsibility that was, of course, my mother's. When I left home for boarding school, my affair with my baby brother and the maternal passions and ambitions which fuelled it easily survived our separation. Though at home my male friends were being transformed into 'dates', I was in a girls' school free from the manipulativeness and hypocrisy of teenage sexual life. It was the perfect setting for dreaming of motherhood without confronting the realities of mothers' lives. If at eighteen anyone had asked me *why* I wanted children, I would have replied in astonishment *Why not*!

Indeed, when I had my first child ten years later I experienced a kind of total joy in which body and soul, even pleasure and pain, seemed one and complete — the kind of joy we experience only when our earliest, most primitive childhood longings are satisfied in the world. However, by that time I was surprised and threatened by my own pleasure, had no words to name it and no strategies for incorporating it into adult life. For during the years since I was eighteen, I had many times over relinquished, repudiated, finally blotted out and lost contact with my desire for children. Not surprisingly, in losing contact with such a deep desire I lost contact with and partly destroyed some aspect of my deepest self. How had this come about?

The story is all too familiar. While I was safely dreaming of motherhood in a school run by women in the interests of girls, I was also experiencing the pleasures of creation, independence and achievement. I rode horses, organised against McCarthy, sermonised from the chapel pulpit, wrote poetry, invented a future for myself. Girls were the normal case, as different from each other as boys are. I learned to work and play with them without the fear that any boy who came along could put our projects and affections in second place. The shadow of adult-hood, where girls became wives and mothers, and Interesting Women were a species apart, scarcely darkened my dreams. This lively, esteem-inducing life should have been an excellent preparation for sturdy, rewarding parenthood. However, it was no preparation at all for parenthood's apparent prerequisite, for the self-denial, dependence and vicarious living expected of middle-class wives.

In an undergraduate college which honoured the sexual division of lives, work and privilege, I learned that I would have to make a choice. There were three possibilities: Wife-and-Mother; Professional; Interesting Woman. Each was unlivable. Wives-and-Mothers were non-people. I saw them trailing after their runny nosed children. They were kind to me when I visited their husbands. With distaste, I stared straight through them and their lives. An Interesting Woman was more than a Wife-and-Mother, less than a Professional. There were many ways for a woman to become Interesting: she could have interesting talents, parents, neuroses, lovers; she could make interesting living rooms, dinners, tapestries, gardens and trips to Europe; she could even have children so long as they were sufficiently well behaved, well spaced and interesting, so long as they didn't clutter up the place. Only two things were necessary for the Interesting Woman. She had to have money and she couldn't be Professional. She was to work just long enough and hard enough to show that she was talented; never so hard or single-mindedly that she became boring. I believe now that I was in fact expected to be and prepared to be an Interesting Woman. However, at the time, the Interesting Woman seemed to offer both too little and too much. I was intimidated by her glamour, competence and apparent ease in her social world. But I scorned her lack of seriousness. Out of timidity and pride, I chose Professional.

In my mind, in the world's mind, in my teachers' minds, professionals were men. If they had children, they had wives. I tried: I chose to study a 'hard' male subject; I applied to graduate schools where all of the faculty were men; I rejected 'feminine' decoration and courted my male teachers as I thought a boy would — with brains only. I made a virtue of my incompetence with children, though I had spent high school summers in a daycare centre, work I'd enjoyed and done well. I scorned anyone who studied child psychology, one of the best departments in the college at the time. But the future would show that my efforts were to no avail. I wasn't a man. Nor did I have the courage of women who, even then, attempted to break down sexual stereotypes and create new ways of living for themselves. There were many reasons for my failure of nerve. Important among them was my refusal to acknowledge and to act upon my desires for children. By 'acting' I mean either to relinquish their fulfillment consciously and admit the loss or to devise strategies for incorporating parenting into a self-respecting, purposive adult life. I simply denied the existence of my desires while they remained intact ready to reassert their power.

I went to graduate school in the late fifties when professional success was its own reward. It was a male world and an unattractive one. People were valued according to their 'promise'; 'promise' was narrowly and amorally defined, tested by its appeal on the academic 'market'. Whatever authentic interest my work had held for me was seriously undermined. My earlier dreams of success seemed to evaporate.

But this was not quite accurate. I wanted, as I always have, to be successful. In the man's world, there were two ways to success. I could still try to be professional or, alternatively, I could marry a professional, the only success wholeheartedly endorsed back home. Marriage to the 'right' man had the further advantage of allowing me to enter a world which for all its faults was freer, more tolerant, more alive than the upper-middle-class suburban world in which I was raised.

I didn't make deliberate choices about my work. In retrospect I seem to have been living in a semi-conscious state. This was partly because I did, quite totally, 'fall' (the verb seems appropriate) in love. Since the man was the 'right sort', this love in no way interfered with the second conventional way to success. But success aside, my actions at the time were wholly dictated by this passion and by my realistic and genuinely self-serving desire to get my way — my lover — permanently. This meant marriage and marriage has, for most of twenty years, worked well for me. It also meant then that I should begin living as 'women' do. This is what it meant to me, not to my husband who was to be quite distressed by the consequences.

What does a woman do? One possibility: she puts all of her energy into teaching which, because it has elements of service and the deadlines of obligation, is conflict free. She reads novels, discusses politics, goes to the movies, learns to cook, looks after her soul. For some women this can last for a lifetime. For me, it lasted about two years. I recovered my premarital consciousness and anxieties when I found myself paralysed and workless in a patriarchal academic community.

In that community there were three classes: wives-and-mothers, people — *i.e.* teachers, doctors and a few other professionals — and a host of workers and servers who more or less invisibly supported the show. I was terrified of becoming one of the wives-and-mothers whose lives were suddenly all too visible. I hoped desperately that it was not too late to become a professional. But I had lived my adult life in graduate school as if I would have no professional future and there was no way of undoing the consequences. Worse, I couldn't even begin to write the dissertation which seemed to offer the only way out of the morass of wifely womanhood. On the other hand, I had become, overnight, an Interesting Woman. I had interesting work (even the possibility of professional work for a woman was an interesting possibility), cooked interesting dinners, had an interesting neurosis. I could have had interesting children. Other interesting women did. In fact, if I continued to be paralysed in my work, the best way to stay interesting would have been to have children whose presence would serve as an excuse for not *finishing* anything while still allowing me to read, talk and start projects in an interesting fashion. Everyone seemed to be talking about children, having children, expecting mine. But for me, children seemed like an invitation to a drowning. I clung to the remnants of my professional identity and resolutely obliterated any returning desires for children which my companionable, reliable sexual life naturally evoked.

In the summer we fled the status-ridden, parochial academic community. In the cool anonymity of the British Museum I read and waited for some returning strength. In *Jacob's Room* Virginia Woolf imagined another woman, a feminist, who also worked in the museum's reading room. Julia Hedge, with considerable anguish, writes what seems to be a first draft of *A Room of One's Own*. Her shoe laces are untied, 'death, gall and bitter dust' are on her pen tip. Near her, 'regal and pompous' young men, the inheritors, apply themselves to their books 'composedly, unconcernedly, and with every consideration', thus arousing the envy and increasing the discomfort of 'poor Julia'. Reading the names of the great men around the dome of the room she laments that they didn't leave room for an Eliot or a Brontë. But Julia does write on, red in her cheek bones, light in her eyes.

I was no feminist that summer, but I like to think I was inspired by Julia's ghost. True, I took comfort in those same male names. They seemed to offer me protection and permission to enter the 'real' world. Despite the evidence of those male names, I still conceived of that world's inhabitants as 'thinking ego(s) . . . ageless, sexless, without qualities and without a life story'. In the real world my gender and its past would be invisible.

Since this was the best world I could then imagine, I tried to pass, tried to appear composed, unconcerned and considerate as any young man. It would be some years before I would have the courage of Julia's sloppiness and anger. But her efforts and her creator's improvements on them allowed me to sit easy in my chair. I found myself with an idea, a thesis for my thesis. That idea became a lifeline by which I could pull myself to a credential and self-respect. Through eighteen months of writing, revising and defending I would never let it go.

After England, we took a short trip to Yugoslavia. I was free of the injuries, ambitions, fears and hopes of academic life. I looked around me and everywhere I saw — families. I saw fathers and children, mothers and grandmothers. One night, in a large empty dining hall, I watched two men, sitting alone, hands clasped, singing. Walking outside, I saw old women sitting in the twilight, chatting and mending. The next morning, picnicking on a nearby island I saw one of the men with several children and their mother – playing together. I didn't know what I was seeing. (I *said* I was seeing socialism.) But I couldn't avoid what I was feeling. I loved those men. I wanted to be those women. I wanted to mother those children. I was deeply certain of my desire and began to act on it. It was four months before I conceived this newly desired child. They seemed unbearably long. I never wavered. I was now as clearly governed by passion as I had been when I steered and lured my lover into marriage.

I say that I never wavered. That is too simple. I was certain and acted on that certainty. But during the long four months I waited I had to keep convincing myself that in fact I wanted what I desperately waited for. Clutching my idea for my thesis I managed to work a little. But most of my time was spent in trying to imagine a future in which my maternal fantasies would be for real. On the day that I learned I was pregnant, I began to write, actually to write my thesis. My work problems disappeared overnight. I now felt whole, complete, healthy and strong. I worked accordingly. When I wasn't working, I took active pleasure in my growing, producing body. I wore maternity dresses before they were necessary. I took long walks through the Vermont countryside, alternating, as mood and fantasy dictated, between the confident stride of a grown woman and the careful steps of a child-mother bearing an infinitely fragile Russian Easter egg.

I did not then make the connections so obvious to me now: my ability to work and my conviction that I would, could mother went hand in hand. In the summer, with the glimmer of an idea for a thesis, came the return of my desire for children. In the winter, with knowledge of conception, came the ability to work. But I kept apart what experience was bringing together. I kept saying to myself and everyone who would listen: this baby won't take as much of my time as you think. I'll work *despite* being a mother. This will be good for me, good for the baby. No child should be the centre of the centre of a woman's life! And then I would spend hours in reverie prodding my belly so I could feel that baby move again.

When that baby was born I fell deeply and passionately in love. I recovered my dissertation (it would be several months before my mildly supportive advisor would look at it) and revised with full energy. I nursed, slept, wrote, slept, walked, slept, read, slept, nursed and slept again. I was living to another creature's rhythms, to new rhythms of my own. As if to help us both, I rented a piano, endlessly played the phonograph, sang songs and read poetry to the sleeping baby. Sometimes I would read the professional journals and plan articles. Often I would tell others (men) that I would soon make up for the time I was 'losing'. I didn't tell the women that. For the first time I actually looked at them, sometimes even listened to them. Their defensive cheerfulness and my defensive ambitions, their limited options and my privileges raised many walls between us. But usually when I could look at them I saw that they saw me. When I could listen, I knew that I had much to learn.

It all sounds implausibly romantic. Maternity was romantic for me. In pregnancy and childbirth I fell in love with a baby, with motherhood, in some small measure with myself. The mood passed, the long haul of raising children soon began. But as in any maturing realistic love, such as parenting and marriage have been for me, those romantic beginnings, when childhood wish and adult expectations are joined, pervade and sweeten the years that follow. For me that sweetness had an unusual poignancy. I was beginning the long return to my mother, my gender, my body, my self — a return which the enraging inequities of patriarchy had almost made impossible.

Parenting is the most common of experiences. This commonality may be threatening or comforting. It allows many female friendships and causes much loss of female identity. Tangentially, the commonality makes it difficult for me to continue this story. The fifteen years that have passed since childbirth are punctuated by the events which characterise parenthood in my subculture. First teeth, first steps, first words; frightening illnesses, nightmares, shynesses and phobias; schooldays, birthdays, examinations, friendships, betrayals; clubs and exclusions from clubs, winning, losing, melting smiles, rending tears.

These greeting-card events, the lives of my children, have shaped my life. They have provoked intensities of pleasure and anxiety which astound non-parents but are recognised by parents as the staple of life. For me, the passions of maternity were so unexpected, unexplored and confusing that to this day I haven't discerned the patterns. I find it impossible to convey either the miracle or the dailiness of children. I was asked to write about the consequences of children for my life. But there is no abstract entity, 'my life', which exists independently. The experience of parenting has been shaped by and has shaped every other aspect of my life.

Most obviously, parenting has shaped the structure and the content of my marriage. Given the nature and limits of technology, it takes two to have a child. It didn't feel that way to me. *I* wanted children. My husband, though briefly opposed to the idea, was mainly indifferent. He wanted me to be happy. If that meant having children, okay. But so far as he knew and I could tell, having children was my business and my desire. We both feared a baby would change the kind of pleasure we took in each other. We were right. We were not only lovers and friends but parented each other, giving and getting the kind of 'spoiling' attention only beloved children and long-loving, child-free couples can count on. A baby would change all that. We knew, he resented it, especially during the last days of pregnancy and the first weeks after birth, so heightened and meaningful to me, so trying and excluding for him. What neither of us guessed was that I had married not only a friend, lover, provider and inseminator but a father as well, a man for whom the cares and loves of parenthood would be as central and obligatory as they are for a mother. I asked for and expected my husband's help. These were his children; he was a good man. I got much more. No task or challenge – bathing, diapering, clothing, feeding, advising, protecting, snuggling, or educating – would or could be mine alone. Although now I am aware of the political and of course the psychological benefits of this sharing, at the time I frequently felt that *my* space was invaded, my competence diminished. In all my fantasies I'd mothered alone, with at most a returning appreciative mate to witness my power. It was not part of my plan actually to raise children *with* someone and the working out of this new way required patience, resilience and a sense of humour.

Today, still, I see mothers around me who appear to be assuming almost all of the daily care of children. Fathers, even those who live with their children, seem like extra-terrestial visitors who 'take' the children – to the movies, to school, to the father's world – fitting them into the interstices of their lives. They are often fine parents – cheerful, sympathetic, entertaining. They should be, since their children require so little from them. This, I suppose is the scene in which, as a young mother, I'd expected to play my part. But now, as a spectator, it fills me with confusion and pain. I am furious with those mothers who cannot or will not shape a life of their own; I am also resentful on their behalf and would take up their cause. But they, usually, do not want my advocacy, fearing rightly that I see their lives too impatiently and, simply, that I veer too close to the woman-contempt in which I had earlier self-protectively steeped myself. And so, though I am angry with the lordly fathers coming and going in their houses at their leisure, I feel helpless and finally disgusted with all of us. These are the confused feelings that led me, for so many years, to bury even the thought of parenting life. If my husband and I had lived out the parts expected of us, those feelings would be crippling me still.

Even my own story bears disconcerting resemblances to the patriarchal domestic scene which fills me, consciously, with disgust. When our baby was born my husband and I largely continued our self-absorbed love affair. Now we loved the parent in each other and the baby plaything that made our love visible. Child-chores were light. My mother-in-law gave me a washer and dryer. We diapered, laundered, fed and dressed our baby with lots of love and little fuss. A second child, city life, troubled ambitions and the greater soul demands of the baby himself changed all that. No *kind* of duty was beneath either of us, no challenge or setback reserved for one of us. Yet gradually the responsibility for juggling the many demands of work and family life became largely mine.

How did this happen? Again the story is all too familiar. I

allowed my husband to plead quite real demands of work in order to renege on family tasks which I still believed to be *rightly* a woman's. I meanwhile was largely workless. I welcomed visible Motherliness as a refuge from ambition and depended upon myriad obligations to excuse worldly failures. Our growing inequality was exacerbated when we began to get helpers so that we would have more child-free time. When the free hours were over, I felt more than ever obligated to the children. My husband took the purchased freedom for what it was – a proper and expected bonus of usable time. He would return to find me intensely engaged with the children. I was both relieved to be safely back home and guilty for having gone out in the first place. I did not seek and would not have welcomed his 'help' at that moment. Not surprisingly, he took the occasion to move off again to his own concerns. Old patterns were repeated; the world watched approvingly.

Given the prevailing politics of childcare, with its flagrant exploitation of women's work and love, to speak of my own contribution to our inequality may seem like blaming the victim.[1] Of course, I would not have been so workless and fearful outside my home, nor so dependent upon my special competences within it, had I not been deeply inhibited by the matter-of-fact denial of significant non-maternal work to women. Nonetheless, I know that during those years I took comfort and even gained some strength from the sexist division of labour and lives that I now realise is so damaging. I offered my husband the temptations of benevolent patriarchy. He was

[1]Just conditions of parental work are not a personal, individual matter. Women will be able to mother well only when the community values and supports their efforts socially, economically, emotionally. For example, humane, free, healthy childcare centres, open to mothers and their children from infancy on, are as important to good parental work as an individual's just relations at home. Nor should we construe 'home' simplemindedly, as a matter of justice between mothers and fathers. As single mothers, lesbian mothers and co-parenting women continually remind us, there are many ways to provide children with examples of caring which do not incorporate the inequalities of power and privilege which so nicely prepare the next generation to find 'natural' a world in which they will either exploit or be exploited.

the best of fathers, yet still master of his time and work. Seeing that he was more involved with the daily details of childcare than any other man around, I counted my blessings and praised his virtues. His 'help' was my luck, not my right. To the extent that I worried at all about the moral character of our joint parental work, I was guilty that I was not still more completely the mother, not still more the supportive, enabling wife. Thinking this way, it is not surprising that I came close to reproducing in my own family the destructive saga of the kind, judgemental returning father, beloved and catered to by women and children, resented and feared by all.

We were saved from this fate by my growing ability to work and by the ever greater importance of feminism in my life. Work/worklessness: they were as much an obsession of my mothering years as they are of this essay. I have already spoken of the interconnections between work and my will to conceive; conception and my ability to work and of the early months of infant care when I lived both to the rhythms of maternity and to the tune of the academic world. A year and a half after childbirth, on my wedding anniversary, I conceived a second child. She was the unplanned, unexpected but wholly willed creature of maternal passion. We were shortly to move to the city where I could surely secure part-time jobs and would soon expect to want a responsible position on the academic ladder. But I couldn't stop with one child; couldn't give up the consuming idyll of child-centred life; couldn't yet forego the passionate experiences of pregnancy, childbirth, and nursing. Meanwhile, the women's movement was taking hold. I was getting permission to take my own work seriously, a permission that I would gradually internalise so that it became an insistent, inspiriting, subjective demand. Most nights I could dampen maternal desire, quell work anxiety, and plan a make-shift 'career'. This night, romantically enough, I couldn't. I had afterthoughts, but I had conceived. When I knew that I temporarily put aside thoughts of a career. But my new sense of women's rights and possibilities forced me to realise that this was only postponement.

Soon the easy times were over. The first child stopped taking naps, the second child arrived. The immediate demands of a thesis had been met and no other job or task shaped my life. Yet I needed work as a fish needs water. Without it, I would become a 'mere woman', a kind of death. So I made up work in unpromising circumstances. My days and large parts of my nights were scheduled according to the unpredictable demands of small children. I felt increasingly isolated not just from professional life but from professional persons and concerns. I kept looking for a 'subject' and fantasised about academic jobs that would not take me too far from home, literally or symbolically.

For I was largely happy and felt largely effective 'at home'. Yet I still operated with the old categories: professional = men = real life = 'outside' work; mothers = women = losers = boring private domesticity. Increasingly, my passions, and often my mind, dwelt among women and the crises and creatures of the women's world.

This split, and the denials and dissociations it required, now seems so literally unlivable that I have difficulty remembering how my days actually went. There was time with the children and time 'free' of them. Some of the free time was spent in part-time jobs — briefly in publishing, then in teaching. Otherwise, I was 'trying to write'. These free hours were always being interrupted by unexpected demands of the children, or because my husband or helpers were not there when they said they'd be. They were interrupted by all sorts of pleasures — movies, eating, novel-reading — the mixed pleasures of anti-war politics. And finally they were sabotaged by my own weird way of thinking about myself.

I thought of the time I spent with the children as duty time taken from 'self-expressive' work. Yet when the time came to work, I spent a large portion of those precious hours coming down off life with the children — their cares and pleasures, our projects. Now, when I try to induce memories of those years, incident after incident, moments of being with the children, come back in poignant detail. By contrast, I can barely remember the content of my work. What I do recall are restless hours at my desk comforted by the litter of books and unfinished essays, remnants of identity as a 'person in my own right'.[2] With other mothers I talked easily of 'having work', though I felt both repelled and excluded by the clever, smug philosophers and academics who should have been my colleagues. My alienation was partly defensive; I denigrated a life I thought I'd lost. It was also the consequence of the Vietnam War. When other women and their children were being bombed out of home and life, it was difficult to respect those professionals who couldn't decide when it was appropriate to speak or what it was appropriate to feel. But neither the war nor my sense of isolation explain the emptiness, the unreality of my working hours – especially when I compare them to my maternal hours so chock full of being.

As the children grew, I became more restless. When I wasn't teaching, I took up and put down many books, many projects. Serendipitously, I rekindled two early undergraduate passions – for Gertrude Stein and Virginia Woolf. The passion for Woolf grew into an intense, disciplined 'amateur'[3] interest in her life and work. My work on both of these women was fueled by 'personal' concerns, including my love for my mother and my fear for her death. These personal connections required me to connect in my *work* with my mother and with her life. Although I was largely leading that life, my mother never had the support nor came to the convictions of feminism. Though not much supported, Woolf, against all likelihood, did come to the convictions.

I sometimes plan short reading lists for prospective mothers: Jane Lazarre's *The Mother Knot*, Tillie Olsen's *Tell Me a Riddle*, Adrienne Rich's *Of Woman Born*. On any short list, I put *To the Lighthouse* and *Three Guineas*. Together these

[2]'Somewhat earlier I had accepted an invitation to do an essay . . . I accepted not because I wanted to do the thing so much as because it lent reality to my erstwhile – and still cherished – identity as an historian. (After all, had not one of the senior historians at Dartmouth once introduced me at a dinner party as a "person in my own right"?)' Marilyn Young, 'Contradictions' in *Working It Out*, edited by Sara Ruddick and Pamela Daniels (Pantheon Books, New York, 1977).
[3]'By amateur I do not mean the popular definition of one who works as a pastime, or in an unskilled, halfhearted way. I mean amateur in the ancient sense of "devotee" – someone who does what (s)he loves and loves what (s)he does.'
Pamela Daniels, 'Birth of the Amateur', *Working It Out*.

books affirm the necessity of mothers' and other women's independent work as well as the value of motherliness for us all. They show war and crippling work to be insupportable horrors for anyone who has nourished and appreciated growing lives. They look unflinchingly at the damage done to mothers, children and men when the practices of motherhood are confined to the 'private house' of capitalist patriarchy with 'its cruelty, its poverty, its hypocrisy, its immorality, its insanity'.[4] And they ridicule and reject the whole panoply of amoral professionalism in which I had been mired, which itself appears as crippling work that fosters war and depends upon the servitude of those in the private house.

Beginning with Gertrude Stein, more certainly with Virginia Woolf, I began to have what Woolf herself might have called 'a work of my own'. By that I mean work which connected with my life and my feelings and made sense of a newly fervent feminist consciousness. Increasingly, women became the subject of my work and my projected audience. I became interested in *mothers'* lives, culture and thought. Although I still felt a stranger among them, I was most committed to those women I had most despised. But I didn't want to romanticise their maternity as I do my own. I wanted to 'love with all my intelligence'[5] which meant acknowledging the damage that mothers' lives wreak on women and children alike. To the nerve it takes to claim the powers men have always had, I was now adding the greater nerve it takes to be a woman, to value as well as to change women's lives.

'Work of my own' affected mothering. More than ever I valued independent, autonomous work. But now I no longer identified 'work' either with 'male' or with 'professional'. Since independent work was a mother's *right*, I was able to make clear, justified demands on my husband's time in work's name. I no longer saw him as an especially good man because he fathered seriously and encouraged my projects. Like me, he was

---

[4]Virginia Woolf, *Three Guineas.*
[5]Adrienne Rich, 'Splittings' in *The Dream of a Common Language* (W.W. Norton, New York, 1978).

a parent doing, or trying to do, his fair share of our work together.

More somberly, now that I was absorbed, even compelled to read, write, think and teach, I had to remind and train myself to set aside enough truly attentive time for children. This has never been easy; I am still frequently unsuccessful. Though I clearly repudiated this life-long, culturally sanctioned opposition between 'real' work and mother's lives, its unconscious force still provokes anxious ambivalence.

On the plus side I found, unexpectedly, that my years of mothering had prepared me for juggling many kinds of demands. I had learned to say 'no' and to set priorities. You cannot keep on talking to a student if you're meeting a child on a street corner. You cannot accept an invitation if a child is ill. You cannot attend a conference on a child's birthday. These many cannots, accumulating over the years, added up to 'can'. I can turn off the phone, stop talking, stay home. I learned how to do it 'because-of-the-children'. Now I *can* do it for my own work – or pleasure.

As I think about my maternal life, as I think about mothers, I feel as if there must be some lessons learned in our private houses which can be integrated into the public world we now enter. In *A Room of One's Own*, Woolf wrote, 'we think back through our mothers if we are women'. Later, in *Three Guineas*, she urged women to 'enter the professions yet remain civilised human beings' by 'refusing to be separated from the four great teachers' of our mothers' houses: poverty, chastity, derision and freedom from unreal loyalties. Woolf used old terms in new ways to rename the political world. She wanted to preserve the 'womanly' at the same time as she transformed it, affirming again and again her connection to maternal life. Her 'new woman' builds a new professional house rather than infiltrating herself into possessive, jealous, greedy, pugnacious professions.

Let the daughters of uneducated women dance round the new house, the poor house, the house that stands in a narrow street where omnibuses pass and the street hawkers cry their wares, and let them sing., 'We have done with war! We have done with tyranny!

267

And their mothers will laugh from their graves, 'It was for this that we suffered obloquy and contempt! Light up the windows of the new house, daughter! Let them blaze!

I too wish to think back through our mothers, to affirm connection to maternal life, to transform rather than to infiltrate economic, political or professional life. But as I try to put these stirring words into political or personal practice, I find many stumbling blocks. Virtue seems at odds with power and, as Woolf herself recognised, women must have their share of effectiveness or they will not be strong enough to transform anything. More poignant for me personally, there are many aspects of mothers' lives which are troubling. Though these 'maternal failures' are not our 'fault', it is we ourselves who must remedy them.

Let me take mothers' alleged conservatism, or at best our political indifference, as one example of 'failure' which recently I have found troubling. Both my own life and my observation of other mothers lead me to believe that there is much truth in this charge. Some familiar defences come to mind. Mothers are very, very busy people, especially those who chose or must take on non-maternal work. Moreover, it can be exhausting to fight even the small daily battles against sexism, racism, class arrogance, poverty, and bureaucratic incompetence. Mothers may well be too preoccupied to engage in the daily work of politicking or too concerned with tomorrow's well-being to contemplate 'deep structural change'. This is not to say that there are not energetic, effective, politically active mothers. It is only to say that they are exceptional.

I believe that there is a deeper side to this conservatism. Maternal work is done in the face of death. The wanton and unacceptable indifference of nature can frustrate even the most devoted maternal care. The possibility of illness, accident, physical and mental damage make up the context of maternal work. Society supplements the indifference of nature by its cruelty, bigotry and violence. War can destroy, in an instant, years of maternal love and hope. Ideological division, moral recalcitrance and political purity can unravel a fabric of family and community life which is largely the creation of mother-artists. If mothers are more frequently wary and protective than non-mothers, if we are inclined to simply supernatural comforts, paternalistic states, and 'peace at any price', this is a hazard of the work situation. For a mother 'life' may seem 'terrible, hostile and quick to pounce on you if you give it a chance'.[6] She may well learn to value keeping over acquiring, to devote herself to preserving what is fragile, to maintaining whatever is at hand and necessary to her child's life.

I do not believe that these characteristics of maternal life require that we be apolitical or conservative. I do believe that, combined with our history of seclusion, ridicule and impotence, they make conservatism a liability. We need to free ourselves from the possessiveness, false pride and restricted loyalties which may be endemic to human life but which are certainly encouraged by capitalism and probably by professional life everywhere. The causes of peace, decent public health, daycare, good schooling – these are obviously mothers' issues. Any mother should prefer that her children be freed from a world in which they must either dominate or submit, exploit or suffer, a world in which master and subject alike are corrupted by varieties of colonisation. We would all like our children to have at least the chance of being both happy and good. To give them that chance we could take a genuinely 'radical' politics as our own. But to do this we must first learn to sustain a creative tension between our fierce, wholly natural desire to foster our own children and the essential but less compulsive demand that children everywhere are well-mothered.

It will not be enough to develop political consciousness. It is notorious that in political life and political organisations women become servers and apologists. This may be especially true of mothers, since maybe we are weakened by our strangeness to public life and repelled by it in its patriarchal forms. We will need the minds and energies of feminists, many of them non-mothers, if we are to articulate ideals and techniques of implementation which truly represent both our fears and our best hopes.

[6]The words are Mrs Ramsay's, in Virginia Woolf's *To the Lighthouse*.

Like everyone else, mothers are corrupted by concerns of status and class. Often our misguided efforts on behalf of the success and purity of our children frighten them and everyone else. Yet when maternal possessiveness is balanced with human inclusiveness, we should be especially able 'to join in loving rather than hating'.[7] For it has been our business to mediate difference and make connection — in our festivals, at our meals, in the classrooms, playgrounds, and living rooms of our communities. We can bring to politics our conviction that the best of human wills is limited. We know how hard we tried, how often we failed, know that even our own children will not be wholly healthy and good.

My babies are now thirteen and fifteen. My daughter will begin her adult life with options of work, love and sexuality that I never dreamed of having. Her cool and confident pride in her sex kindles my own. As a feminist, I often feel like gathering my daughter into a fierce cross-generational separatist circle of women. We would of course include her father, my lover, the exceptional man. I am tempted but because I have a son I don't even try. A boy on the edge of adolescence cannot be accommodated, like my husband whose tenderness and friendship have been tried. A boy's capacity for love and reciprocity does not come easily or all at once. I have tried asking of my son a precocious wisdom and restraint I would never demand of my daughter. But the sheer physical evidence of his future strength and sexuality belied my efforts to predict and control. To accept him meant to accept his gender.

It hasn't been easy. Men have always and everywhere committed violence — physical, social and psychological violence — against women. 'Good' men have stood by and watched. The evidence grows and announces itself; I am increasingly able to hear it. In its light, to be 'separatist' seems a requirement of loyalty, survival, and love. Yet my son, by his

[7]The words are Antigone's in Sophocles' *Antigone*. She obeys the law of love rather than the laws of the state, buries a brother, thus honouring and forgiving him, despite his treacherous and politically reprehensible behaviour.

very existence, demanded something else. Because I have a daughter, because I am a daughter and a woman, I am wholly bound to women and the transformation of our lives. But because I have a son, I must include men, not the individual exceptional lover, but men as such, into my angriest and wildest utopias.

Adolescent children require absolutely honest, unsparing accounts of the world in which they will struggle, combined with a confident parental judgement that their efforts will be morally and psychologically rewarded. This most recent demand on my parenting life sometimes seems the hardest. Once again, I look for help – from my husband, from other women, from feminism, from my own work – and increasingly from my children themselves.